|18-

FIFTY THINKERS WHO
SHAPED THE MODERN WORLD

FIFTY THINKERS WHO SHAPED THE MODERN WORLD

Stephen Trombley

ATLANTIC BOOKS

LONDON

First published in Great Britain in 2012 by
Atlantic Books, an imprint of Atlantic Books Ltd.

Copyright © Stephen Trombley, 2012

1 3 5 7 9 10 8 6 4 2

A CIP catalogue record for this book is available
from the British Library.

Hardback ISBN 978-1-84887-823-5
Trade paperback ISBN 978-0-85789-616-2
E-book ISBN 978-1-78239-038-1

Printed and bound in Great Britain
by the MPG Books Group

Atlantic Books
An imprint of Atlantic Books Ltd
Ormond House
26–27 Boswell Street
London WC1N 3JZ

www.atlantic-books.co.uk

For Peg Culver

Leisure is the mother of *philosophy*.

Thomas Hobbes, *Leviathan* (1651)

Contents

8. Charles Darwin
(1809–82)   65

9. Søren Kierkegaard
(1813–55)   73

10. Karl Marx
(1818–83)   78

11. Arthur Schopenhauer
(1788–1860)   88

12. C. S. Peirce
(1839–1914)   91

13. William James
(1842–1910)   97

14. Friedrich Nietzsche
(1844–1900)   104

15. F. H. Bradley
(1846–1924)   111

16. Gottlob Frege
(1848–1925)   118

17. Sigmund Freud
(1856–1939)   124

18. Émile Durkheim
(1858–1917)   133

19. Henri Bergson
(1859–1941)   139

Introduction

The English philosopher Alfred North Whitehead (1861–1947) once observed that European philosophy consists of a series of footnotes to Plato (*c.* 428/7–*c.* 348/7 BC). If this is the case, then modern philosophy might be more accurately described as a series of footnotes to Immanuel Kant (1724–1804). Plato raised the big questions of philosophy – and Aristotle (384–322 BC) created the first philosophical system – but Kant is the first great system-builder of the modern period, taking into account the impact of the Scientific Revolution and the Enlightenment.

> ... all thought, whether straightaway (*directe*) or through a detour (*indirecte*), must ultimately be related to intuitions, thus, in our case, to sensibility, since there is no other way in which objects can be given to us.
>
> Immanuel Kant, *Critique of Pure Reason* (1781)
> (trans. Paul Guyer and Allen W. Wood, 1998)

For Kant, philosophy is about man having reached the age of intellectual maturity, when the universe can be explained through thinking rather than revelation. He was profoundly influenced by the Scottish philosopher David Hume (1711–76), whom Kant credits with awakening him from a 'dogmatic slumber'. In his *Prolegomena to Any Future Metaphysics* (1783) Kant said that, after reading Hume, 'I could proceed safely, though slowly, to determine the whole sphere of pure reason completely and from general principles, in its circumference as well as in its contents. This was required for metaphysics in order to construct its system according to a reliable plan.' This groundwork led to Kant's masterpiece, his *Critique of Pure Reason* (1781, substantially revised in 1787). Inspired by Enlightenment thinking about freedom – and experiencing the effects of war first-hand when his hometown of Königsberg was under Russian occupation during the Seven Years' War (1756–63) – Kant argued that knowledge and freedom went hand in hand. He explored these themes in two further critiques: the *Critique of Practical Reason* (1788) and the *Critique of Judgement* (1790). The *Critique of Pure Reason* identifies laws that govern science, while preserving free will. The *Critique of Judgement* considers aesthetic judgements, and teleological questions about the purpose of natural organisms and systems.

One of the most enduring aspects of Kant's philosophy is his ethics, with its *categorical imperative*. The categorical imperative says that I must act in such a way that the action I am choosing should become a universal law that should be applied to anyone else finding themselves in similar circumstances. Here Kant argues against a consequentialist ethics like utilitarianism. Utilitarian ethics say the right course of action is that which gives the greatest amount of good to the greatest number of people. Utilitarianism is consequentialist because it urges me to seek the best consequences, which, Kant argues, is no more than my animal self would do. For Kant utilitarianism is not a moral theory because it does not take sufficient account of the difference between animals and persons, i.e., mind. In seeking the categorical imperative for our actions, we are using what Kant calls pure practical reason to arrive at a maxim that would govern our actions. This is called deontological ethics: finding and observing a moral rule, rather than defining good by its consequences.

Kant's philosophy of transcendental idealism – in which the perceiving subject partly assigns meaning to the external world – would set the agenda for the further development of German idealism and much of twentieth- and twenty-first century continental philosophy.

The age of revolutions

The age of Enlightenment was also the age of revolutions. The English civil wars (1642–51) pitted parliamentarians against royalists. The American Revolution (1775–83) saw New World colonists rebelling against the rule of the English king, inspired by the ideas of the English philosopher John Locke and the French philosopher Jean-Jacques Rousseau (1712–78) on the social contract; this was the creation of the United States of America. The French Revolution was fuelled by Enlightenment political ideas about the rights of citizens. King Louis XVI (1754–93)was executed and today France is a democratic republic, although there were several slips twixt cup and lip.

The execution of kings (England executed Charles I in 1649) was the final nail in the coffin of rule by divine right. By 1848 it was truly the Age of Man, but the first cracks in the new post-Enlightenment social organization began to show. New science led to new technology and the Industrial Revolution. Machines now mechanically multiplied the amount of goods that were formerly manufactured by hand. Workers left their agrarian lifestyle (and the agricultural market) and swelled the cities, where the factories were located. Overcrowding, disease and crime followed, all fuelled by poverty as laboured worked long hours for low wages. They suffered a new kind of fatigue, new injuries and new insults to their sense of self-worth. Meanwhile, the owners of manufacture – capitalists – grew richer. The gap in earnings between the rich industrialists and the poor, exploited workers made conflict inevitable.

> The materialist doctrine that men are products of circumstances and upbringing, and that, therefore, changed men are products of changed circumstances and changed upbringing, forgets that it is men who change circumstances and that the educator must himself be educated. Hence this doctrine is bound to divide society into two parts, one of which is superior to society. The coincidence of the changing of circumstances and of human activity or self-change [*Selbstveränderung*] can be conceived and rationally understood only as revolutionary practice.
>
> Karl Marx, 'Theses on Feuerbach' (1845)
>
> (trans. W. Lough, 1969)

Europe in 1848 was the year of revolutions, with uprisings in France, the Italian and German states (those countries were not yet unified), Hungary and Ireland. One result of the Enlightenment philosophy that brought science, technology, politics and jurisprudence was a new capital-based ownership class, a middle class of managers and a working class of the exploited. Philosophy replied. The socialism of Karl Marx (1818–83) and Friedrich Engels (1820–95) was a direct response to the misery that accompanied capitalism and the accumulation of wealth by a few at the expense of the many.

> Because philosophy has its being essentially in the element of that universality which encloses the particular within in it, the end or final result seems, in the case of philosophy more than in that of other sciences, to have absolutely expressed the complete fact itself in its very nature
>
> G. W. F. Hegel, *Phenomenology of Spirit* (1870)
>
> (trans. A. V. Miller, 1977)

After a long run in which Kant was the dominant German philosopher, having been variously interpreted by idealists like Johann Gottlieb Fichte (1762–1814) and F. W. J. Schelling (1775–1854), G. W. F. Hegel (1770–1831) was next to erect a complete system of thought. His focus was on creating a unified theory of everything through reason; his historicism and concern for the interrelationships of social and political entities and questions greatly influenced Karl Marx and Max Weber (1864–1920). This strand of thinking was one of four that would come to dominate the twentieth century: (1) political ideology, (2) biology and genetics, (3) psychology, and (4) post-Newtonian physics.

Fascism

Germany's National Socialists or Nazis were a fascist party – polar opposites of the Karl Marx-inspired socialists. Fascism is sometimes said to be a tendency rather than a systematic programme, and, indeed, it is difficult to point to a coherent *philosophical* explication of Nazi ideology (some attempts are simple catalogues of prejudice). Fascism, as it developed in different countries – Italy, Germany, Spain – was a ragtag assemblage of extremist beliefs, popularized during a time of deep financial crisis. For Germans suffering under the weight of the Versailles treaty, fascism defined itself by its choice of scapegoats: Jews, socialists and US consumerism. Important components of German fascism include extreme nationalism, the idea of Aryans as the 'master race' and a militaristic pursuit of empire. The Nazi leader Adolf Hitler (1889–1945) did not place economics high on his list of priorities, possibly because the industrial demands of world domination would mean plenty of factory work, as well as guaranteed consumption of its products by the military (after the appropriation of the wealth of conquered nations). The libertarian economist Sheldon Richman defined fascism as 'socialism with a capitalist veneer'.

Socialism in practice

The work of Karl Marx and Freidrich Engels culminated in the economic and political philosophy of socialism. Socialism was adopted by Vladimir Ilyich Lenin (1870–1924), who implemented a form of it which became the official socialism of what would eventually become the Soviet Union after Russia's October Revolution of 1917. Marx and Engels viewed social organization as the result of historically determined economic relations. For them the story of modern humankind was the conflict of labour and capital, which, of necessity, demanded a radical politics. The workers' paradise that Marx and Engels had in mind when they wrote *The Communist Manifesto* in 1848 proved in the twentieth century to be an unattainable utopia. The rise of Joseph Stalin (1879–1953) to the leadership of the Soviet Union led to as many as 20 million deaths, as a result of famine, purges and deportations.

> The history of all hitherto existing society is the history of class struggles.
>
> Karl Marx and Friedrich Engels, *The Communist Manifesto* (1848) (trans. Samuel Moore, 1888)

Soviet citizens were guaranteed work, but their quality of life, in terms of material comforts, was nothing like that enjoyed in the West, where capitalism was producing record profits and ushering in a new world of prosperity for Americans and, eventually, Europeans. Also, while the United States and much of Europe enjoyed democratic elections, leadership in the Soviet Union was imposed on the masses. Membership of the Communist Party was restricted to a privileged minority and an elaborate police state kept the population in line.

The price of totalitarianism

With the establishment of totalitarian regimes in Russia and Germany, intellectuals in those countries found themselves in danger. Their role was often simply to agree with a system that was both morally bankrupt and intellectually dishonest. As the Nazi persecution of the Jews began in Germany in 1933, preparing the ground for the horrors of the Second World War, both the United States and Britain benefitted from the arrival on their shores of philosophers and scientists fleeing for their lives. Eventually, the United States would be the first nation to develop a nuclear weapon using the science brought there by German refugees, including Albert Einstein (1879–1955). When the war was over and the US and Soviet victors moved in to cherry pick the best Nazi scientists to come and work for them, the United States got Wernher von Braun (1912–77). Braun was the physicist and rocket designer who created the deadly long-range V-2 rocket that rained death and destruction on London. But he was not merely a rocket designer; he was also a member of the Nazi Party and an SS officer. The Americans grabbed him before the Soviets could, giving them the edge in ballistic missiles with which to project thermonuclear weapons at targets several thousand miles away. Braun was responsible for the rocket science that made the United States the first nation to put a man on the moon.

Communities tend to be guided less than individuals by conscience and a sense of responsibility. How much misery does this fact cause mankind! It is the source of wars and every kind of oppression, which fill the earth with pain, sighs and bitterness.

Albert Einstein, 'The World as I See It' (1934)

Philosophy against fascism

Against the thinkers who designed war may be mentioned four examples, two of whom were students of Edmund Husserl, who defined the moral centre of German philosophy in crisis, and demonstrated how it could be held. They are: Edith Stein, Hannah Arendt, Karl Jaspers and Dietrich Bonhoeffer. Bonhoeffer was a Lutheran theologian whose posthumous *Ethics* (1955), much of which was composed during the Nazi era, imagines a world in which the social and political order is Christian. Acting as a double agent for the German resistance inside the Abwehr (German secret police), Bonhoeffer was part of a plot to kill Hitler. He justified his action as a Christian by acknowledging his guilt and sacrificing himself in an act that, while being a sin, was committed for the greater good. He was arrested, imprisoned for eighteen months and finally hanged at Flossenbürg concentration camp.

Edith Stein struggled doubly as a woman and a Jew in the German university system. She became Edmund Husserl's personal assistant and promised to be one of the leading phenomenologists, but converted to Roman Catholicism and became a nun. For a while she escaped deportation because of her status as a nun; but soon after being transferred to a convent in the Netherlands, the SS came for her (and her sister, who was with her) and deported her to Auschwitz where she perished in 1942. Her work on empathy was influenced not only by Husserl and the Augustinian tradition, but also by her experience as a nursing assistant in the First World War, and by the deaths in that conflict of those she loved.

> The struggle for total domination of the total population of the earth, the elimination of every competing non-totalitarian reality, is inherent in the totalitarian regimes themselves; if they do not pursue global rule as their ultimate goal, they are only too likely to lose whatever power they have already seized.
>
> Hannah Arendt, *The Origins of Totalitarianism* (1951)

Karl Jaspers is the unsung hero of mid-twentieth century philosophy, a Mahler to Heidegger's Wagner. His existentialist philosophy was also, like that of Stein and Bonhoeffer, based on communication through love, and empathic moves towards the other. He steadfastly resisted the Nazis and protected his Jewish wife, with whom he survived the war. He also took over from Heidegger the supervision of Heidegger's former lover and student Hannah Arendt. Once again, the Augustinian theme of love occurs in Arendt's work, and after she fled for her life from Germany, and then from France, she settled in New York to become the foremost political philosopher working in the phenomenological tradition as transformed by Heidegger. In 1948 Jaspers left Germany to take a chair in Basel, where he remained until his death.

Science accelerating

Einstein's theory of relativity gave us a vantage point from which to view the progress of thinking in our time. During the 2,000 years that humans looked at the world through the eyes of Aristotle, Ptolemy (c. 90–168), Copernicus (1473–1543) and Galileo (1564–1642), knowledge was accumulated by quick insights that gave scientists something to think about for several hundred years at a time. Not so in the post-Newtonian world. Since the splitting of the atom, physics, chemistry, engineering and their subsequent contributions to technology have proceeded at a dizzying pace. The increasing specialization of the physical sciences has put paid to the age of enlightened amateurs like Isaac Newton (1642–1727); only specialists can keep up with the pace and detail of advances in, for instance, particle physics or astrophysics. The danger of this massively focused approach, which gives sharp clarity to individual problems in science, is that the bigger picture can go out of focus. The risk is that we could lose our way. While we pursue excellence in science and knowledge for knowledge's sake, we lose sight of the context in which science is carried out – by people, in communities. One of philosophy's roles is to remind science of this broader, social and political context.

It must also be remembered that today knowledge is acquired at the behest of – and paid for by – those in whose interest it is to possess knowledge. In fact, this has always been the case. At the beginning of the scientific age, monarchs – and then later democracies – were the patrons and beneficiaries of scientific knowledge. Now, corporations control much of today's scientific discovery and its future applications, their power unchecked by the regulations that pertain to governments. The power of corporations is less visible than that of governments, and their accountability is only to a bottom line. Science has become, as never before, a political act.

The genetic turn

While physicists were busy blowing up the world and at the same time discovering how it came into existence, biologists and geneticists were turning to the world within. Physics explores the world beyond us, no matter how small or large. Biology – particularly genetics – goes inside our bodies to discover how they work. And with genetics we have the possibility of changing what goes on inside our bodies by tinkering with DNA, the building blocks of all life. Charles Darwin (1809–82) started a trend that would have as great an impact on humankind as did the work of Karl Marx.

> If humankind evolved by Darwinian natural selection, genetic chance and environmental necessity, not God, made the species. Deity can still be sought in the origin of the ultimate units of matter, in quarks and electron shells (Hans Kung was right to ask atheists why there is something instead of nothing) but not in the origin of species. However much we embellish that stark conclusion with metaphor and imagery, it remains the philosophical legacy of the last century of scientific research.
>
> E. O Wilson, *On Human Nature* (1978)

Darwin's theory of natural selection – which, popularly understood, means that humans descended from apes – continues to fuel debate and underline the gulf that exists between knowledge and mythical belief. This disjunction has created an anti-intellectual climate in the late twentieth century that makes progress from the Inquisition seem questionable.

Meanwhile, science proceeds at an extraordinary rate. The work that began with Aristotle's cataloguing of plants and animals according to genus and species was continued with Darwin's publication of *On the Origin of Species by Natural Selection* (1859) and the work by Gregor Mendel (1822–44) and other geneticists to discover the mechanism of inherited characteristics. The explosion of research stimulated by these discoveries – in the fields of biology, chemistry and genetics (and combinations of those subjects) – led to the isolation of DNA as the building blocks of life and, finally, to the work of the Human Genome Project (1990–2003), which mapped the genes that make up the human genome.

The interior voyage

Whereas political ideologies, post-Newtonian physics and biology and genetics deal with the physical world, whether inside us or far out beyond the stars, psychology – the last important strand of modern thought – is concerned with our interior existence, our thoughts and emotions, and our behaviour. The history of Western thought, as far as it involves metaphysics, ethics, aesthetics (and even logic, on occasion), is marked by various attempts to understand human psychology. Philosophers have been fascinated and confounded by the part of us they cannot see, whether it is called mind, soul, psyche or self.

The idealist tradition in philosophy involves psychology at every turn, for the mind plays some role in the constitution of the world beyond the subject; it is equally important to empiricism, where the mind is the recipient of sense impressions. The most dramatic contribution to psychology in the twentieth century was the elaboration by Sigmund Freud (1856–1939) of the role of the unconscious in human behaviour. Freud created a map – a topographical description – of the human mind that has three parts: id, ego and superego. This identification of the 'seats' of various human behaviours was instrumental in his development of psychoanalysis, a type of treatment for neuroses and other conditions in which the patient relates his thoughts to the therapist in a voyage of discovery, uncovering the hidden mechanisms of repression in an effort at self-understanding.

> Obviously one must hold oneself responsible for the evil impulses of one's dreams. In what other way can one deal with them? Unless the content of the dream rightly understood is inspired by alien spirits, it is part of my own being.
>
> Sigmund Freud, *The Interpretation of Dreams*
> (1925 edition, trans. James Strachey)

Whatever the scientific standing of psychoanalysis, it has done as much as Marxism to fuel philosophical investigation, particularly in France. Psychoanalysis and Marxism have been the engines for much philosophy and philosophical thinking in the twentieth and twenty-first centuries, because, while they both have a technical content, they are relatively easily grasped by a broad range of readers, and philosophers have used them as tools for framing and answering philosophical questions. Freudianism and Marxism were also vital forces in the development of critical theory and deconstruction, and they give theoretical coherence to the explication of texts, whether they be literary, artistic or political.

By contrast, biology, genetics and physics require the sort of rigorous and disciplined training that usually puts students on a strictly technical career path: it is a simple economic fact. (Its highly technical nature also guarantees a limited audience.) However, the work of those scientists is highly relevant for philosophers, since it gives rise to questions that philosophers are uniquely qualified to phrase and to answer. The single most important question that psychology raises for philosophers is a fundamental one that has been with us from the time immemorial: is the mind merely a bundle of nerves and vessels charged with electricity and driven by complex chemicals? Or is it something else, the final mystery, the invisible, indivisible, undefinable essence of humanity?

The first philosophers struggled with problems of knowledge versus belief. Today, philosophy and science understand two incontrovertible facts about our world: (1) rather than having been created by God in six days, humans are descended from other mammals, and (2) the universe is 13.75 billion years old, not 6,000. We know the first fact from the fossil record, and the second because a satellite has measured fluctuations in the cosmic microwave background – heat remaining from the Big Bang. These are extraordinary advances. Both Copernicus and Darwin suffered censure from the Church because of their discoveries. Yet both men were Christians and they did not consider their newfound knowledge a threat to their faith; it informed their faith. Today, the leading exponents of evolutionary theory and the Big Bang theory – E. O. Wilson (*b.* 1929) and Stephen Hawking (*b.* 1942) – are atheists. Is religious belief possible in an age of knowledge? Writing in 1931 Albert Einstein, echoing Socrates' view that philosophy is born of wonder, cited the mysterious as being at once the goal of philosophy of science and the most beautiful experience available to humankind.

> The most beautiful experience we can have is the mysterious. It is the fundamental emotion that stands at the cradle of true art and true science. Whoever does not know it and can no longer wonder, no longer marvel, is as good as dead, and his eyes are dimmed. It was the experience of mystery – even if mixed with fear – that engendered religion. A knowledge of the existence of something we cannot penetrate, our perceptions of the profoundest reason and the most radiant beauty, which only in their most primitive forms are accessible to our minds: it is this knowledge and this emotion that constitute true religiosity. In this sense, and only this sense, I am a deeply religious man . . . I am satisfied with the mystery of life's eternity and with a knowledge, a sense, of the marvellous structure of existence – as well as the humble attempt to understand even a tiny portion of the Reason that manifests itself in nature.
>
> Albert Einstein, *The World As I See It* (1931)

1

Immanuel Kant

22 April 1724 – 12 February 1804

German philosopher who is the *central figure in modern thought;
his critical philosophy synthesized religious belief and human
autonomy and influenced all areas of philosophical investigation, from mathematics to aesthetics.*

During the academic year 1927–8 the English mathematician and philosopher Alfred North Whitehead (1861–1947) gave the prestigious Gifford
Lectures at Edinburgh University under the title *Process and Reality*.
In those lectures he famously declared: 'The safest general characterization of the European philosophical tradition is that it consists of a
series of footnotes to Plato.' A more accurate characterization of *modern*
European philosophy might be that it consists of a series of footnotes
to Kant. There is no area of modern philosophy – from mathematical
logic to phenomenology – that Kant does not touch. All who follow
in his footsteps must, at some turn in their careers, define themselves
as for or against Kantian positions. Modern thought begins with Kant.
If Plato introduced the eternal themes of philosophical inquiry and
Aristotle (384–322 BC) devised the first philosophical system, Kant
built the most comprehensive and detailed system of philosophy since

the scientific revolution. His work poses questions that continue to grip the imaginations of philosophers today. His influence is felt in every area of philosophy and spills over into other disciplines as diverse as law and astronomy.

Man's coming of age

In 1784 Kant addressed the issue of God and post-Enlightenment man in his essay 'An Answer to the Question: What is Enlightenment?' In it he asked, what is the present role of church and state authority in relation to individual freedom; what role should religious and secular authorities play in the lives of citizens? In his reply, Kant gave a succinct summary of his highly complex and systematic philosophy, which is ultimately concerned with the question of human freedom: 'Enlightenment is man's emergence from his self-imposed immaturity. Immaturity is the inability to use one's understanding without guidance from another. This immaturity is self-imposed when its cause lies not in lack of understanding, but in lack of resolve and courage to use it without guidance from another.' He went on to summarize his entire philosophy of knowledge and freedom thus: 'Laziness and cowardice are the reasons why such a large proportion of men, even when nature has long emancipated them from alien guidance, nevertheless gladly remain immature for life. For the same reasons, it is all too easy for others to set themselves up as their guardians.'

Knowledge and freedom

The problems of knowledge and freedom go hand in hand for Kant. They also raised the most profound philosophical questions for him:

if, through knowledge, we discover rules or laws that govern the natural world, how can man be free – are man's actions not governed by the rules of cause and effect? Might they even be predetermined? In working through these questions, Kant published three major treatises: the *Critique of Pure Reason* (1781; he made important revisions for the second edition of 1787), *Critique of Practical Reason* (1788) and *Critique of Judgement* (1790).

In his *Critique of Pure Reason* Kant attempts to provide a foundation for the laws of science, while at the same time establishing the human subject as a rational agent characterized by free will. In the *Critique of Practical Reason* he argues that man's free will, though it can be proven theoretically, only *actually* follows from our own consciousness of it emanating from within ourselves. It is our consciousness that binds us to moral law, and our knowledge of moral law is not imposed from outside by God or any other agent. In the *Critique of Judgement* Kant concerns himself with aesthetic judgements and teleological questions, such as 'What is the purpose of natural organisms or systems?' In doing so, he leaves the door open for theological and ethical inquiry. For instance, what role does God play in the world?

Any one of these three treatises would be considered a lifetime's achievement for a philosopher, but Kant published many more titles, ranging from early treatises on the natural sciences (particularly astronomy) to works on the philosophy of history and aesthetics.

Kant's 'Copernican turn'

Kant was born in modest circumstances in Königsberg, East Prussia, but nevertheless had a very good education prior to entering the university there at the age of sixteen. By then Kant had absorbed the key texts of Greek philosophy, as well as Latin history and poetry for amusement. His was a strict Pietist* upbringing, and while the central element of his philosophical legacy was to make man the centre of our world, he still reserved a place for God in man's world.

Kant's contribution to Western thought was the philosophical equivalent of Nicolaus Copernicus's demonstration that the sun, not the Earth, is the centre of our solar system. Kant's assertion that man was the maker of his world was as shocking to his contemporaries as the heliocentric theory was to Copernicus's, and it is often referred to as his 'Copernican turn'. In the *Critique of Pure Reason* Kant argued that space, time and causal relations have no existence apart from our minds which perceive them.

Kant's insistence on the role of man in making his own world and on self-reliance rather than the consolations of religion may be a response to the early deaths of his mother (when he was thirteen) and his father (when he was twenty-two). Kant's mother Regina had encouraged his curiosity, exploring the world on long walks with him and explaining things to the best of her ability. Kant told his student and friend Reinhold Bernhard Jachmann (1767–1843): 'I will never forget my mother, for she implanted and nurtured in me the first germ of goodness; she opened my heart to the impressions of nature; she awakened and furthered my concepts, and her doctrines have had a continual and beneficial influence in my life'. Perhaps Kant's belief in man as the maker of his world and his sense of self-reliance encouraged in him the

---

* A Reformist movement within the Lutheran church, Pietism stressed individual religious devotion, and in his book on Kant the English philosopher Roger Scruton (*b*. 1944) has argued that Pietism's 'vision of the sovereignty of conscience exercised a lasting influence on Kant's moral thinking'.

quality of persistence. He constantly modified and updated his thinking, so that each of the three *Critiques* is a further development of his thought.

After graduating from the University of Königsberg, where he studied philosophy and physics, Kant worked as a private tutor. He did not obtain a university teaching post until he was thirty-one, and then taught an astonishing range and number of courses, including mineralogy, anthropology, moral philosophy, natural law, geography, natural theology, logic, pedagogy, mathematics, physics and metaphysics. He only did this because he was in straightened circumstances and needed the money: under the system that then prevailed, university teachers were paid by the number of students that subscribed to their lectures. He was only appointed to a professorship (in logic and metaphysics) in 1770, when he was forty-one.

War and poverty

In the early 1760s Königsberg was under Russian occupation during the Seven Years' War. Life was tough economically and to make ends meet Kant took on a second job as a sub-librarian of the natural history collection in the Royal Library. He also took in lodgers and was forced to sell books from his library to make ends meet. But as the world changed around him, Kant remained a man of habit and reliability. His schedule of daily walks, said the poet Heinrich Heine (1797–1856), was so reliable that the residents of Königsberg set their clocks by him.

The transcendental ego

Despite the fact that Kant included in the second edition of *The Critique of Pure Reason* (1787) a chapter entitled 'The Refutation of Idealism', the central concept of his philosophy remains the doctrine of transcendental idealism. By this Kant does not mean idealism in the sense of George Berkeley (1685–1753), who did not believe that matter exists – Berkeley's theory was famously criticized by Samuel Johnson (1709–84), who kicked a stone and exclaimed: 'I refute it thus!' Nor does Kant follow René Descartes' (1596–1650) brand of problematic idealism, which argues that the only existence we can prove by immediate experience is our own.

Kant argues that the transcendental ego (his concept of the human self) imposes categories upon sense impressions and thus constructs knowledge of them. He summarized this position in his last work, the *Opus Postumum* (1804), by saying that man 'creates the elements of knowledge of the world himself, *a priori*, from which he, as, at the same time, an inhabitant of the world, constructs a world-vision in the idea'. What this means, in essence, is that the elements of knowledge, the categories by which we understand the world, exist *a priori*, which is to say, without reference to experience. *A priori* knowledge is *in* us, as a given. So, Kant argues in the *Critique of Pure Reason*, 'We are perfectly justified in maintaining that only what is within ourselves can be immediately and directly perceived, and that only my own existence can be the object of a mere perception.'

As a consequence of this, 'the existence of a real object outside me can never be given immediately and directly in perception, but can only be added in thought to the perception, which is a modification of the internal sense, and thus inferred as its external cause.' Kant argues that we never actually perceive external things, but only infer their existence, although external objects are the proximate cause of the inference of their existence. So, Kant's transcendental idealism differs from that of Berkeley or Descartes. It is also, Kant reminds his critics, not an absurd, contrarian worldview. 'It must not be supposed,' he writes in the *Critique of Pure Reason*, 'that an idealist is someone who denies the existence of external objects of the senses; all he does is to deny that they are known by immediate and direct perception.'

Categorical imperative

Kant's concern with questions of knowledge and freedom naturally led him to ethics and the ultimate question: 'What is the right thing to do?' Kant rejected the utilitarian ethics of Jeremy Bentham and John Stuart Mill, which hold that actions resulting in the greatest amount of happiness (Bentham's 'hedonistic calculus') for the largest number of people are good actions. In his *Groundwork of the Metaphysics of Morals* (1785) Kant argued against utilitarianism by proposing that if we allow our behaviour to be governed by utilitarian motives, then we might value other people in the light of what 'good' they can be used for – that is to say, treating them as means to an end, rather than ends in themselves. He also objected to the doctrine of moral absolutism, which holds that there are absolute standards of conduct resulting in 'right' and 'wrong' behaviour, regardless of context. Kant's reply to utilitarianism and moral absolutism was to develop the categorical imperative, a rule by which man should act ethically: 'Act only according to that maxim whereby you can at the same time will that it should become a universal law.' The categorical imperative is well illustrated by the famous 'is/ought' distinction in ethics. For Kant, our ethical behaviour ('ought') should not necessarily follow from a particular state of affairs ('is'). Our sense of ethical duty should never include what is impossible for us to do; in this way, 'ought' implies 'can'. Kant's deontological ethics are a can-do affair: if I *ought* to do such-and-such, then it is logically possible for me to do it; and therefore, I *can* do it.

Kant as scientist

If Kant had never written his three great treatises, nor any of his other important works, such as the 'Prolegomena to any Future Metaphysics' (1783), *Metaphysical Foundations of Natural Science* (1786) or *Metaphysics of Morals* (1797), he would have found a place in the history of science for his development of the Kant-Laplace theory to describe the formation of the universe. One only mentions this to make the point that Kant's influence is to be felt *everywhere* in modern thought. In his *Universal Natural History and Theory of Heaven* (1755) he theorized that our solar system formed as a result of a rotating nebula, whose gravitational force compressed it into a spinning disk, throwing off the Sun and the planets. Kant's theory was largely ignored in his lifetime. Then in 1796 the French astronomer and mathematician Pierre-Simon Laplace (1749–1827) developed a similar theory, quite independently of Kant's work. Later scientists, noticing Kant's precedent, called it the Kant-Laplace hypothesis. It is the basis for the generally accepted nebular hypothesis that scientists use today to explain the formation of the solar system. In the *Critique of Practical Reason* Kant said: 'Two things fill the mind with ever new and increasing admiration and awe, the more often and steadily we reflect upon them: the starry heavens above me and the moral law within me.' These words are carved on his tombstone.

Kant's legacy

Kant represents the culmination, the perfection, of the Enlightenment. In Kant all traces of religious, medieval thinking are cast aside and man is placed at the forefront of his own situation. His freedom extends from his perception of himself as an autonomous agent; and from this understanding flows his role as a political actor and ethical being. With his theory of transcendental idealism Kant demonstrated how man *makes* his world; how knowledge and experience do not exist apart from him, but by and through him. His importance and influence cannot be overestimated.

> Experience is without doubt the first product that our understanding brings forth . . . Nevertheless it is far from the only field to which our understanding can be restricted. It tells us, to be sure, what is, but never that it must necessarily be thus and not otherwise. For that very reason it gives us no true universality, and reason, which is so desirous of this kind of cognitions, is more stimulated than satisfied by it. Now such universal cognitions, which at the same time have the character of inner necessity, must be clear and certain for themselves, independently of experience, hence one calls them *a priori* cognitions: whereas that which is merely borrowed from experience is, as it is put, cognized only a posteriori, or empirically.
>
> Immanuel Kant, *Critique of Pure Reason* (1781/1787)
> (trans. Paul Guyer, 1998)

Ancient philosophy adopted an entirely inappropriate stand-point towards the human being in the world, for it made it into a machine in it, which as such had to be entirely dependent on the world or on external things and circumstances; it thus made the human being into an all but merely passive part of the world. Now the critique of reason has appeared and determined the human being to a thoroughly active place in the world. The human being itself is the original creator of all its representations and concepts and ought to be the sole author of all its actions.

Immanuel Kant, *The Conflict of the Faculties* (1798), trans.

Mary J. Gregor, 1992

2

John Stuart Mill

20 May 1806 – 8 May 1873

British philosopher who defined nineteenth-century British empiricism's application of utilitarian principles to political, economic and social questions.

John Stuart Mill was an advocate of utilitarianism, the doctrine developed by Jeremy Bentham (1748–1832) that the greatest good for the greatest number of people should be the guiding force in ethics and government. Mill's utilitarianism differed from that of Bentham, who stressed the *quantity* of pleasure as a measure of social justice; instead Mill emphasized the *quality* of happiness as a better index. (His position came to be known as the 'greatest happiness principle'.) Mill's *A System of Logic* (1843) dominated the period between Immanuel Kant and Gottlob Frege. His logic formed the basis for a theory of how the laws of science are discovered, a position that was promoted (but not acknowledged) by Karl Popper (1902–94). He also prefigured T. S. Kuhn's (1922–96) view that science proceeds by a series of revolutions or ruptures that shift prevailing paradigms. Mill's enduring contributions to political discourse are his classical liberal defence of individual freedom in *On Liberty* (1859) and of women's rights in *The Subjection of Women* (1869).

Nervous breakdown and recovery through poetry

Electing not to study at Oxbridge because he refused to take Holy Orders (as was then required), Mill was educated at home by his father, the Scottish philosopher James Mill (1773–1836), who was Bentham's strongest supporter. Mill's upbringing was exceptionally rigorous, and successful in that it helped produce Britain's most important philosopher of the period; but it was also overly strict and Mill suffered a nervous breakdown when he was twenty, an event he describes in his *Autobiography* (1873). Mill would eventually become godfather to Bertrand Russell (1872–1970), placing him at the epicentre of a British philosophical dynasty.

Mill's influences are various and, for a logician, unusually broad. The poetry of William Wordsworth (1770–1850), with its emphasis on transcendental consciousness, was an aid to recovery from his nervous breakdown. Indeed, Mill's devotion to Wordsworth made him a philosopher with heart; for all his expertise in logic and empiricism, Mill's work shows a deep sympathy with his fellow man. Although Mill and Kant represent different philosophical traditions, Mill's affinity for Wordsworth – whose long poem *The Prelude* (1798–1850) may be regarded as a meditation on Kant's transcendental idealism – indicates a certain predisposition to the *Kantian spirit*.

Mill was also a Francophile, spending much time there (indeed he died and was buried in France at St Véran). He closely followed the work of the father of positivism Auguste Comte (1798–1857), but could not agree with his positions to the extent that Comte wished him to. In Paris Mill was exposed to the early socialist ideas of Henri de Saint-Simon (1760–1825). He also knew the English political economist David Ricardo (1772–1823), who was a close friend of his father's, and he observed Ricardo's thinking as he developed the first systematic economic theory, including the labour theory of value (which states that the values of commodities are measured by the labour cost of their production) – an idea that much influenced Karl Marx. Mill himself made a distinguished contribution to political economy with his own book *The Principles of Political Economy*, which was published in 1848, the year of European revolutions.

A System of Logic

Underlying his popular thought is a corpus of more specialist work in logic, of which *A System of Logic* (1843) is the most important. Mill was a radical empiricist and believed that the truths of logic and mathematics – what he called 'necessary truths' – could be derived from experience and the psychological process of *associationism*.

Associationism is an epistemological doctrine that says the association of ideas or experiences with things or events in memory accounts for our understanding of them. Mill's associationist psychology, which underpinned his system of logic, was inherited from his father, who was the main nineteenth-century exponent of an idea first developed by Plato and Aristotle, and then by the British empiricists John Locke (1632–1704) and David Hume (1711–76). Mill distinguished between connotation ('real' meaning) and denotation (attributive function, which refers to a description such as a *good* book, a *cold* drink). Then Mill broke down propositions into those that are verbal/analytic or real/synthetic, rejecting any appeal to a priori assumptions. For Mill, mathematics could be reduced to generalizations from previous experience.

Mill's politics: liberalism and radicalism

The subject of Mill's *On Liberty* is 'the nature and limits of the power which can be legitimately exercised by society over the individual'. For Mill each individual is sovereign 'over himself, over his own body and mind'. He identified various manifestations of tyranny that threatened individual liberty, including the tyranny of political rulers, social tyranny and the tyranny of the majority. Even where society guards against the tyranny of political rulers, individual liberty can be threatened by social tyranny: 'Society can and does execute its own mandates: and if it issues wrong mandates instead of right, or any mandates at all in things with which it ought not to meddle, it practices a social tyranny more formidable than many kinds of political oppression.' Mill established the view that individuals ought to be free to act as they wish, provided they do no harm to others. A cornerstone of his liberalism was the concept of free speech, of which he was a passionate defender. His views were held to be so fundamental by the authors of the Constitution of the United States (1789) that they form the First Amendment to that document: 'Congress shall make no law respecting an establishment of religion, or prohibiting the free exercise thereof; or abridging the freedom of speech, or of the press; or the right of the people peaceably to assemble, and to petition the Government for a redress of grievances.' A consequence of Mill's free-speech position was his rejection of censorship.

While James Mill was a political radical who advocated universal male suffrage, Mill *fils* went much further and argued – indeed, agitated for – universal female suffrage. Mill was familiar with the work of the feminist and first woman sociologist Harriet Martineau (1802–76), who, apart from her own work as a commentator on politics and social issues, translated the works of Comte into English. For many years Mill enjoyed a friendship with Harriet Taylor (1807–58), whom he married upon her husband's death. Taylor and Mill worked together to develop the ideas that Mill would publish in *The Subjection of Women*. 'With regard to the fitness of women, not only to participate in elections, but themselves to hold offices or practise professions,' he wrote, 'this consideration is not essential to the practical question in dispute: since any woman who succeeds in an open profession proves by that very fact that she is qualified for it.' Mill's ability to imagine and to promote the positions of women, blacks and people of modest origins was partly developed by his cultivation of the sensibilities of poetry that he got from reading Wordsworth and Samuel Taylor Coleridge (1772–1834).

Mill is unique among English philosophers in that he combined themes of the Enlightenment and Romanticism – a tendency that imbues his writing with a concern for others that is best characterised by the term decency. As a Liberal member of parliament Mill exemplified his view that action is the natural articulation of thought. In this way he influenced the American pragmatists, including C. S. Peirce, William James and John Dewey. While his logic and epistemology hold historical interest, Mill's political views and his feminism continue to be relevant today.

Mill's presence in nineteenth-century politics and culture is so powerful, his writings so diverse and detailed, that it can be hard to see his thoughts as a whole. Yet there is a very strong unifying theme: it is his lifelong effort to weave together the insights of the Enlightenment in which he had been reared, and the nineteenth-century reaction against it, a reaction sometimes romantic, sometimes historical and conservative, and often both.

John Skorupski, *Why Read Mill Today?* (2006)

As it is useful that while mankind are imperfect there should be different opinions, so is it that there should be different experiments of living; that free scope should be given to varieties of character, short of injury to others; and that the worth of different modes of life should be proved practically, when any one thinks fit to try them. It is desirable, in short, that in things which do not primarily concern others, individuality should assert itself. Where, not the person's own character, but the traditions or customs of other people are the rule of conduct, there is wanting one of the principal ingredients of human happiness, and quite the chief ingredient of individual and social progress.

J. S. Mill, On Liberty (1859)

3

Johann Gottlieb Fichte

19 May 1762 – 27 January 1814

Developed German idealism after Kant, and was often cited by German nationalists as a forecaster of that country's destiny in the nineteenth and twentieth centuries.

In 1792 Fichte published his first work, *Attempt at a Critique of All Revelation*. He was aided by Immanuel Kant, whose support – financial and otherwise – he had sought. The work was anonymous and was put out by Kant's publishers after an introduction by him. In one of the most successful stunts in the history of philosophy, Fichte allowed it to appear that the *Attempt* was in fact the work of Kant. When Kant loudly and publicly distanced himself from Fichte's work, it drew even more attention, guaranteeing Fichte's fame. He argued that revealed religion is a critical element in the education of man, regarding God, not man, as fixing the moral order of the world. He was closely associated with Friedrich Schlegel and the German Romantics who regarded him as a major influence. Of Fichte, Schlegel remarked in his 'Fragment No. 216' (1798), 'The three greatest tendencies of the age are the French Revolution, Fichte's *Wissenschaftslehre* [see p.135] and Goethe's *Wilhelm Meister.*'

Fichte used Kant's transcendental idealism as groundwork for a philosophy that made the subject – the 'I' – supreme. He further developed the Kantian idea of freedom and attempted to identify a unity of knowing and doing that he claimed was the foundation of all branches of philosophy. He is also famous for supporting the French Revolution (1789–99); but when Napoleon invaded Austria, Fichte wrote a series of fiercely nationalistic essays that identify race as a key component of being German.

Fichte and Kant

Fichte was a child prodigy born into modest circumstances in Saxony. He attracted the interest of a clergyman who became his benefactor after learning that Fichte could recite from memory an entire sermon after hearing it once. Fichte was sent to the famous boarding school at Pforta, where Friedrich Nietzsche (1844–1900) would later be a pupil. Though Fichte attended the Universities of Jena and of Leipzig, the death of his benefactor left him without funds and he did not take a degree. Fichte worked unhappily as a tutor teaching Kantian philosophy, but two years after the publication of his *Attempt* he was appointed to the Chair of Critical Philosophy at Jena.

In Kant's transcendental idealism there is a world outside the subject that includes 'things in themselves' (*noumena*), in addition to things as they appear to us in our experience (*phenomena*). For Fichte this isn't so. Consciousness isn't grounded in the world of things outside itself, but rather in its own consciousness of itself. It is from this situation that all understanding arises. Fichte began to elaborate his system in the ambitiously titled *Foundations of the Entire Science of Knowledge.* (1794/5, 2nd ed. 1802). This was the first of several works in which

Fichte would develop the notion of *Wissenschaftslehre*, variously understood as his doctrine of science or theory of knowledge, in which all philosophy is grounded in radical subjectivity. Fichte attempted to systematize idealism, making all knowledge dependent upon consciousness of what he called the absolute ego – his concept of God. From the absolute ego our individual – or historical – empirical egos emerge. The goal of *Wissenschaftslehre* is to discover the individual ego from its source in the absolute ego.

German nationalism

While Fichte may be regarded as a difficult and highly technical philosopher he was, at the same time, a popularizer of ideas and an accomplished orator. He paid close attention to the French Revolution, which he supported until Napoleon's occupation of Prussia in 1806. This prompted his series of 'Addresses to the German People', which were enormously influential in developing a growing sense of German national identity. In defining a good German, Fichte began by saying what a good German isn't: a Jew, for instance. In his address 'Contribution towards Correcting the Public's Judgement of the French Revolution' (1793), Fichte referred to Jews as a 'state within a state', a view whose history Hannah Arendt traced in *The Origins of Totalitarianism* (1951). By describing Jews as a 'state within a state' Fichte fed the idea that Jews are unreliable at best and disloyal at worst. He said that the only conditions that would be acceptable for giving Jews civil rights would be 'to cut off all their heads in one night, and to set new ones on their shoulders, which should contain not a single Jewish idea'.

Martin Heidegger's sense of Germany's historical purpose was influenced by Fichte. Heidegger believed that the German people were special because, like the ancient Greeks, they shared a primordial language: German was the basis of a culture defined by poets like Johann Christian Friedrich Hölderlin (1770–1843) and philosophers of destiny like Friedrich Nietzsche. In his 'Thirteenth Address to the German Nation' (1806) Fichte argued that the natural boundaries of states are linguistic rather than geographical: 'Those who speak the same language are joined to each other by a multitude of invisible bonds by nature herself, long before any human art begins.' The nation, made up of people bound by a common language, must be kept whole and pure. 'Such a whole, if it wishes to absorb and mingle with itself any other people of different descent and language, cannot do so without itself becoming confused.' The German nation is blessed, in Fichte's view, by being separated from others by 'a common language and a common way of thinking', as well as by geography ('sharply enough severed from the other peoples – in the middle of Europe, as a wall to divide races not akin'). Race, language and culture are identified and gathered together by Fichte as key elements of German nationalism, which would play a role in fostering an extreme sense of German nationalism after that nation's defeat in the First World War, and provide a rallying point for the Nazis during their rise to power.

Schelling: overcoming the 'I'

After Fichte, Friedrich Wilhelm Joseph von Schelling (1775–1854) is the philosopher who continues to develop Kantian idealism until its primacy is challenged by Hegel. Schelling's purpose, as outlined in his *System of Transcendental Idealism* (1800), was to create a philosophy of nature from which he would deduce an objective system of reason. He thought nature to be the 'I' (mind) in the process of becoming. In his late work Schelling developed a theology in which ideas emanate from God, while man's quest is defined as breaking loose from God and then returning to him. These ideas reappear in the work of Arthur Schopenhauer and influenced Friedrich Nietzsche. Schelling's *Philosophical Inquiries into the Essence of Human Freedom* (1809) had an enormous impact on Martin Heidegger; the existentialist theologian Paul Tillich (1886–1965) was also deeply influenced by Schelling.

Like his contemporary Johann Wolfgang von Goethe (1749–1832) he was against all forms of reductionism or attempts to portray and understand the world by mechanical or quantitative means. Rather, reason is seen as an infinite determination of the conscious by the unconscious. Everything proceeds towards the Absolute, which is realized in art. In this, both Fichte and Schelling set the stage for Hegel.

Our task is to *discover* the primordial, absolutely unconditioned first principle of all human knowledge. This can be neither *proved* nor *defined*, if it is to be an absolutely primary principle. It is intended to express that Act which does not and cannot appear among the empirical states of our consciousness, but rather lies at the basis of all consciousness and alone makes it possible. In describing this Act, there is less risk that anyone will perhaps thereby *fail* to think what he should – the nature of our mind has already taken care of that – than that he will thereby think what he should not. This makes it necessary to *reflect* on what one might at first sight take it to be, and to *abstract* from everything that does not really belong to it.

Johann Gottlieb Fichte, *The Science of Knowledge* (1792)

(trans. Peter Heath and John Lachs, 1970)

There is nothing more common regarding philosophy lectures than to hear complaints about their unintelligibility . . . where the subject is *in itself* unintelligible and muddled, the highest art of oratory would still be incapable of making it intelligible.

F. W. J. Schelling, 'On the Academic Study of Philosophy' (1842)

4

G. W. F. Hegel

27 August 1770 – 14 November 1831

The greatest system builder in philosophy, whose work marked the climax of German idealism and had a great influence on Karl Marx.

Georg Wilhelm Friedrich Hegel was the last in the line of great German idealist philosophers that included Fichte and Schelling. His goal was to create a system to explain everything. By everything he really did mean *everything*: from solar systems to microbes, from God to man. Hegel tried for a unified system of understanding in which reason would replace faith – the ultimate Enlightenment effort. His quest was that of the first philosophers when they turned away from mythical belief and applied their reasoning powers to the universe. More than any other philosopher since Aristotle (384–322 BC), Hegel stressed the importance of dialectical reasoning. Karl Marx claimed to be a Hegelian, although he rejected Hegel's idealism. Marx 'stood Hegel on his head' and used his thought to make a materialistic philosophy that would be developed into *dialectical materialism*. One of the main challenges in getting to grips with Hegel is that he is very difficult to read. His prose is dense, his books are long. In *A History of Western Philosophy* (1945)

Bertrand Russell, whose German was very good, said of Hegel: 'he is, I should say, the hardest to understand of all the great philosophers'.

Key works in the Hegelian oeuvre are: *The Phenomenology of Spirit* (1807), *The Science of Logic* (1812–17), *Encyclopedia of the Philosophical Sciences* (1817) and *Elements of the Philosophy of Right* (1820) in which he progressively outlines a philosophical programme that begins with an understanding of individual consciousness and proceeds to a description of how individuals form groups, and what are the duties and responsibilities of individuals and the state. Hegel himself changed the way man was to be understood in relation to himself, to others and to history. But through his influence on Marx, Hegel also had an enormous influence on the practical politics of the nineteenth and twentieth centuries.

Hegel was the dominant influence in British philosophy before Bertrand Russell and G. E. Moore (1873–58) turned against idealism and embraced the *logicism* of Gottlob Frege (1848–1925) and the *logical atomism* of Ludwig Wittgenstein. He was the force behind British idealism – a somewhat misleading term since many philosophers in British universities were followers of Hegel in one guise or another; so it would be more accurate to say that, during the second half of the nineteenth century, British philosophy was Hegelian as much as it was empirical. The most important British idealist was F. H. Bradley (1846–1924), whose *Appearance and Reality* (1893) was the subject of the poet T. S. Eliot's (1888–1965) doctoral dissertation at Harvard.

Hegelian historicism

Born into a bourgeois household in Stuttgart, Hegel thought he was destined for the clergy; but at the Protestant seminary attached to the

University of Tübingen he made two close friends with whom he would turn towards other interests: the poet Friedrich Hölderlin (1770–1843) and the philosopher Schelling. All three were enthusiastic followers of the French Revolution (1789–99). They were hungry for change. The way to a new understanding, according to Hölderlin and Schelling, was through studying the work of Immanuel Kant and his doctrine of transcendental idealism, which Hegel was initially reluctant to do.

The three young thinkers were key members of the movement that came to be known as German Romanticism. Like all 'schools' that contain a large number of major talents across numerous disciplines, the definition gets fuzzy fairly quickly. But in general one can note a resistance to mechanistic and rationalist explanations of the world, a sense of the importance of the perceiving subject (promoted by Kant's transcendental idealism) and, in Germany, a nationalistic pride in the German language and people (*das Volk*).

Hegel earned his qualification in theology and went to work from 1793 to 1796 as the private tutor to a wealthy family in Bern. During his Swiss period, Hegel was concerned with two things: Christianity and history. There, in 1795, he wrote 'The Life of Jesus' and *The Positivity of the Christian Religion*. After a disagreement with his employer Hegel moved to Frankfurt to take up another tutoring post. He stayed there from 1797 to 1801, renewing his friendship with Hölderlin and writing further essays on Christianity. Hegel was attracted to the humanity of Christ and the mystery of his divinity through God the Father. While Hegel would ultimately refer to an absolute 'Spirit' rather than God, he would attribute to Spirit a teleological purpose. Here in these early writings on Christianity one can find the roots of Hegel's historicism, which he would develop more fully in his mature work.

Hegel's philosophy of history

In the last year of his life, in a series of lectures given in 1830–1, Hegel talked about the idea of God and divine purpose guiding history (these lectures would be published after his death as *The Philosophy of History*). He talked of God as 'not a mere abstraction, but a vital principle capable of realising itself'. Moreover, God determines history: 'God governs the world; the actual working of his government – the carrying out of his plan – is the History of the World.' It is the job of philosophy to understand the divine plan; only the results of the preordained plan have what Hegel called 'bona fide reality'. There are no random acts, no accidents, for Hegel. All is planned. 'Before the pure light of this divine Idea – which is no mere Idea – the phantom of a world whose events are an incoherent concourse of fortuitous circumstances, utterly vanishes.'

It is easy to see how Marx refashioned Hegel's philosophy of history to suit his materialistic purposes by simply replacing 'God' with 'class struggle'. The most vocal twentieth-century opponent of Hegelian historicism was Karl Popper, who, in *The Open Society and Its Enemies* (1945), declared Hegel one of three forefathers of totalitarianism, along with Plato and Marx, because, says Popper, Hegel took a deterministic view of history. One can equally argue that Hegel had an optimistic view of history and thought that real progress was possible.

Hegel's method

In *The Phenomenology of Spirit* (*Phänomenologie des Geistes*) Hegel plays on the double meaning of the German word *Geistes*, which can mean 'spirit' or 'mind' (the book has been translated both ways in

English). This work is the first part of Hegel's attempt at a systematic, scientific account of knowledge. Its subtitle – *Science of the Experience of Consciousness* – lets us know that Hegel wants to take the subject of consciousness beyond the purview of metaphysics and fully into the realm of scientific investigation.

In his phenomenology of mind Hegel dismisses the epistemologies of Enlightenment thinkers from René Descartes (1596–1650) to Kant because of their foundationalism (their desire to find a firm base upon which knowledge can be progressively understood). By taking consciousness itself, its objects, and consciousness being conscious of having objects, Hegel opens up a new way of understanding knowledge. It is in this context that his famous dialectical method comes into play. The formulation of the triad *thesis-antithesis-synthesis*, often cited in discussions of Hegel, was actually the work of the German philosopher and Hegelian commentator Heinrich Moritz Chalybäus (1796–1862). This triad describes the motion by which consciousness, as it studies itself, moves progressively forward to new syntheses.

For Hegel the dialectic is a never-ending process, the first mover of thought. But his characterization differed from Chalybäus's in that the terms he used were *abstract-negative-concrete*. This formulation is far more critical than the thesis-antithesis-synthesis, because it allows that all initial theses are flawed. As the *abstract* moves through the *negative* stage of the dialectic it undergoes a process of *mediation*; only then do we arrive at the *concrete*, at which point the whole exercise begins again. Hegel called the motor which drives this process *sublation*.

The key to Hegel's thought is his elaboration of the individual consciousness becoming conscious of itself and its objects, and how each individual consciousness becomes aware of other conscious beings. By being conscious of the other recognizing my consciousness

I become a social being, and this becomes the foundation of all social relations and the precondition for freedom (which may be seen as the main subject of Hegel's thought).

In the *Phenomenology* Hegel introduces the theme of the *master/slave dialectic*. When two people meet there is a struggle between their subjectivities, with one trying to gain ascendancy over the other. Ultimately the master/slave relationship resolves itself because both parties recognize their interdependence. In this parable that Hegel calls 'Lordship and Bondage', he describes how subjectivities, confronting one another, engage in a 'struggle to the death' for ascendancy over the other. But the master can never really gain ascendancy over the slave, upon whom he depends (for services, goods). Equally, the slave eventually sees that he is not a slave, because the fruits of his labour create the world in which he and the master live. In the Hegelian dialectic, these contradictions are sublated in self-consciousness that leads to intersubjectivity and a shared world that is the basis for social organization.

For Hegel the *Phenomenology* was a prelude to *The Science of Logic* (1812–17). Taking Kant's transcendental idealism further, Hegel argued in the *Phenomenology* that what we call reality is so influenced by our perception of it that, ultimately, it *is* mind. Everything in the world can be explained by the underlying order that consciousness makes of reality. This order is logic. The science of logic, for Hegel, is an attempt to understand the underlying structure of the world we make.

Philosophy of right

In *Elements of the Philosophy of Right* (1820) Hegel combined his understanding of consciousness and the logic that organizes our world to address himself to the practical business of law and politics. Hegel believed that law was of primary importance to the organization of a society that would avoid despotism. He viewed human freedom as only realizing itself through participation as a citizen in civic and social life.

Hegel identified three spheres in which 'right' operates: *abstract right*, *morality* and *ethicality*. Abstract right concerns our relations with others, and Hegel outlines the basic principle of 'non-interference' to describe how we should respect the rights of others (and what we expect in return). Morality involves our understanding of our own subjectivity (or 'particularity'), as outlined in the *Phenomenology*, as the basis upon which we can acknowledge the subjectivity of others and therefore respect their rights as if they *were* us. Hegel describes three aspects of the problem of morality: purpose and responsibility; intention and well-being; and 'the good' and conscience. In the third sphere, 'ethicality', Hegel synthesizes the subjective experience of the individual with the progressively larger groups in which he or she exists: the family, civil society, the state. It is a uniquely inclusive survey of how the individual subject relates to the wider world.

Hegel had an enormous influence on the development of British idealism and European philosophy throughout the nineteenth and twentieth centuries. Friedrich Nietzsche developed the theme of *master morality* and *slave morality* in *On the Genealogy of Morals* (1887). Martin Buber's *I and Thou* (1923) owes much to the master/slave dialectic and Simone de Beauvoir made extensive use of it in *The Second Sex* (1949), her survey of woman's position in history. Perhaps the most important elaboration of this theme can be found in the philosophy and psychiatry of the German philosopher Karl Jaspers, who refines the concept of separate, self-conscious subjectivities and their relation to other subjectivities through what he calls the 'loving struggle'. Perhaps because Hegel is so closely associated in the popular mind with his appropriation by Marx, he has suffered the same fate as Marx in the post-Marxist, post-communist world of the twenty-first century. But, just as Marxist analysis will be revived by searchers for a solution to the crisis of late capitalism, so Hegel's ideas about consciousness may offer a palliative to those dissatisfied with overly reductive accounts of who we are and how our social relations are constructed.

The goal, which is Absolute Knowledge or Spirit knowing itself as Spirit, finds its pathway in the recollection of spiritual forms (*Geister*) as they are in themselves and as they accomplish the organization of their spiritual kingdom. Their conservation, looked at from the side of their free existence appearing in the form of contingency, is *History*; looked at from the side of their intellectually comprehended organization, it is the *Science* of the ways in which knowledge appears. Both together, or History (intellectually) comprehended (*begriffen*), form at once the recollection and the Golgotha of Absolute Spirit, the reality, the truth, the certainty of its throne, without which it were lifeless, solitary and alone.

G. W. F. Hegel, *The Phenomenology of Spirit* (1807)
(trans. J. B. Baillie, 1967)

The fact is that interest, whether in the content or in the form of the former metaphysics, or in both together, has been lost. Remarkable as it is if a people has become indifferent, for instance, to its constitutional law, to its convictions, its moral customs and virtues, just as remarkable it is when a people loses its metaphysics — when the spirit engaged with its pure essence no longer has any real presence in its life.

G. W. F. Hegel, *The Science of Logic* (1832)

(trans. George di Giovanni, 2010)

Each pathway into philosophy depends on certain underlying assumptions about what is to be taken as a starting point. But what if we made no such assumptions? Would all of our inquiries then be devoured by sceptical doubts and come to naught? Hegel . . . did not think so. His response — a refreshing and invigorating one — was that it matters little where we start or whether we assume anything; our philosophical journey will inevitably be a prolonged process of self-examination in which thought interrogates itself and remedies its deficiencies as it progresses.

Michael Allen Fox, *The Accessible Hegel* (2005)

5

Auguste Comte

19 January 1798–5 September 1857

French thinker who originated positivism and laid the ground-work for sociology.

Auguste Comte is the originator of a line of thought that rejected the metaphysics of Immanuel Kant, and G. W. F. Hegel, in favour of an approach that excluded from study anything that could not be directly observable. This approach, which became known as positivism, led Comte to develop what he called 'The Law of Three Stages', which argued that man's historical intellectual journey, which ends in positivism (the third stage) begins with the 'Theological State', characterized by belief in Gods, passing through an intermediate 'Metaphysical Stage'. He sought to understand social behaviour through his positivist method, borrowing an evolutionary metaphor from Charles Darwin. His highly original contribution paved the way for Émile Durkheim's creation of sociology as a formal academic discipline, and Max Weber's elaboration of it as a non-empirical methodology which took account of subjectivity in sociological research.

Secretary to Saint-Simon

After being expelled from the École Polytechnique in Paris for participating in a student protest, and then briefly studying medicine at Montpellier, Comte worked as secretary to the socialist Henri de Saint-Simon (1760–1825) from 1817 to 1824. With Saint-Simon, Comte had the opportunity to develop his own thinking and to publish unsigned articles in Saint-Simon's periodical *L'Organisateur*. In 1823 Saint-Simon, who had been acting erratically for some time, attempted suicide by shooting himself six times in the head. This left him blind for the last two years of his life. In 1824 Comte cut off relations with Saint-Simon. Various of Comte's essays had been published under Saint-Simon's name, but he drew the line when Saint-Simon attempted to publish the first part of his *Course of Positive Philosophy* (6 vols, 1830–42) under his own name. (Henceforth, Comte would publicly reject Saint-Simon.)

The pairing of Saint-Simon and Comte was a particularly unhappy one as Comte himself suffered from depression. In 1826 he was treated in an asylum run by the psychiatrist Jean-Étienne Dominique Esquirol (1772–1840), who diagnosed him as suffering from mania; he prescribed cold-water treatments and blood-letting. In 1827 Comte released himself from Esquirol's care and attempted suicide several times, most notably by leaping from the Pont des Arts in Paris.

Law of Three Stages

Comte's Law of Three Stages, outlined in his *Course on Positive Philosophy*, presents an evolutionary idea of man's intellectual development: 'The law is this: that each of our leading conceptions, each branch of our knowledge, passes successively through three different theoretical conditions: the Theological or fictitious; the Metaphysical or abstract; and the Scientific or positive.' The theological stage is broken down into three parts, characterized by *fetishism*, *polytheism* and, finally, *monotheism*. In the Metaphysical or abstract stage of thinking man tries to explain phenomena through 'forces' and 'essences'. This thinking is more sophisticated, but does not give certain, measurable results. It is only in the scientific stage or the positive stage that our understanding of the world is obtained through observation. Comte likened this evolution of European thinking to that of individual human development: childhood (theological stage), youth (metaphysical stage), adulthood (scientific stage).

Comte's second law is known as the Encyclopedic or Epistemological Law. Again, it takes an evolutionary approach, this time to describe the order in which the sciences developed, each laying a foundation for the next. The first is mathematics, from which is derived (in increasing order of complexity) astronomy, physics, chemistry, biology and, finally, sociology (the scientific study of society). The six volumes of Comte's *Course* is just that, an entire course in all of these subjects.

Positivism and sociology

Comte saw positivism as a way to combat the uncertainty that reigned after the French Revolution. Everything had come into question: the institution of the Church, individual belief in God, the monarchy, the state, the role of the people. Sociology would discover the laws behind human social interaction. It would identify how social institutions and groups worked, allowing sociologists not only to understand but to predict what happens in social systems.

Comte's success outside France is due to the translation and abridgement of the six volumes of his *Course* by the English social theorist

Harriet Martineau (1802–76) as *The Positive Philosophy of Auguste Comte* (2 vols, 1853). Martineau was the first female sociologist, and an activist who used a positivist approach to oppose slavery and demand the emancipation of women. In England Comte's work was championed by John Stuart Mill, but only up to a point. Comte continually sought Mill's approval, but Mill could not follow him when he attempted to elevate his positivism to the status of a 'religion of humanity'.

Comte created a positivist calendar that divided the year into thirteen months named after great men like Archimedes and Dante (1265–1321), while the days of the week were named for other men of distinction. (He proposed that leap years had a festival to celebrate the lives of holy women.) Adherents of Comte's religion of humanity built a Chapel of Humanity in France at the end of the nineteenth century, and there are three in Brazil – indeed, the Brazilian flag carries the motto of Comte's positivism: 'Ordem e Progresso' (Order and Progress). Comte's motto was *vivre pour altrui* or live for others; it is the source of the word *altruism* and a fitting epitaph for a thinker whose influence extends into the twenty-first century.

In thus studying the total development of human intelligence in its different spheres of activity, from its firsts and simplest beginning up to our own time, I believe that I have discovered a great fundamental law, to which the mind is subjected by an invariable necessity . . . This law consists in the fact that each of our principal conceptions, each branch of our knowledge, passes in succession through three different theoretical states: the theological or fictitious state, the metaphysical or abstract state, and the scientific or positive state.

Auguste Comte, *Introduction to Positive Philosophy* (1830)
(trans. Frederick Ferré, 1970)

[Comte] maintained that positivism and its principal component, sociology, would profoundly change the way people think. This intellectual revolution would lead to a revival of moral order and then a political transformation that would usher in a new era of consensus.

Mary Pickering, *Auguste Comte: An Intellectual Biography* (1993)

6

Henry David Thoreau

12 July 1817 – 6 May 1862

American transcendentalist who advocated civil disobedience and was an influence on environmentalism.

The enduring influence of Kant's, transcendental idealism is evident in the work of the American philosopher, diarist and essayist Henry David Thoreau. Thoreau is best known for two works: 'Civil Disobedience' (1849) and *Walden, or Life in the Woods* (1854). Thoreau wrote 'Civil Disobedience' after he was imprisoned for refusing to pay a poll tax in protest against the Mexican-American War (1846–8). His essay laid the groundwork for peaceful resistance to government based on conscience, paving the way for civil rights leaders in the twentieth century, such as Mohandas Gandhi (1869–1948) and Martin Luther King (1929–68). *Walden* is the diary of a two-year experiment in self-reliance, when Thoreau withdrew from society and lived alone near Concord, Massachusetts, on woodland owned by his mentor Ralph Waldo Emerson (1803–82). In *Walden* Thoreau reflects on man's place in relation to the state, society, nature and himself.

Transcendentalism

Thoreau was a leading member of the American transcendentalist movement, which had arisen as a response to the intellectualism of the prevailing Unitarian doctrine at Harvard (and more generally in New England society). The American transcendentalists resisted church teaching and argued in favour of an individual intuition that would lead to a state of spiritual transcendence over the physical world. Transcendentalism was an anti-empiricist movement.

One of transcendentalism's founders was Ralph Waldo Emerson. Thoreau's philosophy cannot be understood without reference to Emerson, who toured the Continent in 1832, before seeking out some of the leading British intellectuals of the day, including William Wordsworth, Samuel Taylor Coleridge, John Stuart Mill and the Scottish satirist and essayist Thomas Carlyle. Wordsworth in particular had been imbued with the transcendental idealism of Kant, and his long poem *The Prelude* demonstrated Kantian ideas of how the subject constitutes the world. While Emerson and the American transcendentalists rejected Mill's empiricism, they embraced his theory of justice, with its emphasis on individual resistance to state control, as well as his positions against slavery and in favour of female emancipation. Carlyle introduced Emerson to the work of Johann Wolfgang von Goethe (1749–1832) and encouraged him to pursue transcendental ideals in an age of increasing rationalism and scepticism. Invigorated by his European journey, Emerson returned to the United States where he would perform an important role as Carlyle's literary agent.

Emerson's work is not systematic, but focuses rather on recurrent themes that characterize the American tradition, particularly a focus on the subjects of individualism and freedom. As a transcendentalist

Emerson's theme is the relationship of man and his soul with the natural world – a theme that would be further explored by Thoreau. Emerson's best-known work is the essay 'Self Reliance' (1841), in which he presages Thoreau's Walden experiment: 'There is a time in every man's education when he arrives at the conviction that envy is ignorance; that imitation is suicide; that he must take himself for better for worse as his portion; that though the wide universe is full of good, no kernel of nourishing corn can come to him but through his toil bestowed on that plot of ground which is given him to till.'

At the time Emerson was writing, the United States was in its infancy; in many ways it was still dependent upon Europe for culture. Emerson, and then Thoreau, began to reverse the trend. The most compelling example is Emerson's influence on Friedrich Nietzsche (1844–1900). Here we find a home-grown American philosopher influencing an Old World thinker, who would earn a place in the first division of German thought, and whose work continues to be widely read. Nietzsche's journals record his admiration for Emerson and contain passages from the essays 'History' and 'Self-Reliance', which he copied out from German translations. Scholars have recently discovered more than a hundred direct references to Emerson in Nietzsche's notebooks, and Emerson's influence on Nietzsche's *The Gay Science* (1882) was significant. With Emerson, the United States was no longer just an importer of European culture; it was now an exporter too. Emerson's work is a significant milestone in America's intellectual coming of age.

Walden and methodology

After graduating from Harvard in 1837 Thoreau worked unsuccessfully as a schoolteacher for several years, before taking employment with Emerson as a tutor to his children. He also took on the roles of Emerson's editor, gardener and all-round factotum; Thoreau regarded physical or intellectual work that was well done for oneself or properly rewarded by an employer as a transcendental activity. He prefigured Marx's theory of alienation, in which work loses its value in-itself for the subject and becomes a forced activity that must be done to meet material needs. Indeed, need and necessity are central themes of *Walden*.

Thoreau's experiment in simple living in a forest near the shores of Walden Pond began on 4 July 1845 and lasted for two years and two months. His method is to reduce himself to the position of a subject with no material comforts who must remake his place in nature. In this condition Thoreau rediscovers the basic needs of man: shelter, food and society. He sets out to make these things for himself by building a small house, gathering his own food. He lives mostly alone, but allows himself some company and social intercourse. In reporting his thoughts and actions Thoreau identifies and elaborates upon themes that would become central to twentieth-century philosophy, such as the role of the subject in scientific observation and the nature of man's interaction with the environment. He prefigured late twentieth-century interest in Indian philosophy in the West with his readings of the *Bhagavad-git* (*c.* 1000 BC) and the *Laws of Manu* (*c.* 500 BC), whose influences can be traced in *Walden*.

Thoreau's methods for exploring need and necessity in *Walden* are unique. If Descartes's (1596–1650) *Meditations on First Philosophy* (1641) was a mental reduction, stripping knowledge back to the *cogito ergo sum* ('I think therefore I am'), *Walden* is a mental *and* physical reduction in which Thoreau starts from a savage state and progressively restores human needs. This analysis leads him to a deep scepticism of the state's ability to meet or even to accommodate those essential needs; in fact, the state may prove to be inimical to them. Thoreau's reflections on the role of the individual in relation to the state are an example of how, while his philosophy is forward-looking, it also restores a connection with the past: particularly the works of Plato, specifically *The Republic* (*c.* 380 BC). There is a unique satisfaction in reading Thoreau because of the manner in which his work can be seen to be flowing from the past and into a future that has become our own present. Environmentalism owes a good deal not only to Thoreau's philosophical work, but also to his scientific observations as a naturalist, particularly on seed dispersal and forest regeneration (a particular interest of his after he accidentally started a forest fire that consumed 300 acres).

Civil disobedience

In 1848 Thoreau presented a series of lectures entitled 'The Rights and Duties of the Individual in Relation to Government', the key ideas of which would emerge in his essay 'Resistance to Civil Government' (renamed 'Civil Disobedience' in 1849). 'Civil Disobedience' is a classic defence of conscience that succinctly describes Thoreau's view that a line must be drawn between the duty of the individual and the demands of the state. He regarded the United States' war against Mexico as an attempt to expand slavery, a view that was shared by former US president John Quincy Adams (1767–1848). As a consequence, Thoreau refused to pay a poll tax and was jailed for one night in June 1848 (it appears that an aunt might have paid the tax and secured Thoreau's release from jail, where one imagines he would have preferred to have stayed a little longer).

Martin Luther King cited 'Civil Disobedience' as one of the primary inspirations in his development of the civil rights movement in the United States. The Indian civil rights activist Mohandas Gandhi regarded 'Civil Disobedience' as a key text not only for its irrefutable logic, but because it documented a plan of action as well as a mode of thought, and so set an example of how effectively to confront state power in a peaceful way. The practical aspect of Thoreau's philosophy, in combination with its reflective nature, gives it a whole view of the world without actually being a 'system'.

Between them, Emerson and Thoreau developed the first significant American philosophical style. While transcendentalism may have lost its appeal over the centuries, Americans still find in the work of these two men an expression of ideas upon which their nation is founded: individualism, self-reliance and self-determination.

Government is at best but an expedient; but most governments are usually, and all governments are sometimes, inexpedient. The objections which have been brought against a standing army, and they are many and weighty, and deserve to prevail, may also at last be brought against a standing government. The standing army is only an arm of the standing government. The government itself, which is only the mode which the people have chosen to execute their will, is equally liable to be abused and perverted before the people can act through it. Witness the present Mexican war, the work of comparatively a few individuals using the standing government as their tool; for, in the outset, the people would not have consented to this measure.

Henry David Thoreau, 'Civil Disobedience' (1849)

A hundred years ago Henry David Thoreau was looked upon as a minor disciple of Ralph Waldo Emerson. Fifty years ago he was thought of as an 'also-ran' who was rapidly and deservedly being forgotten. Yet today he is widely rated as one of the giants in the American pantheon and his fame is on an upward rather than a downward curve. It is universally agreed that he speaks more to our day than to his own.

Walter Harding, *The Days of Henry Thoreau:*
A Biography (1965)

7

Ludwig Andreas von Feuerbach

28 July 1804 – 13 September 1872

German philosopher and young Hegelian who broke with his master, and as a radical materialist and critic of religion was a major influence on Karl Marx.

Feuerbach's criticism of religion, formulated in *The Essence of Christianity* (1841), was the most trenchant of any Western philosopher to date. He said that God existed only as a projection of mankind's need. We pervert love by first embodying it in an objectified repository called God, from which it is then returned to our fellow man. In Feuerbach's view this process leads to alienation and it compromises human autonomy. The young Karl Marx was much influenced by Feuerbach, as can been seen from his later portrayal of religion as the 'opium of the people'. Feuerbach challenged the metaphysical attitude of Hegelians who chased a theory of everything; he also rejected the socialist attitude that group action was the answer to social problems. His focus was on the individual and the possibility for intersubjective relations. He occupies an important place in the history of Western thought as a bridge between Hegel and Marx.

From theology to Hegel

Born the son of a diplomat, Feuerbach entered Heidelberg University to study theology with Karl Daub (1765–1836), a protestant whose goal was to reconcile the teaching of theology with philosophy. Feuerbach soon tired of this and expressed a desire to study with Hegel at Berlin, a move of which his father disapproved. Feuerbach went to Berlin anyway, telling his father he was going to study with the great theologian and hermeneuticist Friedrich Schleiermacher (1768–1834), but followed Hegel instead. After a period with Hegel, Feuerbach studied natural science at the Friedrich-Alexander-University. Feuerbach's gradual conversion from theology to anthropology was complete. Man is of central importance to himself, said Feuerbach, and is the source of his own divinity and transcendence. There is no salvation to be found in God or religion. All that exists is rational, sensual humankind. He observed in his self-published collected works: 'Truth, reality and sensation are identical. Only the sensuous being is a true and real being.' (Vol. II, 1844–6).

Feuerbach published several philosophical works in quick succession while a lecturer at Erlangen, but his academic career ended when he was revealed as the author of the anonymously published *Thoughts on Death and Immortality: From the Papers of a Thinker, along with an Appendix of Theological Satirical Epigrams* (1830). In this book Feuerbach argued against the survival of a personal soul after death (for him the individual consciousness returned to a sort of universal group consciousness). He also said that our humanity is our unique quality and that it is not eternal, and his satirical epigrams mocked prominent theologians of the day. The university responded by dismissing Feuerbach; he would not teach again.

Religion demystified

The loss of his position did not immediately trouble Feuerbach, for he made a good marriage to the heiress of a porcelain factory. Freed from the restrictions and proprieties of a university appointment he was able to concentrate on the full formulation of his anthropocentric philosophy. *The Essence of Christianity* (1841), with its focus on man's ability to create himself and his place in the universe, had an immediate and dramatic effect on the intellectual life of Germany. Thirteen years later it was translated into English by the novelist George Eliot (1819–80), where its influence not only on philosophy but on popular thinking was further magnified. Feuerbach was now a must-read for a post-Hegelian public that was beginning to consider a world without God.

The Essence of Christianity starts with a simply stated proposition in the manner of Hegel: 'Man – this is the mystery of religion – objectifies his being and then again makes himself an object to the objectivized image of himself thus converted into a subject.' The importance of this beginning cannot be overstated, because it was the lure that enabled a new generation of thinkers to retain the rational rigour of Hegel's *Phenomenology of Spirit* (1807), while rejecting the metaphysical and Christian orientation of Hegel's philosophy. Using what he called *transformative method*, Feuerbach 'stands Hegel on his head' where religion is concerned (as Marx would 'stand Hegel on his head', replacing idealism with materialism). In Hegel's *Phenomenology of Spirit* it is Absolute Spirit's objectifying of itself that leads to self-knowledge; in Feuerbach's *The Essence of Christianity* the *finite* spirit – temporal, not eternal – objectifies itself in the form of God, then understands that this objectification is actually the realization of its own essential nature.

Feuerbach and Marx

At bottom, religion alienates man from himself: this is what Marx took from Feuerbach when he characterized religion as 'the expression of real distress and the protest against real distress. Religion is the sigh of the oppressed creature, the heart of a heartless world, just as it is the spirit of a spiritless situation. It is the opium of the people' (*Critique of Hegel's Philosophy of Right*, 1843). But Feuerbach, unlike Marx, did not think the time was right for revolution. Marx famously criticized him in his eleven 'Theses on Feuerbach' (1845), the seventh of which states that Feuerbach 'does not see that the "religious sentiment" is itself a social product, and that the abstract individual that he analyses belongs in reality to a particular social form.'

Feuerbach contradicted Marx in the great revolutionary year of 1848, arguing for a form of personal revolution in which individuals take stock of their own consciousness. By acknowledging one's sensuousness and the power of love in interpersonal relations, change on a larger scale would follow. In this Feuerbach offers a prelude to the alternative cultures of the 1960s and, in particular, the thought of Herbert Marcuse (1898–1979), who argued for human emancipation through a Freudian grasp of sexuality and a Marxist understanding of politics.

For all his rejection of God as divine, Feuerbach has had a profound influence on modern theology. His later philosophy focused on I–Thou relations, the recognition of each individual of the other's consciousness, and the common humanity we share. This concept was so important for the Jewish Austrian philosopher Martin Buber that *I and Thou*

(1923) became the title of his most popular work. Buber did believe in God, arguing that God was most easily found in the moment of I–Thou relations.

> Religion is the disuniting of man from himself; he sets God before him as the antithesis of himself: God is not what man is – man is not what God is. God is the infinite, man the finite being; God is perfect, man imperfect; God eternal, man temporal; God almighty, man weak; God holy, man sinful. God and man are extremes: God is the absolutely positive, the sum of all realities; man is the absolutely negative, comprehending all negations.
>
> But in religion man contemplates his own latent nature. Hence it must be shown that this antithesis, this differencing of God and man, with which religion begins, is a differencing of man with his own nature.
>
> Ludwig Feuerbach, *The Essence of Christianity* (1841)
> (trans. Marian Evans (George Eliot), 1854)

> Feuerbach is the first and the greatest of the modern critics of philosophy outside the positivistic tradition. His is a devastating critique of professional and professorial philosophy. Moreover, it is a systematic and thorough one, and not merely rhetorical or aphoristic, like that of Schopenhauer or Nietzsche. Though Feuerbach is easily quoted in his aphoristic asides (e.g., 'My religion is no religion; my philosophy is no philosophy'), what is more striking and more substantive is the detail and the character of his critique of philosophy. It is a historical critique, which gives it range and an extraordinarily rich content.
>
> Marx W. Wartofsky, *Feuerbach* (1977)

8

Charles Darwin

12 February 1809 – 19 April 1882

British naturalist and father of the modern theory of evolution by natural selection.

With the publication of *On the Origin of Species by Natural Selection* (1859) Charles Darwin changed our understanding of our place in the *natural world* more than any other thinker in the past two hundred years. Darwin's theory of evolution is based on his discovery of the process of natural selection, in which organisms better suited to their environment than others produce more offspring, while those less suited to their environment do not survive. The originally random genetic traits of a species change as a result of natural selection, so that those which are beneficial for survival predominate, while others decrease.

Of the three modern thinkers whose work transformed our understanding of the human subject in his *social milieu*, the work of Charles Darwin stands with Karl Marx's explanation of social and economic structures and Sigmund Freud's mapping of the unconscious mind. It is true that Albert Einstein's theory of relativity explained time and matter in a way that changed our understanding of the *physical world*; but the importance of Darwin, Marx and Freud is that they changed the way we understand our *selves*. Darwin's theory of evolution provided a scientific explanation of the origin of species that countered miraculous 'explanations', so bringing science to the attention of many ordinary people for the first time.

In *The Descent of Man* (1871) Darwin traced the origins of the human being through natural selection to show common ancestors with the chimpanzee. The conclusions to be drawn from this shattered more than three millennia of belief that man was created by God in the sense portrayed in the Book of Genesis. If the creation myth was shown to be just that, a myth, then the idea of a natural, teleological movement towards perfection was called into question; and, as a result, many felt that the foundations of Christianity – and belief in God itself – had been destroyed. Additionally, since man was shown to be a mammal (although a superior one), everything about him could now be studied (and possibly explained) scientifically – even zoologically. Areas that previously had belonged to religion or metaphysics – mind, consciousness, moral sensibility – now fell under the purview of scientific enquiry. Darwin's theory posed in the Victorian period (as it does today) the supreme challenge of how to evaluate *knowledge* (science) and *belief* (religion). However, it also posed problems for thinkers who, while respectful of science and reason, feared that an overly reductive approach to the study of man would exclude an appreciation of spiritual, psychological and other existential aspects of man that eluded scientific study.

The voyage of HMS *Beagle*

Darwin was born into wealth. His father Robert Darwin was a wealthy doctor who married Susannah Wedgewood, the daughter of Josiah

Wedgewood, the man responsible for industrializing the manufacture of pottery. The young Darwin was a delicate child and he suffered throughout his life from extremely debilitating bouts of ill health. Ironically, he began his studies as a medical student at Edinburgh, but his constitution was not up to the rigours of the profession and his studies ultimately bored him. He then went to Cambridge, where he took an ordinary degree, devoting much of his time to collecting and studying insects. The combination of an inherited fortune and ill health allowed Darwin to spend most of his life – apart from the long voyage he took aboard HMS *Beagle* – working as a naturalist in the quiet seclusion of his home.

In 1831 Darwin accepted an invitation to join an expedition charting the coast of South America. Darwin's five-year service as a naturalist during the voyage of HMS *Beagle* (1831–6) allowed him to collect the bone and fossil data which, when studied in Cambridge and London after the journey, led him to develop his theory concerning the origin of species. During his journey on the Beagle, Darwin read George Lyell's (1797–1875) *Principles of Geology* (3 vols, 1830–3). Lyell championed the idea of *uniformitarianism*, which holds that the Earth has been shaped over a long period of time by forces which have been in operation since its formation and which are present today (as opposed to *catastrophism*, the idea that the Earth's features are the result of sudden, cataclysmic events). Lyell sharpened Darwin's interest in geology and therefore in fossils. Fossils were important evidence for Darwin because they provided a record of plants and animals distributed across vast distances and over a very long period of time. The uniformitarianist slogan, 'the present is the key to the past', resonated deeply with Darwin, as pieces in the puzzle of how species form began to arrange themselves in his mind.

Descent with modification

The fossil evidence collected during his journey on the *Beagle* gave Darwin the idea of *descent with modification*, suggested by his observation of variations among related species on the Galápagos Islands. The clear timeline evidence afforded by fossils not only showed the progression of life, but also provided evidence of *diversification* of life, as animal and plant forms appeared at specific places and times, and not somewhere else; and of *extinction*, as the record goes quiet. The other element in Darwin's reading of the fossil record was his study of the morphology of plants and animals. By tracing similarities among groups Darwin was able to form the idea of a common ancestor.

Darwin needed an explanation of the actual means by which species evolved. He initially turned to the work of the French naturalist Jean-Baptiste Lamarck (1744–1829), who offered the hypothesis that species *acquired* character traits which promoted their survival and passed them on to future generations. This position, known as *Lamarckism*, argues for the heritability of acquired characteristics. As a scientific explanation, Lamarckism was wanting. What was required was an explanation of the actual mechanism by which characteristics passed from one generation to the next. The answer lay in the new science of genetics.

Genetics

The Austrian monk Gregor Mendel (1822–84), working in relative isolation, had conducted experiments in plant hybridization using peas. He discovered the laws that govern the inheritance of characteristics, laying the foundation for the science of genetics. Mendel's discoveries provided a scientific understanding of how particular traits were passed from one generation to another, ensuring that a particular organism would reach sexual maturity and reproduce, so preserving itself from extinction. Mendel's work was unknown to Darwin, so the next step in the solution of the evolutionary puzzle, including an understanding of the role played by genetic mutation, would have to wait until Mendel's conclusions were independently rediscovered in the 1890s by the Dutch botanist Hugo Marie de Vries (1848–1935) and also by the German botanist Carl Erich Correns (1864–1933).

Work in genetics would dominate the life sciences in the twentieth century, and inform Julian Huxley's (1887–1975) *Evolution: The Modern Synthesis* (1942). Two key moments in genetics are the discovery in 1953 of the double-helix structure of the DNA molecule by James Watson (*b.* 1928) and Francis Crick (1916–2004) and the completion of the entire sequencing of the human genome in the Human Genome Project (1990–2003) started by Watson and completed by the American geneticist Francis Collins (*b.* 1950).

Prior to genuine scientific work in genetics, an oversimplified version of Darwin's theory was often used for political purposes in the late nineteenth and early twentieth centuries. Herbert Spencer (1820–1903) coined the term 'survival of the fittest' after reading *On the Origin of Species* – a phrase much used by imperialists and right-wing theorists to promote *laissez-faire* capitalism and to justify the suppression of groups on the basis of social class and race. In the late nineteenth century the term 'social Darwinism' became popular to justify various applications of the survival of the fittest idea, particularly the perfectibility of the human race through struggle and competition. Darwin's half-cousin Francis Galton (1822–1911) coined the term *eugenics* – the 'improvement' of 'the race', as Galton and other eugenicists would say, by breeding from the 'fittest' (positive eugenics) or sexually sterilizing the 'unfit' (negative eugenics). As a result a number of countries – the United States in particular – compulsorily sterilized the 'unfit' in the first half of the twentieth century. In Germany Hitler's first act after making himself Führer was a 1933 decree ordering the sterilization of Jews, homosexuals and other 'unfit' persons.

Darwin's discoveries set the agenda for the work of leading biologists in the late twentieth and early twenty-first centuries. E. O. Wilson (*b.* 1929) coined the term sociobiology – the 'extension of population biology and evolutionary theory to social organization' – which he outlined in *Sociobiology: The New Synthesis* (1975). Wilson refers to the 'evolutionary epic', signifying that science has supplanted myth in its explanation of the world, but that the explanation nevertheless has a dramatic, epic quality about it. In *The Future of Life* (2002) he notes that most of the species on Earth have yet to be discovered.

Endurance of creationism

Prior to Darwin the dominant explanation of the natural world was creationism, based on the biblical account given in the Book of Genesis: God created the world and everything in it. According to creationism, the world is about 6,000 years old (the earliest fossil is 2.7 billion years old). Religious opposition to Darwin's theory was immediate and continues today, particularly in the United States. In 1925 the theory of evolution found itself on trial in Tennessee *v* Scopes or the Scopes Monkey Trial. High-school biology teacher John Scopes was accused of violating a federal law that prohibited the teaching of evolution. It was a remarkable case because, in effect, *science* was on trial. The ruse backfired on the creationists: the trial received wide publicity and a majority of Americans came down in favour of Scopes and evolution.

One hundred years later the situation is reversed. Creationism has been repackaged as 'creation science' or 'intelligent design' with its proponents arguing that it should be given equal time with evolution in school curricula.

Darwin's disciples

Stephen Jay Gould made one of the most important contributions to our understanding of evolution in 'Punctuated Equilibria' (1972), a paper co-authored with the palaeontologist Niles Eldredge (*b.* 1943). Gould and Eldredge proposed the theory of *punctuated equilibrium*, observing that evolution occurs in fits and starts rather than at a constant rate (gradualism), thereby accounting for the apparent 'gap' in fossil records. Gould's main work is *The Structure of Evolutionary Theory* (2002). He is well known for having led a critical movement against sociobiology for its deterministic view of human behaviour. Richard Dawkins argues in *The Selfish Gene* (1976) that the principal unit of selection is the gene. In *The Blind Watchmaker* (1986) he describes the attempts of creationists to claim 'equal time' with evolutionary theory. He argues for atheism in *The God Delusion* (2006), pointing out that belief in the miraculous is incompatible with science.

Recent polls in the United States show that 87 per cent of people believe in some form of creationism; only 13 per cent 'believe' in evolution with no 'guiding hand of God' in the process. More than any other visionary idea, Darwin's theory of evolution pits science and knowledge against religion and belief. It draws attention to the fact that many people in the twenty-first century subscribe to a pre-scientific belief system that significantly pre-dates the Dark Ages.

There is grandeur in this view of life, with its several powers, having been originally breathed into a few forms or into one; and that, whilst this planet has gone cycling on according to the fixed law of gravity, from so simple a beginning endless forms most beautiful and most wonderful have been, and are being, evolved.

Charles Darwin, *On the Origin of Species by Natural Selection* (1859)

The old argument from design in Nature, as given by Paley, which formerly seemed to me so conclusive, fails, now that the law of natural selection has been discovered. We can no longer argue that, for instance, the beautiful hinge of a bivalve shell must have been made by an intelligent being, like the hinge of a door by man. There seems to be no more design in the variability of organic beings, and in the action of natural selection, than in the course which the wind blows.

Charles Darwin: His Life Told in an Autobiographical Chapter, and in a Selected Series of His Published Letters (1892)

He embraced a terrifying materialism. Only months before he had concluded in his covert notebooks that the human mind, morality and even belief in God were artefacts of the brain . . . Working through the implications gave him migraines, left him writhing on his sick bed, fearing persecution.

Adrian Desmond and James Moore, *Darwin: The Life of a Tormented Evolutionist* (1994)

9

Søren Kierkegaard

5 May 1813 – 11 November 1855

Danish thinker who established key themes of existentialism and argued that truth was to be found in subjective experience of the world, which could not be understood purely by objective methods.

Søren Kierkegaard identified and explored the main themes of existentialism more than a hundred years before the leading figures of that tendency had published a word. The concepts of nothingness, anxiety and dread had all been described by Kierkegaard long before Martin Heidegger (1889–1976) – with scarcely a nod to their source – elaborated them in *Being and Time* (1927). Jean-Paul Sartre's (1905–80) view of man as 'a useless passion', which he describes in *Being and Nothingness* (1945), is also drawn from Kierkegaard.

'Insane' upbringing

Kierkegaard's father was a wealthy, gloomy, guilt-ridden man who so affected the young Kierkegaard that he referred to his upbringing as 'insane'. Kierkegaard initially studied theology in order to please his father, but eventually abandoned it in favour of the life of a *boule-*

vardier. Upon his father's death Kierkegaard took up the formal study of philosophy, earned his degree and became engaged to marry. After a year Kierkegaard broke off his engagement and his anguish over the matter became a driving force behind his early works, three of which were published in 1843: *Either/Or, Fear and Trembling* and *Repetition.* Kierkegaard's output was prodigious, but the works that had the most influence in his lifetime were *Philosophical Fragments* (1844), *The Concept of Anxiety* (1844), *Stages on Life's Way* (1845) and *Concluding Unscientific Postscript* (1846). Two posthumous works continue to have an influence in the twenty-first century: *The Sickness unto Death* (1849) and *Training in Christianity* (1850).

Pseudonyms and indirect communication

After breaking off his engagement Kierkegaard lived a bachelor existence of hard work and deep reflection. However, the gravity of his themes of faith and despair is undercut with a serious playfulness. In many of his works Kierkegaard adopted pseudonyms: Victor Eremita, Johannes de Silentio, Constantin Constantius, Johannes Climacus, Vigilius Haufniensis, Anti-Climacus and H. H. The use of pseudonyms was part of his method of indirect communication, in which Kierkegaard encouraged readers to think for themselves – to discover their own subjectivity, rather than merely to receive the 'truth' as handed down by authority (the 'author'). Rather than proselytize, Kierkegaard uses different personae to offer competing perspectives on a problem, leaving the reader to decide what he thinks.

Subjectivity, paradox and the 'leap to faith'

Kierkegaard is the philosopher of subjectivity. He regards the self as *free to create choices*, to *make* itself. To fail to be conscious of oneself and the possibilities for freedom is to be in a state of despair. Everyone, however, at some time in their lives, falls into despair, which can present the opportunity to *be* oneself. In *The Sickness Unto Death* (1843) Kierkegaard writes: 'Despair is a sickness in the spirit, in the self, and so it may assume a triple form: in despair at not being conscious of having a self (despair improperly so called); in despair at not willing to be oneself; in despair at willing to be oneself.'

Kierkegaard's concept of being and subjectivity allowed him to accept paradox as a foundation of religious faith. Kierkegaard formulated the concept commonly referred to as the 'leap of faith' (although his literal phrase was 'leap *to* faith'). The mysteries of Christianity cannot be explained by reason, Kierkegaard said, and they do not need to be. They exist outside reason. They are *paradoxical*. One must believe, but one cannot prove. One must believe like Abraham, who was prepared to sacrifice his only son at God's command.

Kierkegaard's thinking is in stark contrast to that of Hegel. Hegel proposed a grand logical system of pure reason by which man and his world would be understood objectively, as if from a God-like perspective. Kierkegaard argued that this would never be possible; that the human subject is always situated in the perspective afforded by his body, his location in space, his own consciousness. This rejection of a God-like perspective and the pseudo-objectivity that results from it, along with a tolerance for paradox, greatly influenced the twentieth-century French thinker Maurice Merleau-Ponty — see p. 266 — and these ideas are central to his *Phenomenology of Perception* (1945). Kierkegaard has had an enormous influence on Protestant theology in the twentieth and twenty-first centuries. Martin Buber's 'I–Thou' philosophy owes much to Kierkegaard; so does Rudolf Bultmann's (1884-1976) *demythology*, the position that the only necessity for Christian faith is the fact of the crucified Christ. The enormously influential German-American theologian Paul Tillich (1886–1965) advanced Kierkegaard's concept of 'being' as the key to understanding man's relationship with God.

How barren is my soul and thought, and yet incessantly tormented by vacuous, rapturous and agonizing birth pangs! Is my spirit to be forever tongue-tied? Must I always babble? What I need is a voice as penetrating as the glance of Lynceus, terrifying as the sigh of the giants, persistent as a sound of nature, mocking as a frost-chilled gust of wind, malicious as Echo's callous scorn, with a compass from the deepest bass to the most melting chest-notes, modulating from the whisper of gentle holiness to the violent fury of rage. That is what I need to get air, to give expression to what is on my mind, to stir the bowels of my wrath and of my sympathy. – But my voice is only hoarse like the cry of a gull, or dying away like the blessing upon the lips of the dumb.

What is to come? What does the future hold? I don't know, I have no idea. When from a fixed point a spider plunges down as it its nature, it sees always before it an empty space in which it cannot find a footing however much it flounders. That is how it is with me: always an empty space before me, what drives me on is a result that lies behind me. This life is back-to-front and terrible, unendurable.

Søren Kierkegaard, *Either/Or: A Fragment of Life* (1843)

(trans. Alastair Hannay, 1992)

The difficulties for a reader of Kierkegaard's writings are due in part to the multiplicity of pseudonymous writers who present their own views in a complex dialogue. Avoiding a conclusive system, Kierkegaard lets each pseudonymous writer have his voice . . . The reader is thereby in the position of entering, if he so pleases, into the complex dialogue and putting it all together. The pseudonymity also discourages the diversionary tendency to commit the genetic fallacy of psychologizing and historicizing the works as autobiography and thereby supposedly 'explaining' them. There is also a pedagogical aim in the complexity: 'The task must be made difficult, for only the difficult inspires the noble-hearted' [*Concluding Unscientific Postscript*].

Howard V. and Edna H. Hong,
The Essential Kierkegaard (2000)

10

Karl Marx

5 May 1818 – 14 March 1883

German creator of a methodology that uses politics, philosophy and economics to analyse man's historical situation and develop agendas for change.

Karl Marx is often judged by the activities of those who call themselves Marxists, an error akin to judging Jesus Christ by the actions of those who call themselves Christians. Marx represents a grand conclusion to the idealist tradition descending from Kant and ending in Hegel. Taking his cue from Feuerbach, who criticized Hegel's belief that God is the ultimate truth, Marx dismissed both God and the state as the highest authorities and replaced them with the self-conscious human subject, who, collectively, is both the maker of the state and the creator of his history.

Socialism before Marx

Marx focused the disparate ideas of nineteenth-century socialism into a coherent theory and laid the groundwork for a philosophy of action. His most popular work is *The Communist Manifesto* (1848), co-written with his lifelong collaborator and benefactor Friedrich Engels (1820–95). In *Das Kapital* (1867) Marx offered an analysis of how capitalism works and labour's relation to it; he predicted that collective action would lead to the replacement of capitalism by socialism. Marx's contribution was to fuse the study of politics, philosophy and economics into a method of inquiry that identified the status of man's place in history and gave him the tools not only to analyse his situation, but also to change it.

A bourgeois upbringing

Marx came from a bourgeois background. His parents were Jews living in Trier in the Mosel wine-growing country of Germany and his father was obliged to convert to Lutheranism in order to maintain his position as a lawyer. Marx had found a benefactor in the first Baron von Westphalen and married his daughter Jenny. Despite his father's exhortations to frugality Marx's profligate ways would be a source of money troubles throughout his life. As a result he knew at first hand the effects of poverty: economic want, poor health and infant mortality. On 18 June 1862 he wrote to his friend Engels: 'Every day my wife says she wishes she and the children were safely in their graves, and I really cannot blame her.' Of Marx's seven children, one died at birth, two died before reaching their first birthdays and one died aged eight.

At seventeen Marx went to the University of Bonn to study law, but devoted much of his time there to writing volumes of romantic poems dedicated to Jenny von Westphalen. After a year he went to the University of Berlin, where he joined the Young Hegelians in their critique of Hegel's views on God and the state. In 1841 the Prussian king Frederick William IV (1795–1861) summoned Schelling – see p. 36 – to take over

Hegel's old chair in philosophy with the order that he 'root out the dragon-seed of Hegelianism'. In a great philosophical moment, Marx, Engels, Kierkegaard and Mikhail Alexandrovich Bakunin (1814–76) were present in the same lecture hall in Berlin to hear the first of Schelling's anti-Hegelian lectures. The Prussian king was prescient in his fear of the Young Hegelians: their fervour was a prelude to the socialism of Marx and Engels, and the anarchism of Bakunin.

Collaboration with Engels

Marx and Engels met briefly in 1842 while Marx was editor of the *Rheinische Zeitung*. They met again in Paris in 1844 and thereafter became lifelong collaborators. Engels's father owned shares in a Manchester textile factory where Engels worked, first as a clerk, later as a partner (work that he hated, but undertook to help support Marx). Engels's first book was *The Condition of the Working Class in England in 1844* (1845) in which he described such economic iniquities of capitalism as poverty, child labour and the destruction of the environment. The two were a perfect partnership: Engels had an elegant prose style and Marx a highly original mind and a capacity for deep scholarship. After Marx's death, Engels edited volumes two and three of *Das Kapital*.

Marx was influenced by Hegelian dialectic – the concept of thesis-antithesis-synthesis – but rejected Hegel's idealism, putting the final nail in the coffin of a German philosophical movement that had held sway since Kant. (While he rejected Hegel's conclusions, Marx retained his method, always maintaining that he was a student of Hegel – indeed, that Hegel was his master.) The end of German idealism was signalled by Feuerbach's criticism of Hegel, and Marx declared in 1845 in his 'Theses on Feuerbach' (published in 1888): 'The philosophers have only interpreted the world, in various ways; the point is to change it.'

Socialism and philosophy

While Marx may have quarrelled with philosophers, the attention he paid them throughout his life showed that respect outweighed contempt; though his goal was to change the world through action that was informed by an understanding of first principles and of history (including the thinking that accompanied successively present historical epochs). Marx organized the ideas of the Welsh socialist Robert Owen (1771–1858) and his French counterpart Henri de Saint-Simon (1760–1825) into a coherent programme of thought and action. In *The Communist Manifesto* Marx codified his materialist conception of history (his followers later called it historical materialism) in the claim that 'The history of all hitherto existing society is the history of class struggles.' This short book also included a ten-point plan for the creation of a communist state that included the abolition of private property and the centralization of credit.

Classical origins of Marxism

Marx's doctoral thesis *The Difference Between the Democritean and Epicurean Philosophy of Nature* (1841, published 1902) laid the groundwork for his materialist philosophy by examining the atomism of Epicurus (341–270 BC) and Democritus (460–c. 370 BC). Here Marx argues that a material world exists independently of any human perception of it. He later refined this idea in *Das Kapital*, claiming that 'The ideal is nothing else than the material world reflected by the human mind, and translated into forms of thought.' Marx's famous criticism of religion as 'the opium of the people' is part of a rather more complex analysis of social relations and the need for illusion that appears in his *Critique of Hegel's Philosophy of Right* (1843):

> Man makes religion, religion does not make man. Religion is, indeed, the self-consciousness and self-esteem of man who has either not yet won through to himself, or has already lost himself again. But man is no abstract being squatting outside the world. Man is the world of man – state, society. This state and this society produce religion, which is an inverted consciousness of the world, because they are an inverted world. Religion is the general theory of this world, its encyclopaedic compendium, its logic in popular form, its spiritual *point d'honneur*, its enthusiasm, its moral sanction, its solemn complement, and its universal basis of consolation and justification. It is the fantastic realization of the human essence since the human essence has not acquired any true reality. The struggle against religion is, therefore, indirectly the struggle against that world whose spiritual aroma is religion.
>
> Religious suffering is, at one and the same time, the expression of real suffering and a protest against real suffering. Religion is the sigh of the oppressed creature, the heart of a heartless world and the soul of soulless conditions. It is the opium of the people.

Alienation

Marx described the worker's predicament under capitalism as *alienation*. The object of his labour, the product, is alienated from him (meaning it is not for his use). Additionally, the worker is alienated from himself by his work because it is not part of what Marx called his 'species-life' or 'species-being'. In his *Economic and Philosophic Manuscripts of 1844* (1932) Marx wrote: 'Man is a species-being, not only because in practice and in theory he adopts the species (his own as well as those of other things) as his object, but – and this is only another way of expressing it – also because he treats himself as the actual, living species; because he treats himself as a universal and therefore a free being.' Production takes away the species-life of man, which is his social essence, ultimately alienating him from other men.

Alienation occurs because of the way capitalism is structured. In volume three of *Das Kapital* Marx talks of the 'invisible essence' of capitalism: *surplus value*. When a worker produces goods from raw materials, they acquire a new value that creates profit for the capitalist at the expense of the unpaid labour of the worker: surplus value. Surplus value is the means by which owners accumulate capital. The phenomenon is succinctly described by Marx's biographer David McLellan: 'surplus value was not created by exchange but by the fact that the development of the means of production under capitalism enabled the capitalist to enjoy the use-value of the worker's labour-power and with it to make products that far exceeded the mere exchange-value of labour-power which amounted to no more than what was minimal for the worker's subsistence'.

What is Marxism?

Using the term 'Marxist' is as problematical as using the term 'Christian'. Marxists, like Christians, come in many different flavours, some of which bear no resemblance to the original. Marx's main contribution to thought was a method for analyzing economic, political and historical events.

His method of thinking was dialectical and therefore open-ended. The thesis-antithesis-synthesis process was continuous and not fixed; and while Marx did establish certain core principles (like alienation and surplus value) his work has no finished, cut-and-dried conclusion.

The process by which Marx's thought was fixed as 'Marxism' has much in common with the way the Church fixed Christ's thought as 'Christianity'. Christ's simple command 'love one another' and his teachings in the Gospel of the New Testament are not the same as the rigid decrees that the Catholic Church laid down in the Council of Trent between 1545 and 1563. Similarly, the communist state ideology created from aspects of Marx's thinking by Joseph Stalin (1878–1953) is a rigid and oppressive artefact that Marx would have rejected. There can be no doubt that, had Marx been a twentieth-century Russian, Stalin would have had him shot.

Mao Zedong and Chinese communism

Mao Zedong (1893–1976) adapted Marxism to suit the economic and cultural situation of China. While Europe had become industrialized and its workers mainly factory labourers, China was still an agrarian economy. Marx saw revolution starting with the proletariat, but for Mao it would be the work of peasants. A veteran of the 1911 uprising that overthrew the Qing dynasty, Mao began studying Marxism while he was a library assistant at Beijing University. Combining his modified Marxist ideas with brilliant military strategy that saw off the Nationalists in the civil war (1947–9), Mao established the People's Republic of China in 1949.

Mao expressed his reworking of Marxist philosophy (Maoism) in *Quotations from Chairman Mao Tse-Tung* (1964), a brief collection known in the West as *The Little Red Book*. While Marx advocated a questioning spirit, Mao offered programmatic answers with forbidding chapter titles, such as 'The Correct Handling of Contradictions Among the People' and 'Correcting Mistaken Ideas'. *The Little Red Book* sold 800 million copies, second only to the Bible in book sales. By contrast, Marx and Engels's *The Communist Manifesto* has sold 10 million copies, about the same number as Adolf Hitler's (1889–1945) *Mein Kampf* (1925–6). The appropriation and adaptation of Marxist ideas by Mao and Vladimir Ilyich Lenin resulted in totalitarian regimes that – like the Nazi regime of Adolf Hitler – killed millions of their own citizens.

Marx's Western European legacy

The end of the Second World War left an enormous vacuum in philosophical and economic thinking in universities across Western Europe. It was filled – in France in particular – by Marxist-based theorizing of various kinds. Half of Germany's professors of philosophy had been Nazis and their post-war extirpation from academic life meant that contemporary German philosophy – with the exception of Heidegger and a few others – no longer ruled the discipline as it had since the time of Kant. Most French existentialists were Marxists to begin with, and schools of thought led by Marxists began to flourish throughout Europe.

The Hungarian philosopher and literary critic Georg Lukács (1885–1971) established a tradition known as Western Marxism with the publication of *History and Class Consciousness* (1923), advocating Marx's methods as opposed to the dogmas associated with 'Marxism'. The Italian thinker Antonio Gramsci (1891–1937) further developed Western Marxism with his elaboration of the idea of hegemony, in which capitalism controlled society not only through ownership of the means of production and violence, but also by the more subtle means of a hegemonic culture which made bourgeois values dominant. Benito Mussolini (1883–1945) considered Gramsci such a threat to his fascist regime that he had him imprisoned for twenty years. The prosecutor underlined the state's fear of this intellectual when he proclaimed 'for twenty years we must stop this brain from functioning'. Gramsci was released in ill health after serving eight years and died shortly thereafter. His *Prison Notebooks* (1948, 1951) were published posthumously and continue to be widely read. In France Louis Althusser (1918–90) led a movement called structural Marxism which sought to integrate Marxist method with the structuralism of Claude Lévi-Strauss (1908–2009). Althusser's career came to an end after he strangled his wife in 1980.

Marx was a dominant force in the academic study of philosophy, politics and economics in the twentieth century, and no philosopher can be said to have had a greater impact on world events. The creation of socialist states and communist regimes are a direct result of his thinking and writing. There is no greater event in modern history than the conflict between the Soviet Union and the United States, which dominated geopolitics from the end of the Second World War in 1945 to the fall of the Soviet Union in 1991. For much of the twentieth century the dominant trend in European thinking and to some degree in the United States was Marxist or a variation on it. The rise of American conservatism that began with the presidency of Richard Nixon (1913–94), combined with the demise of the Soviet Union combined to sideline Marx as force in political philosophy and other university disciplines. However, the banking collapse of 2008 in the United States and Europe sent worried economists scurrying back to Marx in search of some explanation for the Great Recession. It is safe to say that, as the crisis of capitalism continues in the twenty-first century, Marx will remain a relevant theorist of its organization and predictor of its fate.

It is not the consciousness of men that determines their being, but, on the contrary, their social being that determines their consciousness.

Karl Marx, *Das Kapital* (1859)

The history of all hitherto existing society is the history of class struggles. Freeman and slave, patrician and plebeian, lord and serf, guild-master and journeyman, in a word, oppressor and oppressed, stood in constant opposition to one another, carried on an unin-terrupted, now hidden, now open fight, a fight that each time ended, either in a revolutionary reconstitution of society at large, or in the common ruin of the contending classes . . . The commu-nists everywhere support every revolutionary movement against the existing social and political order of things . . . They openly declare that their ends can be attained only by the forcible over-throw of all existing social conditions. Let the ruling classes tremble at a communistic revolution. The proletarians have nothing to lose but their chains. They have a world to win.

Workers of the world, unite!

Karl Marx and Friedrich Engels,
The Communist Manifesto (1848)

Karl Marx was right, socialism works, it is just that he had the wrong species. Why doesn't it work in humans? Because we have reproductive independence, and we get maximum Darwinian fitness by looking after our own survival and having our own offspring.

E. O. Wilson, interview at Harvard University, 27 March 1997

11

Arthur Schopenhauer

22 February 1788 – 21 September 1860

German anti-rationalist who advocated asceticism as the only tenable posture in a universe hostile to the insatiable strivings of the human will.

German philosophy since Kant was represented by a distinguished line of thinkers descending through him and culminating in Hegel. This idealistic tradition was marked by a high-minded effort to create systems that explained everything from logic to metaphysics, while retaining a belief in God and the state. In contrast, Schopenhauer was an iconoclast who regarded Hegel as a hot-air merchant whose overly complex language masked the vacuousness of his thought. Schopenhauer was equally dismissive of Schelling and Fichte. Plato and Kant were his masters and Schopenhauer was the first Western philosopher to incorporate ideas from Eastern philosophy in his work. He read the *Upanishads* daily, studied Buddhism and practiced meditation. Schopenhauer's interest in Eastern philosophy is an important link with the American transcendentalist philosopher Ralph Waldo Emerson (1803–82), whose thought fascinated Nietzsche.

Like Nietzsche, Schopenhauer had a doctorate (although his *was* in philosophy) but did not thrive in the academic environment, prefer-ring to work as an independent scholar (he had inherited wealth). His thesis *On the Fourfold Root of the Principle of Sufficient Reason* (1813) challenged the prevailing philosophical orthodoxy that reason, and reason alone, is the right path to knowledge. In *The World as Will and Representation* (1818) Schopenhauer proclaimed: 'no truth is more certain, more independent of all others, and less in need of proof than this, namely that everything that exists for knowledge, and hence the whole of this world, is only object in relation to the subject, perception of the perceiver, in a word, representation.' This is one source of Nietzsche's perspectivism.

Schopenhauer is most often referred to as a pessimist, a view supported by an aside in *The World as Will and Representation* in which he remarks, 'I do not know what eternal life is, but this present life is a bad joke.' However, Schopenhauer is more than a pessimist, and his concept of the will is complex. It is, at base, synonymous with Kant's being-in-itself. Schopenhauer's concept of will forms part of a sophis-ticated elaboration of ontology and epistemology. He defines matter as 'the *visibility* of the will in general'. Will inhabits and animates nature, independent of man – a phenomenon described by Heidegger's notion of being-in-the-world. Additionally for Schopenhauer, 'the whole body is the will itself, exhibiting itself in the perception of the brain'. Nietzsche would go on to characterize the will as those urges which dominate human behaviour: the will to live and the sexual impulse. If these ideas resemble those of Freud, it is because Freud was profoundly influenced by Nietzsche and Schopenhauer.

'The world is my representation': this is a truth valid with reference to every living and knowing being, although man alone can bring it into reflective, abstract consciousness. If he really does so, philosophical discernment has dawned on him. It then becomes clear and certain to him that he does not know a sun and an earth, but only an eye that sees a sun, a hand that feels and earth; that the world around him is there only as representation, in other words, only in reference to another thing, namely that which represents, and this is himself.

Arthur Schopenhauer, *The World as Will and Representation* (1818) (trans. E. F. J. Payne)

A philosopher who, far ahead of his time, brought together the three great affronts to human megalomania and thought them through to the end. The cosmological affront: our world is one of countless spheres in infinite space, with a 'mildew of living and sentient beings' existing on it. The biological affront: man is an animal, whose intelligence must compensate for a lack of instinct and for inadequate adaptation to the living world. The psychological affront: our conscious ego is not master in its own house.

Rüdiger Safranski, *Schopenhauer and the Wild Years of Philosophy* (1989) (trans. Ewald Osers)

12

C. S. Peirce

10 September 1839 – 19 April 1914

American logician and scientist who established the principles of pragmatism.

There is no American philosopher more diversely talented than Charles Sanders Peirce. His contributions to logic, scientific method and semiotics have had an enduring effect on how thinkers think about those subjects. Like his master and mental sparring partner Immanuel Kant, Peirce sought a systematic understanding of the world and everything in it. He devoted his life to achieving clarity of thought, a task he worked at daily.

Unlike most of the fifty thinkers treated here, one cannot point to a few publications of Peirce's as 'recommended' reading. His life's work is a patchwork of articles and essays that have been variously collected, but a definitive and useful edition of his work awaits.* Jacob Bronowski (1908–74) once defined a genius as someone with two great ideas. Peirce had at least three: predicate logic, semiotics and pragmatism. In addition, he also made lasting and practical contributions to

---

* The Peirce Edition Project of the Indiana University-Purdue University at Indianapolis is in progress with *Writings of Charles S. Peirce: a Chronological Edition*.

mathematics, astronomy, chemistry, geodesy, surveying, cartography, meteorology, spectroscopy, psychology, philology, lexicography, the history of science and mathematical economy.

Peirce was largely educated at home by his father Benjamin Osgood Peirce (1854–1914), who held the Hollis Chair of Mathematics and Natural Philosophy at Harvard from 1888 until his death and is credited with having largely created the Harvard mathematics department. In addition to his academic achievements, Pierce's father was a practical man who co-founded the Smithsonian Institution and the US Coast and Geodetic Survey (at which Charles would be employed for most of his working life). The origins of Peirce's pragmatism may be found in the style of his father's instruction, which included the setting of difficult mathematical and scientific problems, the answers to which were subjected to rigorous scrutiny. Peirce graduated from Harvard at the age of twenty with a bachelor of science degree in chemistry. For the next two years he worked as a scientist for the US Coast and Geodetic Survey, and from 1879 until 1884 he was also a teacher of logic in the Department of Mathematics at Johns Hopkins University.

Rejected by academia

In spite of his genius – for Peirce was undoubtedly a genius, perhaps the greatest American philosophical mind ever – he lost his position at Johns Hopkins and would never again have an academic appointment. Peirce was an unconventional man and after his first wife left him he cohabited with a woman who would become his second wife. Juliette Pierce had been previously known as Annette Froissy and also Juliette Pourtalai; her origins were obscure and the authorities at Johns Hopkins considered her to be a gypsy. Peirce's scandalous relationship with Juliette lost him his job.

He could also be a difficult and abrasive colleague, perhaps because he suffered from trigeminal neuralgia, a chronic condition that causes stabbing pains in the face. Peirce used cocaine, morphine and alcohol to treat himself, and no doubt this contributed, indirectly, to his dismissal from the university. Despite his prolific output – he left 100,000 pages of unpublished manuscript – Peirce achieved very little recognition in his lifetime, and died in poverty and illness.

Continuation of Kantian ideas

Peirce first read Kant's *Critique of Pure Reason* (1781) when he was sixteen – he studied it for three years, mastering the text and taking issue with it (he would continue to study it throughout his life, returning to Kant time and again as he developed his own thought). Peirce's early and precocious thinking about logic led him to dismiss Kant's as 'puerile'; and he rejected Kant's *a priorism* and his position that space was subjective. Despite these objections, Peirce had much in common with Kant. Both sought explanations of phenomena ranging from the concept of matter to the origins and physical laws of our universe; and perhaps more than any of our fifty thinkers, Peirce is the leading modern heritor of Kant. Peirce's thought was not affected by the division that occurred in philosophy at the beginning of the twentieth century, when it split into the two seemingly irreconcilable tendencies of analytic and continental. He travelled his own road as an independent thinker. Peirce was a logician, a theorist of scientific method and no defender of 'soft' metaphysics; but his hard and common-sense thinking in logic and science would ultimately lead him to embrace some of the metaphysical principles of Kant, Hegel and other idealists.

Peirce's epistemology defined against Kant's

For Peirce experience was everything and all of our knowledge must be based on it. Consequently, he rejected Kant's concept of the thing-in-itself (*Ding an sich*) as something that could not be 'indicated' or 'found' in experience. 'Therefore, all references to it must be thrown out as meaningless surplusage' (*Collected Papers, Vol. 4*). All knowledge must refer back to experience and, as a consequence, all meaning – there can be no meaning, no significance, independent of experience. It is in this sense that Peirce is sometimes called a Kantian realist: 'nothing can be more completely false than that we can experience only our own ideas' (*Collected Papers, Vol. 6*).

Pragmatism

Peirce's greatest contribution to modern thought is *pragmatism*, which holds that propositions are true if they work, so that unpractical ideas should be rejected. Apart from the transcendentalism of Emerson and Thoreau, pragmatism is the other uniquely American school of philosophical thought. While William James was the first to publish the term 'pragmatism', he credited its first use and elaboration to Peirce, who outlined its basic ideas in two articles published in 1878 in the accessible *Popular Science Monthly*. The first article, 'How to Make Our Ideas Clear', defined a clear idea as 'one which is so apprehended that it will be recognized wherever it is met with, and so that no other will be mistaken for it. If it fails of this clearness, it is said to be obscure.' The means by which ideas are made clear is *inference*. In 'The Fixation of Belief' Peirce wrote: 'We come to the full possession of our power of drawing inferences, the last of all our faculties; for it is not so much a natural gift as a long and difficult art.' It is through the use of logic and the accretion of demonstrable conclusions that can be shared by a community of observers that knowledge – reality, our objective understanding of the world – arises.

Unlike most philosophers of the modern period, Peirce was a working scientist all of his life (in this he was rather like the Pre-Socratics, who did not draw the distinction between philosophy and science that we do today). For Peirce, philosophy *is* the philosophy of science, and this is demonstrated by his pragmatic method. Apart from William James, some key pragmatists include Josiah Royce (1855–1916), John Dewey, George Herbert Mead (1863–1931) and George Santayana. Pre-eminent among twenty-first-century pragmatists is Susan Haack (*b.* 1945), who is often referred to as Peirce's intellectual granddaughter.

Semiotic

For Peirce, logic provided the underpinning of a more general and inclusive study that he called 'semiotic' or the theory of signs as distinct from what Ferdinand de Saussure and his followers termed 'semiotics'. Like much in Peirce's systematic thinking, the theory of signs was triadic. The three elements are the *sign* itself; its *object* or that to which it refers; and the *interpretant*. What Peirce meant by the interpretant is the subject of much contemporary debate. The role of the interpretant is to determine how the sign represents the object. It may be regarded as the meaning of the sign, but it is also seen as a process, product and effect. An interpretant becomes another sign in itself, and so the semiotic process goes on. This is a key difference between Peirce's semiotic and the semiotics of Saussure, which posits a dualistic tension between the *signifier* and the *signified*, whose relationship may be arbitrary. Peirce's semiotic is radical and an essential part of his philosophical edifice, which includes his logic and pragmatic method. 'Peirce held that not only do humans engage in semiosis as they endlessly represent and interpret reality, they themselves are signs' (Robert W. Preucel, *Archaeological Semiotics*).

Peirce left 80,000 unpublished manuscript pages at his death, and the task of organizing and publishing them in a way that makes the architecture of Peirce's thought clear is a long and daunting one. It is a sure bet, however, that when the task is complete, Peirce's work will give future thinkers much to consider.

But *how can* I know what is going to happen? You certainly do not think that it is by clairvoyance . . . Still, it remains true that I *do know* that that stone will drop, as a *fact*, as soon as I let go my hold. If I *truly know* anything, that which I know must be *real*. It would be quite absurd to say that I could be enabled to know how events are going to be determined over which I can exercise no more control than I shall be able to exercise over this stone after it shall have left my hand, that I can so peer into the future merely on the strength of any acquaintance with any pure fiction.

I know that this stone will fall if it is let go, because experience has convinced me that objects of this kind always do fall; and if anyone present has any doubt on the subject, I should be happy to try the experiment, I will bet him a hundred to one on the result.

C. S. Peirce, *Pragmatism as a Principle* (1903)

13

William James

11 January 1842 – 26 August 1910

*American psychologist who defined the nature of consciousness
as a stream, introduced the ideas of pragmatism to a wide audience and explored the varieties of religious experience.*

In his *Principles of Psychology* (1890) William James provided the first
comprehensive and original modern account of the subject in English.
He popularized and developed in his own style the pragmatism of
C. S. Peirce and was viewed by the general public as the originator of
the doctrine (although Peirce was its unsung progenitor). James
addressed the phenomenon of religious belief in the age of scientism,
publishing *The Varieties of Religious Experience* in 1902. He described
our perception of time as a 'stream of consciousness'. This discovery
had a profound effect on the writing styles of his student Gertrude
Stein (1874–1946) and the novelists Marcel Proust (1871–1922), Virginia
Woolf (1882–1941), James Joyce (1882–1941) and William Faulkner
(1897–1962). As a result, a wide public came to be acquainted with this
seminal idea of the twentieth century.

Born into a wealthy New England family, William James was a
nervous child whose youth was marked by bouts of deep depression;

on several occasions he contemplated suicide. His father, Henry James Sr (1811–82) was a theologian who followed the views of the Swedish philosopher and Christian mystic Emanuel Swedenborg (1688–1772); he was also a friend of Ralph Waldo Emerson (1803–82), who would become William's godfather. William benefited greatly from frequent European journeys, during which he was introduced to the intellectuals and writers of the age, many of whom also visited the James's salon in New York –William's younger brother was the novelist Henry James (1843–1916). Originally intending to train as a painter, James settled on medicine. He never practised as a physician, but his scientific training, combined with a taste for metaphysics, led him to create a unique body of work that has left a lasting impression on contemporary thought.

Science and religion

The importance of William James and his role in the rise of American philosophy must be seen in its historical context. The increasing influence of science (and its resulting technologies) at the end of the nineteenth century presented a number of crises for European philosophy. In Germany, home of idealism, science seemed to elbow aside the philosophy of Kant and Hegel and all its attendant metaphysics. It caused Edmund Husserl (1859–1938) to reflect, in his unfinished *Crisis of European Sciences and Transcendental Phenomenology* (1954), that the rise of scientific empiricism threatened the effort to understand our world in other, non-reductive ways. Martin Heidegger was distrustful of science and technology, which he associated with the decadent materialism of the United States.

In nineteenth-century France scientific ideas continued to clash with the teachings of the Roman Catholic Church, which still had enormous influence. Even in mainly Protestant England, Charles Darwin's (1809–82) theory of evolution deeply divided intellectuals, many of whom found it incompatible with Christian belief. If one had to describe William James's contribution in one sentence, he developed a style of thinking that allowed the inquiring mind to follow where science led, without fear of having to let go of religious belief.

Pragmatism: hypotheses and truth

In a public lecture James addressed the situation of 'a common layman' at the beginning of the twentieth century. He asked: 'What does he find his situation to be, in this blessed year of our Lord 1906?' His situation, says James, is this: 'He wants facts; he wants science; but he also wants religion.' James spent his entire career trying to give his hypothetical layman both, and pragmatism is the key to how he did it.

The point of pragmatism, according to James, is to know what effects a thought or action will have, and how one will react to those effects. Pragmatism defines truth as a hypothesis that corresponds with reality. We can establish the fact that it is raining because our clothes are wet from walking in it. This is a directly verifiable truth. Additionally, pragmatism allows for establishing a belief through *indirect* verification: for instance, I do not have to verify *directly* the fact that Belgium is a northern European country bordered by France, Germany and the Netherlands – I know it is the case by referring to a map, and so can make further hypotheses based upon the fact.

Psychology

James's *The Principles of Psychology* (1890) is remarkable not only because its author provides a coherent and systematic account of the subject, but also because of its explication of method. He used four methods in *Principles*: experimental, analytical, statistical and introspection. James created experimental psychology as a discipline at Harvard, and *Principles* opens with a section on brain function that includes experimental evidence starting with the nerve centres of frogs and progressing to experimental results from human beings. James also used an *analytical* approach, in which he surveyed and criticized the theories of his predecessors – Immanuel Kant's innatism; Jeremy Bentham's associationism; Herbert Spencer's (1820–1903) materialism; the scholastic philosophers' spiritualism; and Hegel's metaphysical idealism. His analytical survey of work by his predecessors was designed to identify what he called 'the methods and the snares of psychology'. He employed *statistical method* in a comparative study to determine norms and anomalies. But James's most original contributions come from his use of *introspection*. By looking inside his own mind and investigating how we perceive and understand the world James offered explanations of how we experience time, how memory functions, and the role of imagination, instinct and the will in our psychology.

James's influence on Bergson

James continued the export of American philosophical ideas to Europe which began with Emerson's influence on Nietzsche. James's views on the will influenced Husserl's perspective on that subject, which he expressed in his 'Lectures on Ethics and Value Theory' (1914). But James's deepest impact was on the work of Henri Bergson. The two met in 1908 and remained lifelong friends; James introduced Bergson's work to the United States, where the Frenchman would become an extremely popular lecturer.

Though their philosophies differ in detail, Bergson and James were interested in the same questions and, in a general way, their method-ologies and conclusions were similar. James called his pragmatic approach to research *radical empiricism* – a 'philosophic attitude' not very far removed from Bergson's approach, which Gilles Deleuze called *transcendental empiricism*. In his 1903 essay 'Introduction to Metaphysics' Bergson wrote: 'A true empiricism is the one which purposes to keep as close to the original itself as possible, to probe more deeply into its life, and by a kind of spiritual *auscultation*, to feel its soul palpitate; and this true empiricism is the real metaphysics.' Less poetically, but in the same spirit, James's radical empiricism took into account not only that which is experienced empirically, but also the relations that obtain among the objects of study (including the observer and the act of observing).

Ethics and Religion

James's interest in religion is deeply bound up with his sense of ethics, which is based on the notion of sympathy. In 'The Moral Philosopher and the Moral Life' (1891) James says that the precondition of moral life is to be able to imagine and sympathize with the plight of others. Moral life is that which has a purpose, from which it derives its meaning. Purpose is expressed and achieved through the exercise of free will. James echoes Søren Kierkegaard's *Fear and Trembling* (1843) when he writes that free will allows us to 'seek incessantly, with fear and trembling, so to vote and to act as to bring about the very largest total universe of good which we can see'. James himself was a generous man whose ability to sympathize with others prompted him to provide financial assistance to the impoverished inventor of pragmatism C. S. Peirce, to whom he always gave credit for his ideas.

In *The Varieties of Religious Experience* James followed the method that had proved successful in *The Principles of Psychology*. He begins with a review of reductive, materialist accounts of religious belief provided by neurology and other sciences, before moving on to explore aspects such as mysticism. James limits his original study to individual *religious experience*, not the history of religious sects; this gives much greater scope for discussing the power of religious feeling, including saintliness and mysticism. While he did not subscribe to conventional Christian belief and was certainly not a mystic, James sympathized with those who hold such beliefs and have mystical expe-riences. In *Varieties* he confessed: 'Whether my treatment of mystical states will shed more light or darkness, I do not know, for my own constitution shuts me out from their enjoyment almost entirely, and I can speak of them only at second hand. But forced to look upon the subject so externally, I will be as objective and receptive as I can; and I think I shall at least succeed in convincing you of the reality of the states in question, and of the paramount importance of their function.'

In stressing the paramount importance of experiences and beliefs he does not share, James underlines the most enduring aspect of his thought: that the sciences and religious beliefs are 'genuine keys for unlocking the treasure-house of the universe to him who can use either of them practically'. In James's view, the world is 'so complex as to consist of many interpenetrating spheres of reality, which we can thus approach in alternation by using different conceptions and assuming different attitudes'.

> Philosophy is at once the most sublime and the most trivial of human pursuits. It works in the minutest crannies and it opens out the widest vistas. It 'bakes no bread', as has been said, but it can inspire our souls with courage, and repugnant as its manners, its doubting and challenging, its quibbling and dialectics, often are to common people, no one of us can get along without the far-flashing beams of light it sends over the world's perspectives. These illuminations, at least, and the constrast-effects of darkness and mystery that accompany them, give to what it says an interest that is much more than professional.
>
> William James, *Pragmatism* (1907)

14

Friedrich Nietzsche

15 October 1844 – 25 August 1900

*German philologist and philosopher who proclaimed the death
of God and showed how man must revalue existing values.*

Friedrich Nietzsche trained as a philologist, so he is sometimes dismissed by those who require a philosopher to have a degree in philosophy. However, he is the most popular and influential German philosopher of the late nineteenth century, in part because his aphoristic writing style made him (deceptively) accessible to a general audience. He is most famous for declaring the death of God – a recognition that man must take responsibility for his life through striving and will. The main themes of Nietzsche's philosophy have thrived outside the academy and, like those of Karl Marx and Sigmund Freud, have entered the public consciousness.

In *The Birth of Tragedy* (1872) Nietzsche contrasted what he called the *Apollonian* and *Dionysian* impulses in Ancient Greece. By Dionysian he meant the irrational, chaotic and creative aspect of man's existence. The Apollonian, by contrast, refers to the critical distance of reason, which separates man from his vital experience of the Dionysian. Building on ideas first elaborated by Arthur Schopenhauer, Nietzsche formulated the concept of the *will to power*, a life force that both precedes human existence and drives it. The *death of God* necessitated what Nietzsche called a *revaluing of all values*. He argued for the relative nature of perception and understanding, questioning the notion of objective or absolute 'truth'. His concept of the *eternal return* is premised on the idea that each moment should be lived as if it will occur again for ever, in an endless circle. Perhaps his most famous construct – the 'overman' (*Übermensch*) – referred to Nietzsche's view of man as existing between the animal kingdom and a new, elevated state of being that can be reached by exercising the will to power.

The death of God

Nietzsche came across Arthur Schopenhauer's *The World as Will and Representation* (1818) accidentally in a book shop. He reportedly read it at one sitting. Here he found confirmation of ideas that were brewing inside him: that the world is not reasonable, and that historical meaning and morality are relative. All of this, Nietzsche concluded, proceeds from the fact that God is dead. What does he mean by this? In *The Gay Science* (1882) Nietzsche asks: 'Do we not hear the noise of the gravediggers who are burying God? Do we not smell the divine putrefaction? – for even gods putrefy! God is dead! God remains dead! And we have killed him! How shall we console ourselves, the most murderous of all murderers?' The answer would be the 'consolation' of philosophy, of thinking. Man now had to think for himself, rather than believing blindly in the 'truths' of the Church (or the university).

Nietzsche is often classed as a nihilist, but he is better understood as a critic of mid-nineteenth-century European nihilism, as the rise of nationalism emphasized the secular over the divine, and as science began to trump metaphysics and religion. Nietzsche didn't kill God; he was merely the messenger. The death of God began with Copernicus (1473–1543). 'What did we do when we loosened this earth from its sun?' Nietzsche asks in *The Gay Science* (1882). 'Whither does it now move? Whither do we move? Away from all suns? Do we not dash on unceasingly? Backwards, sideways, forwards, in all directions? Is there still an above and below? Do we not stray, as through infinite nothingness? Does not empty space breathe upon us? Has it not become colder?'

But Nietzsche's criticism went further than science or politics; he blamed Christianity for devaluing life by holding out the idea of an afterlife. The very idea of heaven made life on earth not worth living. In this way, Christianity was a corrupter of man's will, a debasement of all values. It is from this position that man must take responsibility for himself. Furthermore, it is a task that must be undertaken against certain odds. While critical of Darwin – whom he probably did not read, Nietzsche saw man as existing in the midst of an evolutionary drama, halfway between apes and angels.

The *Übermensch*

The man who attempts to get past his present position, through exertion of his will, is the *Übermensch* or 'overman'. The overman must also be the creator of his own values. The ready-made values of Christianity and bourgeois morality were anathema to Nietzsche – stultifying, life-destroying. In *Beyond Good and Evil* (1886) and *On the Genealogy of Morals* (1887) he explored the history of morality from a perspective that greatly enriched the study of ethics. This work was taken up and extended by Michel Foucault, who, of twentieth-century philosophers, was perhaps most influenced by Nietzsche. Although they did not directly influence one another, there are also sympathetic corre-spondences between the work of Nietzsche and Henri Bergson (1859–1941); they are both concerned with what was called *Lebensphilophie*, the consideration of life lived as a whole.

Eternal recurrence

At the centre of Nietzsche's ethics is the theme of the eternal return. It is a teaching hinted at rather than boldly stated in *Thus Spoke Zarathustra* (1883–5). (Nietzsche's Zarathustra is modelled on the ancient Persian deity known in English as Zoroaster, who goes to the top of a mountain to meditate, then descends to teach his 'children'.) Nietzsche was enchanted by and then rejected the music of Richard Wagner (1813–83), the composer of the four-opera cycle *The Ring of the Nibelung*, and with whom he had a long and stormy friendship. Nietzsche has Zarathustra cry out: 'Oh! how could I fail to be eager for eternity, and for the marriage ring of rings, the ring of recurrence? Never yet have I found the woman by whom I should have liked to have children, unless it be this woman I love. For I love thee, O Eternity!' This refrain is repeated several times in the book, and finds the answer: 'But delight wanteth not heirs, nor children. Delight wanteth itself, wanteth eter-nity, wanteth recurrence, wanteth everything to be eternally equal unto itself.'

What Nietzsche calls for with the doctrine of eternal return – which observes that everything in the universe is constantly moving, constantly changing – is a kind of post-theist categorical imperative. If Kant urged that one should act only according to the maxim whereby an act should become universal law, then Nietzsche urged one to act as if that act would be repeated eternally. This is the great seriousness of purpose that is the lot of man, post-God. It is Nietzsche's antidote to the nihilism of his day, and it is a light by which he opened the new territories of human experience and understanding that would be explored by the phenomenologists and existentialists. Nietzsche lays the groundwork for Sartre's ontology and for the themes he explores in his literary works. Nietzsche's constant challenge is to show us the abyss; at every turn he asks us: *Now what?*

Mania, syphilis and death

Nietzsche's life was untidy. He was prone to illness and went out of his way to offend the sensibilities of the intellectual and cultural establishment of his day; in his devotion to thinking, he destroyed his teaching career. After ten years of university teaching he gave himself over to writing and to roaming about Europe. He was involved in an unhappy love triangle with Lou Andreas-Salomé (1861–1937), a Russian-born femme fatale who became an associate of Freud's, and eventually a psychoanalyst, and his friend, the German philosopher Paul Rée (1849–1901). He also had a stormy relationship with his sister Elisabeth Förster-Nietzsche, an extreme anti-Semite who travelled to Paraguay in 1886 to help found a pure Aryan colony.

During the last ten years of his life Nietzsche wandered from spa to mountain, constantly writing. On 3 January 1889, while staying in Turin, he witnessed a man whipping a horse. Nietzsche threw his arms around the animal's neck to protect it, then collapsed. His mother brought him to Basel, and then to a clinic in Jena. Upon her death, Nietzsche lived with his sister in Weimar. He suffered terribly from the effects of tertiary syphilis, and a series of strokes ended his life in 1900.

The traducing of Friedrich Nietzsche

Elisabeth Förster-Nietzsche took control of her brother's publishing and established an archive of his work. She edited his writings to give them a cast that appealed to the Nazis. Adolf Hitler (1889–1945) had his photograph taken with a bust of Nietzsche. The reality is that Nietzsche detested German nationalism and anti-Semitism. His 'politics' – if he had any at all – were those of an aesthete, a snob. He worshipped art. One of his chief tools was irony and, to some extent, Nietzsche was a great humorist. He shouted and laughed from the mountaintop, sometimes in his own voice, sometimes in the voice of one of his 'characters'. In this and other respects, Nietzsche resembled his Danish predecessor in the development of existentialism, Søren Kierkegaard (1813–55).

Nietzsche's aphoristic style, which gave his philosophy a pungent, biting character, is easily quoted out of context. The worst misinterpretation of Nietzsche is that he was an anti-Semite, when he was, in fact, the opposite: an anti-anti-Semite. Nietzsche's biographer Rüdiger Safranski tellingly quotes the Nazi philosopher Ernst Krieck: 'All in all, Nietzsche was an opponent of socialism, an opponent of nationalism, and an opponent of racial thinking. Apart from these three bents of mind, he might have made an outstanding Nazi.'

Nietzsche's great contribution was to show us how to think. He examined problems from several perspectives and turned them on their heads to see if that angle offered any solution. Music and dance is everywhere in his philosophy, leading the reader in a Dionysian quest for knowledge; and, withdrawn from society in his final years, Nietzsche was once observed by his landlady through the keyhole of his door, dancing naked. In *Thus Spoke Zarathustra*, Nietzsche wrote: 'I could believe only in a God only who would know how to dance.'

God is dead. God remains dead. And we have killed him. How shall we, murderers of all murderers, console ourselves?

Friedrich Nietzsche, *The Gay Science* (1882)

(trans. Walter Kaufman, 1974.)

All philosophers share this common error: they proceed from contemporary man and think they can reach their goal through an analysis of this man. Automatically they think of 'man' as an eternal verity, as something abiding in the whirlpool, as a sure measure of things. Everything that the philosopher says about man, however, is at bottom no more than a testimony about the man of a very limited period. Lack of a historical sense is the original error of all philosophers.

Friedrich Nietzsche, *Human, All Too Human* (1878)

(trans. R. J. Hollingdale, 1963.)

15

F. H. Bradley

30 January 1846 – 18 September 1924

British idealist who rejected the native empirical tradition in favour of the one descending from Kant through Hegel.

In the second half of the nineteenth century British philosophy was largely idealist, developing the German line that extended from Kant through Hegel. To that extent, one might say it belonged then to what is now called 'continental philosophy'. But it also had a peculiarly British cast, being a reaction against the reigning empiricism of J. S. Mill and his predecessors John Locke (1632–1704) and David Hume (1711–76).

The most popular of the British idealists was Francis Herbert Bradley, who published *The Principles of Logic* in 1883 and his metaphysical treatise *Appearance and Reality* in 1893. The latter remained in print and went through several editions until the 1930s. The poet T. S. Eliot wrote his doctoral thesis on Bradley at Harvard, which he submitted in 1916 but did not did not defend; it was published in 1964 as *Knowledge and Experience in the Philosophy of F. H. Bradley*.

Bradley occupied a position of extreme monism, which meant he viewed the world as a unity, with no mind-body split (dualism). For him, logic, metaphysics and ethics were all attempts to describe this unity, which, following Hegel, he called the Absolute. His work was largely devoted to grappling with what he called 'the great problem of the relation between Thought and Reality'. His approach combined an openness to contradiction with a highly developed rationality. In this he opened a line of inquiry that would be profitably advanced by Henri Bergson, Gaston Bachelard (1884–1962) and Maurice Merleau-Ponty (1908–61). It is interesting to speculate how philosophy would have developed in the twentieth century if Bradley and his idealist colleagues had not been put out of business by Bertrand Russell and G. E. Moore. Moore's essay 'The Refutation of Idealism' (1903) and Russell's logicist programme marked the end of idealism in Britain.

Keeping Kant alive

Bradley's philosophy, influenced by that of T. H. Green, had kept the Kantian line of inquiry alive and drew on Hegel for a rational metaphysics that could incorporate secular thinking – the problem of Darwin and evolution was crucial then – and the religious sensibility allowed by Hegel's concept of Spirit. Most important for this 'what if?' speculation is that Bradley and his colleagues were open to the ideas of Edmund Husserl and Gottlob Frege. Both men were mathematicians. Frege went on to set the agenda for the logicist account of arithmetic that marked the beginning of the analytic movement. Husserl moved from mathematics and logic to create phenomenology, and so was the father of modern continental philosophy. Instead of being at daggers drawn, as they have been post-Moore and post-Russell, the two trends of continental thought might have been allowed to make complementary contributions to British philosophy, rather than reducing it to one approach.

In his *Ethical Studies* (1876) Bradley argued against the utilitarianism of Jeremy Bentham (1748–1832) and James Mill (1773–1836) on the grounds that community takes precedence over the individual, and that the individual gains his identity through membership of the community. Good is achieved by the individual's contribution to the community and its effort for what is collectively agreed as the common good. Bradley developed a system of logic to defend these claims, and *The Principles of Logic* promotes the idea of wholeness and unity as opposed to a reductive, atomistic understanding of the world. He rejected the idea of language as a basis for logic, since it offered only partial truths. In this Bradley was in stark contradiction to thinkers like A. J. Ayer, who believed that verifiable statements using language were the only basis on which to establish logical truths.

In *Appearance and Reality* Bradley employed an argument subsequently known as 'Bradley's regress' to claim that relations – including thought – are contradictory. They are appearance only and not reality. Appearances for Bradley are contradictory because they are removed from the experience of which they are a part by the fact of our thinking about them. Nevertheless, the whole world, made up of appearances, is experience; and this unity is what Bradley calls the Absolute. In his insistence that consciousness have an object, he shares the tendency of Husserl who argued that all consciousness is consciousness of *something*.

Green, Bosanquet and McTaggart

While Bradley is remembered as the major figure among British philosophers of the period, he was strongly influenced by T. H. Green, an Oxford idealist who began the movement against empiricism and utilitarianism. He was a Kantian in that he believed everything in the world, including objects and feelings, is to be understood as constituted by human consciousness; but he did not follow Kant in thinking that the noumenal world, or things-in-themselves, cannot be known. They *can* be known, said Green, because there exists a single, eternal Mind that unifies everything. In this view everything is related, all is connected. This approach is anti-reductive because it argues that no part can exist except in relation to the whole. In this Green anticipates the theme of multiplicity in Bergson.

Bernard Bosanquet (1848–1903) was a colleague of Bradley's and, like him, was influenced by Green. He took seriously Green's call to 'active citizenship': after being elected a fellow of University College, Oxford, he resigned in 1881 to devote himself to social work in London, and to teach adult education classes. In addition to this service he was a prolific writer – his collected works run to twenty volumes. H. H. Joachim (1868–1938) was a student of Bradley who published an important study of Benedict de Spinoza (1632–77) as well as the boldly named *The Nature of Truth* (1906) in which he formulated an important version of coherence theory. This holds that a proposition is true to the extent that it is a necessary constituent of a systematically coherent whole.

J. M. E. McTaggart differs from Bradley and the above-mentioned philosophers because he was at Cambridge rather than Oxford; this fact is important because he was the teacher of both Russell and Moore. It was from McTaggart that Russell caught his early enthusiasm for Hegel, which would eventually give way to a conversion of Damascene proportions when he performed a monumental about-turn and abandoned idealism for logicism. This trio was remembered by their student, the American mathematician Norbert Wiener (1894–1964), as 'the mad tea-party of Trinity'. As they dined at high table, Russell was the Mad Hatter, McTaggart the Dormouse and Moore the March Hare. McTaggart was a systematic metaphysician and an important interpreter of Hegel. His major works include *The Nature of Existence* (2 vols, 1921, 1927) and 'The Unreality of Time' (1908).

The professionalization of philosophy

The contribution of Bradley and the other idealists is better appreciated if viewed in its historical context. In the period between 1850 and 1903 there wasn't a school of British *idealism*, there was simply *British* philosophy, the general tendency of which was idealist. 'British idealism' is better regarded as a pejorative term created by early analytic philosophers to identify the status quo they wished to supplant with their own brand of thinking. The strange death of idealism in British philosophy goes hand in hand with philosophy's transformation from a gentleman's pastime into a profession. Up until the end of the nineteenth century British philosophers had typically been men of independent means whom we would nowadays call public intellectuals. This was true of John Locke in the seventeenth century, David Hume in the eighteenth, and it was true of the empiricist James Mill and utilitarian Jeremy Bentham against whom T. H. Green positioned himself in the nineteenth century. Green's career is a milestone in the history of philosophy because, according to the utilitarian Henry Sidgwick (1838–1900), he was the first *professional* philosopher in the English-speaking world.

The early analytic philosophers' war on British idealism can be seen to involve much more than the desire to supplant neo-Hegelian idealism and metaphysics in its entirety with logicism: they also wanted the idealists' jobs. The analytic side won both battles. The professionalization of philosophy in Britain and the United States resulted in the death of idealism and the erection of analytic philosophy as the official way of thinking; in this way a generation of teachers led by Russell, Moore and Wittgenstein spawned a new generation of followers, who in turn kept the analytic torch burning brightly in the English-speaking world throughout the twentieth century as their students and their students' students took up university teaching jobs. (There are notable exceptions to analytic dominance, such as Edinburgh, Duquesne, Buffalo, Pennsylvania State, Texas A&M and Fordham universities, with sympathetic elements at Yale and several others.)

The work of Bradley and his colleagues was suddenly cut off (in the sense that its replacement by analytic philosophy quashed any criticism and further development of 'British idealism' at the time). Now, it is the subject of rediscovery and fresh investigation by philosophers in the twenty-first century.

> Every aspect of life may in the end be subordinated to the Good, if, that is, we understand the Good in a very wide sense. Everywhere in life we seem forced, sooner or later, to ask the question Why. And the answer to that inquiry seems everywhere to be found in the fact of contentment and absence or suppression of unrest. We may appeal from one thing to another thing, but it is to this aspect of things, and it is to things as more or less possessing this aspect, that we are brought at last. And we are led to conclude that, so far as anything in the above sense is good, there is nothing else in the world which can pretend to stand above it.
>
> The claim of reason and truth to be an exception here will not hold. For, if you ask what is truth, you are led to answer that it

is that which satisfies the intellect. The contradictory and the meaningless fail to be true because in a certain way they do not satisfy. They produce a special kind of uneasiness and unrest; and that on the other side which alters this unrest into an answering contentment, is truth. It is truth, we may say, where the intellect has found its good.

F. H. Bradley, *Essays on Truth and Reality* (1914)

16
Gottlob Frege

(8 November 1848 – 26 July 1925)

German mathematician who founded modern logic and laid the groundwork of analytic philosophy.

The activity of philosophy usually consists of philosophers constructing arguments against the work of their predecessors. In this way philosophy proceeds like music, for example: composers rarely invent completely new forms, but rather build their ideas in response or reaction to the work of their predecessors. In a sense, most 'new' music is an act of criticism, rather than a wholly original composition. So it is with philosophy. Occasionally the philosophical idea is a homage to the predecessor or competitor; sometimes it is a statement along the lines of: *Here is how x did it. Now I will demonstrate the correct way to do it . . .*

But this is not true for the work of Gottlob Frege. Of all philosophers in the modern period, Frege's contribution was perhaps the most original. Other better known thinkers such as Marx, Freud and Darwin have had a more obvious effect on our world, but only Frege took a branch of philosophy – logic – and advanced it from the state where Aristotle (384–322 BC) left it 2,300 years ago. His work effectively created the starting point for modern logic and analytic philosophy.

Frege was born in 1848 in Weimar, Germany. He studied mathematics at the University of Jena and took his doctorate at the University of Göttingen. He returned to Jena where, from 1874 until 1918, he worked his way quietly through the academic ranks, finally becoming Honorary Ordinary Professor of Mathematics. This unremarkable biography is of interest only because, while the work of lesser philosophers brought them fame in their lifetimes, Frege's achievement was largely ignored. But the few readers he did have were a special group: they included the two brightest stars of analytic philosophy – Bertrand Russell and Ludwig Wittgenstein – and one of the founders of logical positivism, Rudolf Carnap.

A quantum leap for logic

Frege's project was to show that arithmetic could be reduced to logic (logicism). In order to prepare the ground for his work he rejected the two prevailing views of the time: psychologism and empiricism. Psychologism holds that the truths of philosophy are founded upon psychology. Empiricism holds that the truths of arithmetic exist apart from logic, as experience. Frege's starting point was Immanuel Kant (1724–1804), with whom he agreed that our knowledge of mathematics is *a priori*. But he did not agree with Kant that our knowledge of mathematics is *synthetic a priori* – that is to say, dependent upon intuition. He argued, rather, that our knowledge of mathematics is *a priori* in an *analytic* sense, dependent only upon logic. In his search for a purely logical grounding for number theory, Frege would also develop an analysis of language as it related to logic and truth.

His first major work was *Begriffsschrift* (*Concept Script*), published in 1879. Philosophers generally agree it is the most important development in logic since Aristotle. Aristotle developed syllogistic logic and the scholastic philosophers like Abelard refined a dialectical style of logic, but Frege's achievement was to construct a system of notation in his effort to derive mathematical proofs from pure logic. Frege's notation was a tool for expressing arguments in a way that avoided problems of clarity inherent in colloquial language. He also developed a propositional calculus and a predicate calculus, which allowed for the representation and analysis of increasingly complex sentences.

Frege's linguistic turn

Frege went on to make what has subsequently been called 'the linguistic turn', in what is regarded as the first work of analytic philosophy, *Die Grundlagen der Arithmetik* (*The Foundations of Arithmetic*) published in 1884. The linguistic turn is a technique in which problems that had previously been regarded as ontological or epistemological are reformulated as questions about language. In *Grundlagen* Frege asserts three fundamental principles. The first is to avoid psychologism by separating the psychological from the logical, and to distinguish between the subjective and the objective. The second, known as the 'context principle', demands that the meaning of a word is never to be sought in isolation, but only in the context of a proposition. The third requires a distinction between concept and object. Frege argued that concepts and related facts are as objective as objects and their facts. In Frege's understanding of 'concept' and 'object', a number is an object. However, when Frege claims a number is an object, he does not want us to think of it in the same way we do a chair or a desk.

Frege's definition of a number as an object is a negative one, in that he makes two declarations as to what a number is *not*: it is not a property of anything; nor is it anything subjective (as in a mental item). It is independent of mind.

Sense and reference

For nearly a decade Frege put off his attempt to reduce arithmetic to logic in order to study problems of language. His goal was to get rid of what he viewed as the messiness and imprecision of metaphysics (for example, Kant and the German idealists). As he had done with arithmetic, Frege began to reduce language to its essential (logical) components. He did this in a series of three short papers published between 1891 and 1892, one of which outlined a distinction between 'sense' and 'reference' in language. For Frege, a precise study of language begins with an understanding of the difference between 'reference' (the object to which language refers) and its 'sense' (the way the expression refers to an object). A single referent can have two different expressions. For example, John le Carré is the *nom de plume* of David Cornwell. Though John le Carré and David Cornwell are one and the same person, an observer familiar with one but not the other might be surprised to learn that they are one and the same. Frege would argue that this is because their modes of presentation differ. So, he concludes, 'it is the sense of expressions that determine the thought expressed by a sentence in which they occur, whilst reference determines its truth or falsity.' Bertrand Russell famously challenged Frege's two-part semantic theory in his 1905 paper 'On Denoting'. Nevertheless, Frege's distinction between sense and reference continues to be relevant in discussion of theories of meaning today.

Russell's Paradox

After working on the philosophy of language Frege returned to his project of grounding the laws of arithmetic on logic. The first volume of his *Grundgesetze der Arithmetik* (*Basic Laws of Arithmetic*) was published in 1893, the second in 1903. Here he further developed the idea of class, and classes of classes in mathematics. Using set theory, Frege had defined the cardinal number of a given class as the class of all classes that are similar. He now began the rigorous task of deriving the foundations of mathematics exclusively from arithmetic and logic with a view to eliminating all contradiction. In 1901, when the second volume of *Grundgesetze* was at the printer, Frege received a letter from Bertrand Russell. Russell had been studying Frege's work closely, as he was in the process of developing his own account of the foundations of mathematics. During the course of his study he discovered an error in Frege's thinking that (in Frege's words) destroyed the foundation of his life's work.

This error, known as Russell's Paradox, is as follows. Some sets are members of themselves, while some are not. For instance, the set of philosophers is not a member of itself, since it is a set and not a philosopher. But the set of non-philosophers is a member of itself. So: is the set of all sets which are not members of themselves a member of itself? If it is, then it is not; if it is not, then it is. Russell's insight was brutally devastating, but it pushed the grounding of mathematics on to the next stage. Frege's contribution effectively came to an end; but it was one of enormous significance and provided a foundation for the work of Russell and Wittgenstein.

Frege disentangled logic from psychology, and gave it the place in the forefront of philosophy which had hitherto been occupied by epistemology. It is this fact which, more than any other, allows Frege to be regarded as the founding father of modern analytic philosophy.

Anthony Kenny, *Frege: An Introduction to the Founder of Modern Analytic Philosophy* (1995)

In the course of developing logic, Frege also, more or less inadvertently, invented the subject of the philosophy of language.

John Searle, 'The Future of Philosophy' (1999)

Hardly anything more unfortunate can befall a scientific writer than to have one of the foundations of his edifice shaken after the work is finished. This was the position I was placed in by a letter of Mr Bertrand Russell, just when the printing of this volume was nearing its completion.

Gottlob Frege, Preface to *The Foundations of Arithmetic*, Volume II (1903)
(trans. Dale Jacquette, 2007.)

17

Sigmund Freud

6 May 1856 – 23 September 1939

Austrian neurologist who emphasized the roles of sexuality and the unconscious as foundations of personality, and developed the method of psychoanalysis.

Sigmund Freud is a member of the great triumvirate of revolutionary nineteenth-century thinkers that includes Charles Darwin and Karl Marx. Each provided a map of essential contours of the human situation. Darwin offered a scientific explanation of how man evolved; Marx provided the theoretical tools for man to locate and create himself in an historical context; and Freud provided a guide to man's psyche, and an explanation of the dynamics of his psychology.

Freud was a revolutionary because he led the way to overcoming taboos about sex by identifying human beings as essentially sexual. (It is impossible to imagine the 'sexual revolution' of the 1960s without Freud.) He posited the existence of the unconscious, a hitherto secret territory that influences our decisions, a place where secrets and unexpressed desires hide. But he also argued that analysis could reveal the workings of our unconscious. Along with Josef Breuer (1842–1925) and Alfred Adler (1870–1937) Freud was the founder of psychoanalysis.

Freud was a prolific author, whose books and essays range from the theory of psychoanalysis to reflections on society and religion. His joint work with Breuer, *Studies on Hysteria* (1895), described hysteria as the proper object of psychoanalytic method. *The Interpretation of Dreams* (1899) claimed to take psychoanalysis into the realm of science. Other key works that develop the theory of psychoanalysis include *Three Essays on the Theory of Sexuality* (1905), *Introduction to Psychoanalysis* (1917) and *The Ego and the Id* (1923). Almost from the start, Freud began to apply his psychoanalytic method beyond the treatment of patients to include a discussion of larger social phenomena. Important works of this kind include *The Joke and Its Relation to the Unconscious* (1905), *Totem and Taboo* (1913), *The Future of an Illusion* (1927), *Civilization and Its Discontents* (1930) and *Moses and Monotheism* (1939).

Freud trained as a physician and a neurologist. While a medical student he was influenced by the German physiologist Ernst Wilhelm von Brücke (1819–92), who developed the theory of psychodynamics or dynamic psychology, which recognized the role of the subconscious in human behaviour, and employed the metaphor of the first and second laws of thermodynamics to describe the behaviour of psychic energy. Freud also spent some months in Paris studying with Jean-Martin Charcot (1825–93), a pioneer in neurology who used hypnosis to treat cases of hysteria. A third key influence was Josef Breuer, Freud's friend and colleague, who famously treated the patient 'Anna O' by the psychoanalytic method. Anna O suffered from hysterical symptoms such as paralysis; when she talked to Breuer about them, they disappeared, hence the term 'talking cure' to describe psychoanalysis.

Freud's mental topography

In his topography of the mind Freud identified three components: *id*, *ego* and *superego*. The id is the instinctual part, driven by the *pleasure principle* to avoid anxiety. It is composed of two elements which he labels Eros and Thanatos. Eros is the life force, driven by the libido; Thanatos represents the death instinct, which is a cause of aggression. The ego is the rational part of the self that takes notice of the *reality principle*, translating instincts into socially acceptable behaviour. The superego is the internalization of external authority and the site of conscience and morality. A function of the ego is to mediate between the impulses of the id and the suppressive action of the superego.

Freud's mental topography further characterized three aspects of consciousness: the *conscious*, *preconscious* and *subconscious*. The smallest region of the mind is the conscious part, where our day-to-day logical thoughts occur. A larger component of mind is the preconscious, where the kinds of memories that can easily be brought back into consciousness reside. The largest area of the mind is the subconscious, which is not readily available to us, except through psychoanalysis. This is the place where the actions of the id, ego and superego occur. It is the place where traumatic experience is hidden to memory; it is the home of savage impulses. It is where our monsters, our nightmares live. These ideas weren't published until relatively late in Freud's career, in the essays 'Beyond the Pleasure Principle' (1920) and 'The Ego and the Id' (1923).

Psychoanalysis: the talking cure

Freud and Breuer's great therapeutic discovery was that by unlocking the subconscious one could treat hysterical symptoms. An early classic case of successful psychoanalysis was that of the patient known as Dora, whose hysterical symptom was aponia or loss of voice: she couldn't speak. Through dream analysis Freud led Dora to understand that what troubled her was her unspeakable sexual desire for her father, and a couple for whom she was a babysitter.

Psychoanalysis developed as a method for dealing with neuroses resulting from various imbalances in the relations between id, ego and superego. When this happens, Freud argued, certain hidden mechanisms come into play. For instance, excessive desire can lead to *repression*, a mechanism by which desires or actions are lost to memory (but may be revealed by psychoanalysis). Numerous defence mechanisms are identified by Freud, including *regression* (to a less threatening, perhaps infantile state); *projection* of one's own feelings on to another; *denial*; *displacement* (turning anger to an object other than its true one, for instance); and *sublimation*, in which impulses (such as sexual ones) are displaced to another activity (for instance, writing a book about philosophy). Freud's defence mechanisms have penetrated the language as deeply as the symbols of Christianity. For instance, while Christianity gives us angels ('she's an angel'), saints ('she has the patience of a saint'), crosses ('it's a cross she has to bear') and the devil ('oh, she's a little devil') Freud gives us regression (an adult indulging in a childish activity or pastime), projection ('he's just projecting his anger on to you') and denial ('she is totally in denial about her drinking').

As Freud developed the psychoanalytic method he discovered structural relations that emerge between the analyst and analysand. Among these, *transference* is the best known and most important. Generally, transference in psychoanalysis means the transference of the feelings one has for a particular person towards another. In the context of analysis, the therapeutic context is made problematical because the person to whom the feelings are transferred is the analyst – who may become the object of a patient's sexual desire, for instance. To further complicate the procedure, the analyst can direct feelings towards the patient, in the phenomenon of *counter-transference*.

Freud's contemporaries

Freud's contemporaries in psychoanalysis included Carl Jung (1875–1961), who identified ruling archetypes in psychology; Otto Rank (1884–1939), for whom legend, myth and art were also important to psychoanalysis; and Wilhelm Reich (1897–1957), for whom orgasm was of central importance to mental health. Freudians explored a wide range of ideas from alchemy to rain-making, which, in the eyes of some sceptics, reveals just how eccentric and undisciplined were these early psychoanalysts. However, Freud's thought was not only original and revolutionary in an intellectual sense, it was also useful: psychoanalysis *worked*. Some patients were relieved of debilitating systems that had made their lives a misery; others were curious about themselves and their motivations, and so welcomed the insights that could be gleaned from psychoanalysis. The self-obsessed found it a perfect opportunity to talk about themselves, and so we have analyses that go on for a lifetime, in contrast with the brief and successful analysis of Dora.

The astonishing spread of Freud's ideas owes much to the efforts of two Englishmen. James Strachey's (1887–1967) excellent English translations of Freud's works helped to make London and New York early and enduring centres of psychoanalysis (there would soon be more psychoanalysts in New York than in the whole of Austria). The neurologist Ernest Jones (1879–1958) was the first English-speaking psychoanalyst, and he was responsible for its further development beyond Austria. Jones helped to ensure Freud's legacy with his masterful three-volume *Life and Works of Sigmund Freud* (1953–7). In an increasingly schismatic world of competing psychoanalytic schools (just as Marxism splintered into countless groups), Jones protected the purity of Freud's teaching in his roles as President of the British Psychoanalytical Society and the International Psychoanalytic Association.

The cultural and intellectual legacy of Freud

The adoption and manipulation of Freud's theories by French philosophers has led to their application in philosophy and the development of critical theory as applied to literary and other 'texts'. It was Freud's influence that caused Jean-Paul Sartre to characterize human existence and its orientation towards the word as primarily sexual. But it was the French analyst and theorist Jacques Lacan, who gave weekly seminars on Freud at the Sorbonne from 1953 to 1980, who was chiefly responsible for making Freud relevant for the late twentieth century. Lacan's primary focus was on the role of language in psychoanalysis, a move which made Freud attractive to the post-structuralist concern with texts. Lacan's student Julia Kristeva (*b*. 1941), a practising psychoanalyst, employs Freudian ideas in her philosophical essays, but she also believes in their curative power. In *This Incredible Need to Believe* (2009) she writes: 'Analysis renders us capable of new *bonds*: this is what most of those involved in it hope for.'

Freud also influenced the Frankfurt School of philosophers. *Eros and Civilization: A Philosophical Inquiry into Freud* (1955) by Herbert Marcuse (1898–1979) was much coloured by his reading of Freud's

Civilization and Its Discontents (1930), fusing Marxist and Freudian theory in a political analysis that was central to the counterculture of the 1960s. The work of Jürgen Habermas (*b.* 1929) on communicative reason recognizes psychoanalysis as a model for a project based on the eradication of unnecessary oppression and the maximization of human emancipation. For Habermas, 'The birth of psychoanalysis opens up the possibility of arriving at the dimension that positivism closed off, and of doing so in a methodological manner that arises out of the logic of inquiry'.

Feminist criticism of Freud

Criticism of Freud by feminists has been one way to trace the development of feminism itself – possibly because before Freud no one had ever theorized so much about female sexuality. In Freud's account, the female's lack of a penis (or possession of a 'little penis', the clitoris) is viewed with abhorrence by the boy, and ultimately by the girl herself, who is in a state of 'penis envy'. As a result, feminine sexuality becomes secondary to – an adjunct of – male sexuality.

Male views on feminine sexuality at the end of the nineteenth century were usually based on an unexamined position of power, and often assigned women to a degraded, passive state. However, Freud's ideas have proved so useful – both in their intended purpose in psychoanalysis and as critical tools for the study of cultures and texts – that they have survived three waves of feminism. They have, however, been modified by female critics and practitioners of psychoanalysis. Melanie Klein (1882–1960) and Karen Horney (1885–1952) were quick to advance the psychoanalytic understanding of women in their practice and in their writings; and Nancy Chodorow (*b.* 1944) and Juliet

Mitchell (*b*. 1940) continue in the role of practitioner-theorist to address Freud and psychoanalysis from feminist and multidisciplinary perspectives. *The Enigma of Woman: Woman in Freud's Writings* (1980) by Sarah Kofman (1934–94) is a thorough examination of these issues.

The influence of Freud on modern thought cannot be overestimated. Whether we 'believe' in psychoanalysis or not, the fact that we admit the role of the subconscious to our everyday discourse and acknowledge without question that we are complex beings whose sexuality plays a major part in who we are is entirely a result of Freud's thinking. Psychoanalysis flourishes and serves millions of patients worldwide. But in a much larger context, Freud's work inform the natural sciences, the social sciences and philosophy; it can be seen as a modern flowering of Fichte's concept of *Wissenschaftlehre* – an entire science of knowledge that goes beyond positivism and embraces subjectivity.

Every dream reveals itself as a psychical structure which has a meaning.

Sigmund Freud, *The Interpretation of Dreams* (1900)

(trans. james Strachey, 1955.)

. . . At the end of the first phase of attachment to the mother, there emerges, as the girl's strongest motive for turning away from her, the reproach that her mother did not give her a proper penis.

Sigmund Freud, 'Female Sexuality' (1931)

(trans. Joan Riviere, 1932.)

No one, probably, will be inclined to deny the sexual function the character of an organic factor, and it is the sexual function that I look upon as the foundation of hysteria and of the psychoneuroses in general. No theory of sexual life will, I suspect, be able to avoid assuming the existence of some definite sexual substances having an excitant action. Indeed, of all the clinical pictures which we meet with in clinical medicine, it is the phenomena of intoxication and abstinence in connection with the use of certain chronic poisons that most closely resemble the genuine psychoneuroses.

Sigmund Freud, 'Dora, Fragments of an Analysis of a Case of Hysteria' (1905) (trans. James Strachey)

18

Émile Durkheim

15 April 1858 – 15 November 1917

French thinker who established sociology as an academic discipline.

Durkheim is the father of modern sociology and an early architect of the social sciences in general, along with Auguste Comte, Karl Marx and Max Weber. Adopting the positivist philosophy of Comte, Durkheim established sociology as a fully fledged academic discipline that, while it owed much to philosophy, would now be separate from it. In 1895 he developed an original methodology for 'doing' sociology, which is strictly laid down in his *Rules of the Sociological Method*; and in that year he also created at Bordeaux the first university department of sociology. For Durkheim, sociology is the understanding of *social facts*: the institutions, beliefs and shared practices that define a society. Durkheim defined social facts as 'facts with very distinctive characteristics: they consist of ways of acting, thinking and feeling, external to the individual and endowed with a power of coercion, by reason of which they control him'.

In contrast to the tradition of German idealism, which saw the individual subject as the maker of his world, Durkheim identified the social phenomena exterior to man as forces forming the larger part of his experience. The positivist aspect of Durkheim's method was to identify social facts, describe the moral prescriptions inherent in them, and then to study the effect of transgressions against them. This meant that for Durkheim sociology was rooted in ethics; in fact, he described sociology as 'a science of ethics'. His best-known work in the twenty-first century, *Suicide* (1897), is an exploration of the social fact that proscribes suicide, and the widespread transgression against it.

Durkheim used a metaphor from chemistry to elaborate his view of sociology as a science of ethics and the positivist method he employed. He viewed the individual as someone who belonged to a social group; and social groups, like chemical compounds, are more than just the sum of their constituent elements. He also used a metaphor from medicine. Having described – diagnosed, if you will – a social fact and the individual's relation to it (accepting or transgressing the implicit or explicit rules of the social fact), Durkheim went on to 'prescribe' a remedy for the social ill indentified. The Durkheim commentator Robert Alun Jones remarked that 'Durkheim always conceived of societies as subject to conditions of moral "health" or "illness", and the sociologist as a kind of "physician" who scientifically determined the particular condition of a particular society at a particular time, and then prescribed the social "medicine" necessary to the maintenance or recovery of well-being.' (*Emile Durkheim*, 1986).

Durkheim as rabbi manqué

Born in Épinal in Lorraine, Durkheim was meant to be a rabbi like his father, grandfather and great-grandfather. He was placed in a rabbinical school, but soon declared himself an agnostic and left. (Despite his rejection of religion, Durkheim would identify it as an important social fact, and devoted much of his later life to the study of religion and its role in society.) Durkheim was a problematical student and it took him three attempts to get a place at the École Normale Supérieure. When he did succeed in 1879 he joined a class that contained the philosopher Henri Bergson and Jean Jaurès (1859–1914), who would become the leading socialist in France. But Durkheim finished second to last in his class, and with no prospect of a university post he taught in lycées for several years before resuming his studies in Germany. There he developed an appreciation for the rigours of empiricism. His first major work, based on his doctoral thesis, was *The Division of Labour in Society* (1893).

Durkheim's description of the division of labour charts the move from an agrarian society to an industrialized one. In this move he finds not only a new concept of the division of labour, but also a new definition of social status based on merit (in contrast, Marx argued that the division of labour in capitalist societies led to alienation, because man was reduced to the status of a machine). Durkheim described the mechanisms by which societies developed moral as well as economic regulations. New social facts arise in the form of social solidarity, collective consciousness and systems of law designed to cope with the new social order.

Anomie: suicide and the breakdown of social norms

In *Suicide* (1897) Durkheim further demonstrated his sociological method and built upon his analysis of the division of labour to describe what happens when there is disruption of the social order (the breakdown of social solidarity, for instance). He borrowed from the French philosopher and poet Jean-Marie Guyau (1854–88) the term *anomie* to describe an individual's ensuing sense of normlessness or unrooted-ness, a sense of detachment from society, of not belonging. The concept of anomie is useful for describing what Durkheim viewed as the social causes of suicide. The experience of alienation that a person feels as a result of normlessness can lead to the despair which causes a person to take their own life. Durkheim's thoughts on suicide are particularly relevant in the current financial crisis, as large numbers of people in the developed world begin to realize that the goals of continued economic growth and social progress – for individuals and societies – are no longer realistic, leaving many of them feeling alienated as they confront the fact that their futures will not be what they thought. It is this sense of dislocation that Durkheim highlights in making the argument that suicide is a social (sociological) phenomenon more than it is a personal (psychological) one.

What Durkheim brought to the study of suicide – and, by implication, to any other sociological inquiry – was a descriptive analysis that avoided the prescriptive taint of religious and philosophical doctrine. While his descriptive approach cannot be said to be phenomenological in the strict sense laid down by Edmund Husserl, it influenced the existential-phenomenological inquiries of psychiatrists like Aaron Esterson (1923–99) and R. D. Laing (1927–89), who located 'madness' in the rupture between the subject's experience and society's expectations.

Like all social phenomena in Durkheim's worldview, anomie has a moral element. In the last of his three major works, *The Elementary Forms of Religious Life* (1912), Durkheim established religion as a social fact. He showed how religious belief and practice fulfilled important societal needs. As societies became more sophisticated, so did their religions. But industrialization brought with it the kind of social fracturing that led to anomie, and Durkheim noticed that this social rupture — breaks with norms, the phenomenon of normlessness — was in part due to the decline of religion as a communal activity that bound social groups together in a common set of beliefs and practices. Durkheim's view is the opposite of Marx's, who criticized religion for distracting man from his economic and political reality. Eventually, however, Marxism itself would become a kind of secular religion, offering its adherents an alternative set of values, a belief in history, a story of how the world works and man's place in it.

Durkheim's great achievement was to demonstrate a positivistic research agenda and method that went beyond reductive analysis to take account of what might be called the purpose of man: why are we here, what should we do, where are going? His contribution was to place man firmly in a social context. But Durkheim didn't just measure and describe the quantifiable outside social forces that shape us; he also drew attention to the moral values that drive us. That is why his work on the role of religion in society refers back to the work on suicide, and on the division of labour. Without the shared experience of religion, individuals in societies face the danger of anomie; and societies face the possibility of widespread social breakdown.

By their very nature social facts tend to form outside the consciousnesses of individuals, since they dominate them. To perceive them in their capacity as things it is therefore not necessary to engage in an ingenious distortion. From this viewpoint sociology has significant advantages over psychology which have hitherto not been perceived, and this should accelerate its development. Its facts are perhaps more difficult to interpret because they are more complex, but they are more readily accessible. Psychology, on the other hand, has not only difficulty in specifying its facts, but also in comprehending them.

Émile Durkheim, *The Rules of Sociological Method* (1895)

As far as social matters are concerned, we still have the mentality of primitives. And yet when it comes to sociology, so many contemporaries are reluctant to give up this old-fashioned idea, though not because the life of societies seems obscure and mysterious to them. Rather, they are so easily satisfied by these explanations that they cling to these illusions which are repeatedly belied by experience, because social matters seem to them the most obvious things in the world; they do not grasp their true obscurity, and they have not yet recognized the need to replicate the painstaking procedures of the natural sciences in order to dispel this darkness. The same state of mind is found at the root of many religious beliefs that surprise us by their simplistic nature. Science, not religion, has taught men that things are complex and difficult to understand.

Emile Durkheim, *The Elementary Forms of Religious Life*
(1912) (trans. Carol Cosman)

19

Henri Bergson

18 October 1859 – 4 January 1941

French philosopher who developed intuition as a philosophical method and described time as it is experienced subjectively.

Perhaps more than any thinker between the two world wars Bergson succeeded in making complex ideas popular with a mass audience. He was the first international superstar of philosophy, the first bestselling author of philosophical texts. Before Bertrand Russell, Jean-Paul Sartre or A. J. Ayer, Bergson brought philosophy to the public, much as Christian Wolff (1679–1754) had in Germany in the eighteenth century. Bergson's 1913 lecture at Columbia University drew such a crowd that it caused the first recorded traffic jam on Broadway in New York City.

Bergson's international popularity was not only a measure of the power of his ideas. It was also a testament to the intellectual adventurousness of what could be called the 'educated classes' of the time. His most popular work, *Creative Evolution*, first appeared in 1907, but by 1918 it had gone through twenty-one editions – an astonishing feat for a demanding philosophical text that required of the reader not only an understanding of Charles Darwin's theory of evolution, but also an ability to follow detailed metaphysical arguments.

A philosopher's courage in the face of Vichy

Bergson enjoyed the advantages of being born to an English mother and French father, acquiring a facility in both tongues. He elected, fatefully, to take French citizenship. His parents were Jews and Bergson remained culturally Jewish, having temporarily abandoned belief in God after encountering the theory of evolution. Bergson was an unusually spiritual man and he later came to feel an affinity for Roman Catholicism, which he thought complemented Judaism. His attraction to Catholicism persisted, even when the Church placed three of his works on the *Index Librorum Prohibitorum*, which identified books forbidden for Catholics to read; indeed, a Roman Catholic priest said prayers at Bergson's funeral. Had Bergson not died in 1941, he would almost certainly have been deported to Auschwitz, where 74,000 French Jews were sent from Paris, beginning in 1942.

The 81-year-old Bergson's reply to the Nazis who occupied France in 1940 was courageous and noble. He was the most celebrated philosopher in France and had held two chairs at the Collège de France: first the chair in Greek and Latin Philosophy, then in Modern Philosophy. He had won the Nobel Prize for Literature in 1927 and had distinguished himself by acting as France's envoy to President Woodrow Wilson in the successful diplomatic effort to bring the United States into the First World War. ('France was saved. It was the greatest joy of my life,' he wrote.) Working with Wilson he had presided over the creation of the League of Nations' Committee for Intellectual Cooperation, which later became UNESCO.

After the German occupation of France in 1940 the French authorities required all Jews to register with the police – a prelude to being stripped of their citizenship and forced to wear the yellow star and, finally, deported to Auschwitz from the Paris concentration camp at Drancy. The French authorities offered to exempt the distinguished Bergson from registration as a Jew, but in a courageous act of solidarity with his fellow Jews, Bergson resigned his posts, returned his honours and stood in line on a cold day at the end of 1940 to register with the police. Two weeks later he died from bronchitis. So it was extraordinarily crass of Bertrand Russell to write in *A History of Western Philosophy* (1945): 'The main effect of Bergson's philosophy was conservative, and it harmonized easily with the movement which culminated in Vichy.'

Transcending positivism

In common with leading continental philosophers like Franz Brentano (1838–1917) and Edmund Husserl, Bergson began his philosophical studies with Greek, Latin and mathematics. Like Husserl, he believed that philosophy was a science, albeit one that transcended simple positivism. His first publication, at the age of seventeen, was the solution to a mathematical problem posed by Blaise Pascal (1623–62) concerning the locus of a sphere in relation to two planes. (It was remarked by one of Bergson's teachers that philosophy's gain was mathematics' loss.) True to his scientific bent, but with a remarkable understanding of how science and metaphysics coexist, Bergson developed his theory of multiplicity after studying the mathematician Georg Friedrich Bernhard Riemann (1826–66). (The Riemann singularity theorem identified the multiplicity of a point.)

Five Bergsonian concepts

Bergson is often cited for three original contributions to philosophy. The first is the concept of *duration* or 'lived time', which accounts for how we experience time as a stream, as opposed to 'clock time', the series of separate moments studied by scientists. The second is the philosophical method of *intuition*, which he defined in *Creative Evolution* (1907) as 'instinct that has become disinterested, self-conscious, capable of reflecting upon its object and of enlarging it indefinitely'. The third concept is that of the *élan vital* or 'vital impulse', which he used to describe those natural phenomena in evolution that could not adequately be accounted for by reductive methods and mechanistic explanations. Contemporary study of Bergson's work has highlighted his treatment of the *embodied subject*, the subject's experience of his body in relation to self, others and time. In the twenty-first century increasing attention is being paid to Bergson's concept of *multiplicity*.

The problem of time

While Martin Heidegger (1889–1976) is often considered the main twentieth-century philosopher who dealt with the issue of time, it would be wrong to overlook Bergson in this regard. In *Being and Time* (1927) Heidegger argues that man occupies the position of *being-towards-death* (his elaboration of Kierkegaard's concept of *anxiety*). This view (often characterized as pessimistic, but not necessarily so) informs Sartrean existentialism and leads to the concept of authenticity, of life having no meaning except that made by man. However, while Heidegger identified technology as the curse of the modern period and had little technical understanding of science, Bergson brought to his exploration of the problem of time an expert understanding of science and a unique talent for metaphysics.

Bergson, like his friend William James, noticed that mathematics and science provided an inadequate account of time (James famously described our experience of time as a 'stream of consciousness'). In *The Creative Mind* (1907) Bergson notes that the instant we attempt to measure a moment it is gone, it has passed us by. In science, time is represented by a line; but a line is static, frozen. One can point to events in time, but the moment one attempts to capture the event it is already in the past. In reality, time is characterized by its movement. It doesn't stand still and our perception of it may include time speeding up or slowing down. Bergson saw that time could only be grasped through the individual's experience of it. It is only through *intuition* – the self-conscious human power of reflection – that time can be comprehended. The concept of duration then leads to the problem of multiplicity.

Multiplicity

In *Bergsonism* (1966) the French philosopher Gilles Deleuze (1925–95) identifies multiplicity as a characteristic of that which cannot be counted or accounted for by logic or reductive methodologies. Bergson identified two types of multiplicity: *quantitative* and *qualitative*. In *Time and Free Will* (1910) he gives the example of a flock of sheep. At first sight they all look alike, although we can isolate individual sheep and even give them a name. The flock represents a quantitative multiplicity marked by homogeneity. In contrast, a qualitative multiplicity involves human consciousness. Bergson gives the example of the human emotion of sympathy that arises, in the duration, from a successive range of other emotions. The act of noticing another's pain may, if we are honest, inspire abhorrence in us, or disgust. But we realize that if we fail to help another who is in pain, then others might fail to help us in a similar situation. Therefore, says Bergson, this perceived 'need' to help others is only pity motivated by fear. Bergson charts what he calls a *qualitative progress*, a 'transition from repugnance to fear, from fear to sympathy, and from sympathy itself to humility'.

Philosophy and the real world

In addition to his highly original contributions to thinking in science and metaphysics, Bergson also found everyday subjects fertile ground for philosophizing. In *Laughter: An Essay on the Meaning of the Comic* (1900) – Bergson's most popular book in his lifetime – he asked the question, 'What does laughter mean? What is the basal element in the laughable?' He notes that philosophers from Aristotle on have tried to tackle this 'little problem' as he calls it; but, for Bergson the problem is not so little. Laughter 'conjures up, in its dreams, visions that are at once accepted and understood by the whole of a social group. Can it then fail to throw light for us on the way that human imagination works, and more particularly social, collective and popular imagination? Begotten of real life and akin to art, should it not also have something of its own to tell us about art and life?'

In addition to being a gifted mathematician, a metaphysician, and a highly original thinker in science, Bergson kept this thinking and its results grounded in the real, practical world of everyday life. He was not a theorist like Einstein, in search of practical, applicable theories that could be used and built upon by other scientists. Bergson was interested in how one could pose and understand questions, so that scientific theories could be built. For all his panache and elan, Bergson was a hard-working, backroom man of philosophy, and an example of what is best in French thought.

As some shooting stars of later twentieth-century philosophy begin to fade, Bergson's earlier light may be seen to shine ever brighter, as his thought is rediscovered in our own age. When the excitement over post-structuralism and deconstruction has died down, a fuller discussion of Bergson's work — which was interrupted by the Second World War and then by existentialism — will be a key part of the twenty-first-century philosophical agenda.

> I pass from state to state. I am warm or cold, I am merry or sad, I work or I do nothing, I look at what is around me or I think of something else. Sensations, feelings, volitions, ideas — such are the changes into which my existence is divided and which colour it in turns. I change, then, without ceasing. But this is not saying enough. Change is far more radical than we are at first inclined to suppose.
>
> For I speak of each of my states as if it formed a block and were a separate whole. I say indeed that I change, but the change seems to me to reside in the passage from one state to the next: of each state, taken separately, I am apt to think that it remains the same during all the time that it prevails. Nevertheless, a slight effort of attention would reveal to me that there is no feeling, no idea, no volition which is not undergoing change every moment: if a mental state ceased to vary, its duration would cease to flow.
>
> Henri Bergson, *Creative Evolution* (1944)
>
> (trans. Arthur Mitchell)

20

Edmund Husserl

8 April 8 1859 – 26 April 1938

German philosopher, the father of phenomenology, who developed a philosophical method of discovering essences through eidetic reduction.

Phenomenology was the dominant trend in twentieth-century continental philosophy and its influence continues in that tradition today. Because of his role in formulating it, Edmund Husserl is the most influential philosopher since Immanuel Kant. Without Husserl there would be no Martin Heidegger, no Jean-Paul Sartre, no Maurice Merleau-Ponty or a hundred other thinkers, including Hans-Georg Gadamer and Jacques Derrida; there would be no existentialism, no hermeneutics, no post-structuralism.

Husserl has the unique privilege of numbering among his pupils a saint. Edith Stein (1891–1942), a phenomenologist and Husserl's assistant, converted from Judaism to Roman Catholicism, became a nun and was murdered at Auschwitz. She was canonized in 1998 by Pope John Paul II, who, as Karol Józef Wojtyła (1920–2005), had studied Husserl at university and published *The Acting Person: A Contribution to Phenomenological Anthropology* (1969). Two of Husserl's celebrated students – Martin Heidegger and Hannah Arendt – became the most notorious pair of secret lovers in the history of philosophy since Abelard and Héloïse: Heidegger became a Nazi and Arendt, a Jew, fled Germany for her life.

From mathematics to phenomenology

The most significant moment for Western philosophy post-Kant came when Gottlob Frege (1848–1925) and Husserl took divergent paths in the study of arithmetic. Frege's pursuit of an analytic *a priori* grounding of arithmetic in logic led to the development of analytic philosophy, the reigning tendency in anglophone universities. By contrast, Husserl's *Philosophy of Arithmetic* (1891) was famously criticized by Frege for its psychologism (Frege objected to Husserl's use of descriptive psychology alongside logical analysis in his attempt to understand the concept of number). Yet modern readings suggest that the Frege/Husserl divergence of opinion was not so great. Modern scholars point to Husserl's explicit statement in the *Philosophy of Arithmetic*: 'Our mental activity does not make relations; they are simply there, and when interest is directed towards them they are noticed just like any other content. Genuinely creative acts that would produce any new content . . . are absurd from the psychological point of view . . . the act can in no way generate its content'.

Husserl's training as a mathematician was critical to the development of his later philosophy and to our understanding of it. His move away from the study of mathematics was an opening up of logical investigation into a new world of experience, from human emotions to the entire lifeworld (*Lebenswelt*). In formulating his phenomenological method, Husserl sought to create a foundation for philosophy as a rigorous science. The analytical tradition that follows from Frege, including Russell and Wittgenstein, attempted to reduce philosophy to a handful of logical concerns that, in effect, did away with philosophy as applied to the world of human concerns. Husserl went in the opposite direction, using his radical methodology to investigate the world in which we live, and all the phenomena contained in it (including ourselves and our mental acts). The title of his *Logical Investigations* (2 vols, 1900, 1901) indicates the tenor of this project.

Husserl's mind was always of a scientific bent. His first studies at Leipzig were in astronomy and optics, and then in Berlin he studied mathematics with Leo Königsberger (1837–1921) and Carl Weierstrass (1815–97). After taking a PhD in mathematics, Husserl studied philosophy with Franz Brentano (1838–1917). Brentano and Husserl were drawn to Christian thought from different directions. Brentano became a Jesuit priest, but left the church over the issue of papal infallibility. Husserl was a Jew who converted to Lutheranism. Brentano had reintroduced St Thomas Aquinas' (*c.* 1225–74) idea of *intentionality* as a key philosophical concept, and Husserl would develop this as a cornerstone of phenomenological method. Husserl's view of intentionality describes the relationship between consciousness and its objects, and can be formulated as *consciousness is always consciousness of something*.

Husserl is the eternal beginner par excellence. He did not attempt to develop a system of thought, but rather focused on method. Phenomenology provides a way of posing questions and opening up philosophical investigations into any conceivable subject (or object). Husserl's early researches were into acts of perception and consciousness itself. At the other end of the scale, his pupil Hannah Arendt used phenomenological method in her major historical-political analyses *The Origins of Totalitarianism* (1951) and *The Human Condition* (1958). In between these poles of types of phenomenological project is Heidegger's *Being and Time*, which studies ontology in its temporal aspect.

Phenomenological reduction

Husserl's rallying cry was *To the things themselves!* By 'things' Husserl did not just mean objects like desks and chairs, but also relations, categories, ideas, the contents of our thoughts. His phenomenology is concerned with thinking about thinking through the phenomenological reduction. René Descartes (1596–1650) is often said to be the father of modern philosophy. If that is the case, then Husserl can be viewed as the son who succeeded Descartes to become the father of postmodern philosophy. Husserl took Descartes' *cogito ergo sum* (I think therefore I am) several steps further in his examination of thinking about thinking (or experiencing) in his phenomenological reduction.

Descartes' method of radical doubt was to suspended belief in God and the material world only to reintegrate them in knowledge after establishing himself as someone who thinks. Just at the point where Descartes begins his re-establishment of God and the material world, Husserl pauses and introduces a new step in the process of reduction. In place of Descartes' suspension of belief, Husserl asks us to 'bracket out' the objects under study. Bracketing out is a process Husserl called the *epoché*, a term used by the Epicurean Metrodorus of Lampsacus the Younger (331–278 BC) and further developed by Arcesilaus (*c.* 315–240 BC), who was the sixth head of Plato's (428/7–348/7 BC) academy and the force behind academic scepticism. By *epoché* Husserl means the suspension of any preconceptions about the object of study. This is called the *eidetic reduction*, the method by which the essence of things may be studied (the word comes from the Greek word *eidos*, meaning essence or form). Husserl went further still and made the *cogito* itself an object of reflection; this he called transcendental phenomenological reduction.

Husserl and Kant

Husserl's development of Kant's concept of the transcendental ego disturbed some of his earlier followers, like Edith Stein, Max Scheler (1874–1928) and the Polish philosopher and literary theorist Roman Ingarden (1893–1970). What had drawn these students and many others to Husserl's early teaching at Göttingen was the fact that it provided an alternative to the Kantian and neo-Kantian idealism that had governed much of German philosophy for the past century. Husserl's early phenomenology as presented in *Logical Investigations* focused on the object rather than the subject (*To the things themselves!*). It replaced Kantian idealism with a renewed interest in scholasticism, first revived by Brentano and further developed by Husserl. In 1916 Husserl moved to Freiburg, where his main focus became the transcendental ego.

In the last work published in his lifetime, *The Crisis of the European Sciences* (1936), Husserl was careful to distance his phenomenology from Kantian idealism. He wrote: 'Our critical reflections on Kant have already made clear to us the danger of impressive and yet still unclear insights or, if you will, the illumination of pure insights in the form of vague anticipations . . . and this also made comprehensible how he was forced into a mythical concept-construction and into a metaphysics in the dangerous sense inimical to all genuine science.' In the *Crisis* Husserl also criticized philosophy for what he regarded as its increasingly narrow, empirical, analytical and naturalistic complexion. Husserl argued that it was an essential task of philosophy to acknowledge and study the mental and spiritual realities that exist independently of the physical world. For Husserl, their study through phenomenology was a truly scientific enterprise and one that would bring about 'a total transformation of the task of knowledge'.

Husserl and the Nazis

Husserl retired from the chair of philosophy at Freiburg in 1928 and was succeeded by his student Martin Heidegger. In 1933 Heidegger joined the Nazi Party and was made rector of Freiburg. Heidegger countersigned a 1933 decree banning non-Aryans from public service. Husserl was exempted from this because of the clause that recognized the military service in the First World War of his two sons. However, after the 1935 Nuremberg Laws Husserl was stripped of his German citizenship and banned from teaching. His children emigrated to the United States, but he declined the offer of a position at the University of Southern California. Husserl died in Germany in 1938. His philosophy of spirit and his own sense of spirituality provided a moral focus rare in Nazi Germany, but it is sobering to reflect that had Husserl lived until 1942 he would have been deported to a Nazi death camp.

Husserl was one of the great methodologists in Western thought. He provides the grounding for any number of important philosophical investigations and the entire Continental tradition in philosophy will forever remain in his debt.

> We ourselves shall be drawn into an inner transformation through which we shall come face to face with, to *direct experience of*, the long-felt but constantly concealed dimension of the 'transcendental'. The ground of experience, opened up in its infinity, will

FIFTY THINKERS WHO SHAPED THE MODERN WORLD

then become the fertile soil of a methodical working philosophy, with the self-evidence, furthermore, that all conceivable philosophical and scientific problems of the past are to be posed and decided by starting from this ground.

Edmund Husserl, *The Crisis of European Sciences and Transcendental Phenomenology* (1936)

(trans. David Carr, 1970.)

21

John Dewey

20 October 1859 – 1 June 1952

American pragmatist whose theories led to the practical reform of education and underlined the need for an informed electorate to protect democratic freedoms.

Along with C. S. Peirce and William James, Dewey is one of three towering figures in American pragmatism. Like them, he was committed to clarity of thought and action based on the idea that the meaning of a doctrine is the practical effect of applying it; but unlike them Dewey put his thought into action in the practical, public sphere. His early work in psychology was the precursor to investigations into ethics, aesthetics, political theory and education that had a deep impact in the United States in the first half of the twentieth century.

As a PhD student at Johns Hopkins University Dewey had the good fortune to be taught logic by Peirce. In his early years, however, his natural inclination was towards idealism, particularly the work of the British idealist T. H. Green (1836–82) who championed 'active citizenship', which Dewey adopted passionately. At Johns Hopkins Dewey was also taught by George Sylvester Morris (1840–89), who had studied philosophy and theology in Germany and encouraged Dewey's interest in Hegel and Kant. Dewey's formation as a philosopher underlines the enduring vitality of the German Idealist tradition descending from Kant, through Hegel and British idealism. Although he would eventually turn away from idealism, Green's influence can still be felt in Dewey's search for holistic explanations and in his liberal conception of politics.

Psychology and experience

Like his fellow pragmatist William James, Dewey was also a psychologist and his early work *Psychology* (1887) finds him still under the sway of idealism. He made his reputation with his paper 'The Reflex Arc Concept in Psychology' (1896) in which he addressed the 'current dualism of stimulus and response' in psychology. Dewey wanted to find a better explanation of the mechanism that governs sensations, thoughts and acts, which he regarded as more than just 'a patchwork of disjointed parts, a mechanical conjunction of unallied processes'. He wanted an explanation that recognized the *organic unity* of phenomena. In contrast to the mechanical stimulus/response model Dewey offered the concept of the *reflex arc*, in which 'sensory stimulus, central connections and motor responses shall be viewed, not as separate and complete entities in themselves, but as divisions of labour, function factors, within the single concrete whole'.

Education theory and reform

Dewey's thinking about psychology led him to educational theory and in 1894 he moved to the newly established University of Chicago. There he founded a laboratory school in which he could apply his theories of education in a real classroom setting. This resulted in several important books, including *The School and Society* (1899), *The Child and the Curriculum* (1902) and *Moral Principles in Education* (1909). Dewey was instrumental in establishing The New School for Social Research in New York City (1919), Bennington College in Vermont and the experimental Black Mountain College in North Carolina. He developed his educational theories into a political belief that freedom depends upon an informed electorate that takes its responsibilities as voters and citizens seriously, ideas he elaborated in *The Public and Its Problems* (1927), *Liberalism and Social Action* (1935) and *Freedom and Culture* (1939).

At Chicago Dewey developed his interest in psychology and turned it to practical use in thinking about how we experience the world: a curriculum, a work of art, our selves – all of these experiences were the focus of Dewey's investigations. He began with education. In *The Child and the Curriculum* (1902) he wrote: 'The source of whatever is dead, mechanical and formal in schools is found precisely in the subordination of the life and experience of the child to the curriculum.' Life and experience are for Dewey the ingredients that, via education, contribute to a vibrant and free society. In educational terms, the prescription he outlined in *The Child and the Curriculum* was this: 'Abandon the notion of subject matter as something fixed and ready-made in itself, outside the child's experience; cease thinking of the child's experience as also something hard and fast; see it as something fluent, embryonic, vital; and we realize that the child and the curriculum are simply two limits which define a single process.'

Classical influences

Dewey extended his educational theories to the political sphere. He studied ancient Greek philosophy as part of his investigation into civil society: how is it constructed and organized? What are the rules that govern it? But his main focus was on the question of the role of the governed: how to become a good citizen. In *Experience and Nature* (1925) he outlined a Greek conception of life that was harmonious and whole. For Dewey, Ancient Greek society was successful because it avoided a false mind-body distinction, but rather educated the whole person. In his view, education was the key to what he called 'the democratic ideal'.

Dewey's epistemology

Dewey's philosophy of education was one part of his thinking about politics and democracy; another was his epistemology. He was influenced by Charles Darwin's theory of evolution and by William James's idea of the stream of consciousness. Dewey combines the two notions in his 'genetic' concept of knowledge, which arises from the experience of the subject's interaction with his environment. As new problems are faced, new solutions emerge and are adopted. By this process, thought acquires an aspect of *instrumentality*: thinking produces ideas which are useful in that they are like paddles than can be used to navigate the stream of experience to create new and better thinking as man seeks to overcome ambiguity. Dewey himself used the term instrumentalism (not pragmatism) when describing his philosophy.

Dewey and the public sphere

Dewey rejected atomistic explanations of social organization and politics, and saw human identity as arising from relations between men. He argued that 'men are not isolated non-social atoms, but are men only when in intrinsic relations' to one another. In *Democracy and Education* (1916) he said that 'democracy is more than a form of government; it is primarily a mode of associated living, of conjoint communicated experience.' Democracy was strengthened by 'widening of the area of shared concerns'. Education was important, but so was a free press, and the work of journalists and others is to do more than simply regurgitate press releases. The journalist's job is to recognize deliberate misinformation. It is the duty of the citizen to be aware of issues and to vote, involving oneself in political action.

More than any other American philosopher of his age Dewey immersed himself in the politics of the time. He co-founded the American Civil Liberties Union and the American Association of University Professors. He also directed the Dewey Commission investigation into charges made by Josef Stalin (1878–1953) against Leon Trotsky (1879–1940) that he and others had promoted armed insurrection (the Commission concluded that Trotsky was innocent). As a public intellectual Dewey showed the relevance of philosophy to the wider world beyond academe. While his star waned in the second half of the twentieth century, Dewey's emphasis on the conversations needed to keep democracy vital has much in common with the post-Second World War German philosopher Jürgen Habermas's (b. 1929) concepts of the 'public sphere' and 'communicative rationality'. Of the three great American pragmatists, Peirce was a troubled genius of exceptional originality; James had an extraordinary range of interests and was a natural theorist and gifted prose stylist; and Dewey was a dogged thinker who measured the value of his work by its practical application.

The only freedom that is of enduring importance is freedom of intelligence, that is to say, freedom of observation and of judgement exercised on behalf of purposes that are intrinsically worthwhile.

John Dewey, *Experience and Education* (1938)

Dewey marks the end of an era in which a single philosopher with a comprehensive view of the world can be acknowledged on a world scale as a spokesman for mankind. The study and practice of philosophy has now become so technical and academic an exercise that even the idea of the philosopher as a thinker capable of developing a view of the world which could influence the course of history has been lost in the thickets of the academy.

George Dykhuizen, *The Life and Mind of John Dewey* (1978).

22

George Santayana

16 December 1863 – 26 September 1952

The first Spanish-American philosopher; a naturalist and prag-matist who believed human beings are animals in a material world, but capable of creating grace and beauty.

Born in Madrid, George Santayana emigrated to the United States when he was nine years old. Although English is his second language, Santayana is held by many to be without equal among American philoso-phers as a prose stylist. He also published a significant body of poetry, along with memoirs, essays and a novel. Santayana is best known for his aesthetics and his radical naturalist account of the world. His book *The Life of Reason* (vol. 1, 1905) contains the widely quoted aphoristic warning: 'Those who cannot remember the past are condemned to repeat it.' He detested transcendentalism in American philosophy and Puritanism in American life.

A popular teacher at Harvard and a close colleague of William James, Santayana was also an undeclared homosexual, who, despite appear-ances – he had impeccable manners and a calm, aristocratic bearing – never really fitted in to the rarefied intellectual world of the univer-sity. He left the United States for good aged fifty because he preferred, in the words of the gay scholar Warren Johansson (1934–94), 'an immersion in a warm humanity and Old World wisdom that American culture and simple prudence both forbade'.

A naturalist and a pragmatist

Santayana is a naturalist – that is, someone who holds that there is nothing but the human and non-human material world. He is also a pragmatist, who believes that the meaning of a proposition is identical to its practical consequences. But he also transcends these simple definitions, creating a philosophical position of nuanced complexity. Santayana rejected the idealism of G. W. F. Hegel and other system builders, and in *The Life of Reason* (5 vols, 1905–6) he heralded a new beginning for philosophy, arguing that its task 'is not to construct but only to interpret' – a view that would not seem out of place coming from the structuralist/post-structuralist Roland Barthes. Although Santayana is not normally linked with the structuralists, his proclamation that 'The age of controversy is past; that of interpretation has succeeded' has a certain correspondence with their agenda. But Santayana's ultimate purpose is pragmatic: the aim of philosophy is 'a gradual mastering of experience by reason'.

Santayana outlines his naturalism in *Scepticism and Animal Faith: Introduction to a System of Philosophy* (1923). The source of knowledge and belief, he argues, is not reasoning but the fact of our animal existence (animal faith). The fact that I am hungry and there is food is sufficient epistemological basis to prove the existence of the self and the external world. Santayana's method involves the attempt to understand the beliefs that attach to actions and things. For him knowledge is 'a true belief rendered in symbolic terms': its pragmatic aspect is expressed in the conclusion that knowledge is a guide to action, giving it an implicitly ethical dimension; and the symbolic aspect of belief gives rise to 'the hauntingly beautiful worlds of the senses, poetry and religion'. Santayana's naturalism was strictly observed; although he was not a religious man he defended the place of religion in *Dialogues in Limbo* (1926): 'Religion in its humility restores man to his only dignity, the courage to live by grace.' Santayana often referred to himself as an 'aesthetic Catholic'.

Santayana's aesthetics constitute a theory of values that he established in *The Sense of Beauty* (1896), which may be seen as the first American treatise on the subject. He dismisses as facile the classical treatment of beauty as truth, and vice versa: 'a definition that should really define must be nothing less than the exposition of the origin, place and elements of beauty as an object of human experience.' The philosopher must not only ask questions like why, when and how, but must also inquire: 'what elements of our nature make us sensible to beauty, and what the relation is between the constitution of the object and the excitement of our susceptibility'. Ultimately, 'aesthetics is concerned with the perception of values.'

A reputation in decline

The case of Santayana is curious. He was a popular success in his lifetime – indeed, one of the few philosophers whose books were selected for the American mail order Book of the Month Club – and he numbered among his influential readers T. S. Eliot, Gertrude Stein and Wallace Stevens (1879–1955); the journalist and political commentator Walter Lippmann (1889–1974); and the sociologist and civil rights activist W. E. B. Du Bois (1868–1963). Yet, he leaves behind no followers.

There is no 'school' of Santayana like there is of his fellow pragmatists C. S. Peirce, William James and John Dewey. Perhaps it is because he left the United States in 1912, the year of his mother's death. He wandered around Europe, finally settling in Italy. He mistakenly thought that Mussolini's Fascist rule would be the correct solution to that country's political chaos. Realizing his error, he tried to leave for Switzerland, but didn't have the right travel documents. He died in a convent in Rome, where he was cared for by nuns during the last eleven years of his life. (This does not suggest a conversion to Christianity; it was common in Italy for nuns to provide care to the elderly.) His last wishes were to be buried in unconsecrated ground.

Much of Santayana's best work was written after his resignation from Harvard. One clue as to why his popularity declined after the Second World War is the fact that he viewed the university as a place overgrown with the 'thistles of trivial and narrow scholarship'; most professional philosophers, tilling that narrow furrow, would take offence at being so dismissed. It is also likely, as American philosophy began to develop its identity, that many of its practitioners resented Santayana's judgment in *Character and Opinion in the United States* (1920) that 'American life is a powerful solvent. It seems to neutralize every intellectual element, however tough and alien it may be, and to fuse it in the native good will, complacency, thoughtlessness and optimism.' Despite his long association with Harvard and American philosophy's claim on him, Santayana never gave up his Spanish citizenship and he did not seek American citizenship. In the end, he was perhaps drawn to a European culture that had more in common with the Ancient Greeks, who respected what Michel Foucault called 'friendship' among men.

The sense of beauty is its realization. When our senses and imagination find what they crave, when the world so shapes itself or so moulds the mind that the correspondence between them is perfect, then perception is pleasure and existence needs no apology. The duality which is the condition of conflict disappears. There is no inward standard different from the outward fact with which that outward fact may be compared. A unification of this kind is the goal of our intelligence and of our affection, quite as much as of our aesthetic sense; but we have in those departments fewer examples of success. In the heat of speculation or of love there may come moments of equal perfection, but they are unstable. The reason and the heart remain deeply unsatisfied. But the eye finds in nature, and in some supreme achievements of art, constant and fuller satisfaction.

George Santayana, *The Sense of Beauty* (1896)

He refused to argue, and argument is the staff of the life of academic philosophy. For his part, Santayana found most conventional philosophy circular and tautological, 'proving' only what it set out to prove and having little to do with anything that mattered.

John McCormick, *George Santayana: A Biography* (1987)

23

Max Weber

(21 April 1864 – 14 June 1920)

German sociologist and political economist who rejected positivism and emphasized our subjective understanding of social phenomena.

Max Weber is the foremost architect of the social sciences in the twentieth century. In *Fundamental Concepts of Sociology* (1920) he defined sociology as 'a science which attempts the interpretive understanding of social action in order thereby to arrive at a causal explanation of its course and effects'; and while his focus was on groups, Weber was concerned about what happens to individuals in groups as a result of social action. As a consequence of this he moved the social sciences beyond the empirical approaches of his forerunners Auguste Comte and Émile Durkheim, developing and refining them into instruments of human understanding. Weber's best-known work, *The Protestant Ethic and the Spirit of Capitalism* (1905), is a founding text in the modern social sciences. It is a brilliant analysis of why Protestants rather than Roman Catholics came to dominate the capitalist enterprise, offering what some critics have called a 'pre-Marxist' account of capitalism. The authority of Weber's analysis of capitalism and the ascetic spirit of Protestantism derives from his early studies in the economic and legal structures of the Middle Ages. Although best known to a popular audience as a sociologist, Weber's chairs were in departments of political economy, first at Heidelberg, then Vienna.

Weber was born in Thuringia to parents who were talented, prosperous and influential. His father (also Max) was a successful industrialist in the textile business, as well as a National Liberal Member of Parliament. The atmosphere at home was at once worldly and ascetic, cosmopolitan and intellectual. Weber attended the universities of Heidelberg and Berlin, and his training was in the law, which he practised briefly. In 1892 he published a social policy document, *Situation of the Agricultural Workers in East Elbian Germany*, which led to an appointment at Freiburg and then his first professorship at Heidelberg. His wife Marianne (1870–1954) was a noted sociologist and feminist and together they hosted what became known as the Weber Circle, which included György Lukács (1885–1971), the founder of the school known as Western Marxism, and a great literary critic. He and Weber would become close friends of Karl Jaspers, and they exerted significant influence upon one another – their common interest being the situation of the human subject in a social context. While we may regard Weber as a sociologist from today's standpoint, at that time his reputation rested upon his work as a political economist.

Retreat from academia

In 1906 Weber suffered a nervous breakdown, brought on by the death of his father. Weber had always been at odds with his father (taking his mother's side in disputes) and, after a particularly heated argument with Weber, his father fell ill; he died two months later. After this Weber's work suffered; he could not teach. In 1903 he resigned his university post and would not return to academic life until 1919.

In this period Weber did his best work as a public intellectual. In addition to research and scholarship in the field of political economy, he also established the sociology of religion as a discipline, and it was both the results of these studies and his methodological approach that led to his masterpiece on Protestantism and capitalism. Unlike Marx, who sought to derive laws of history from his study of empirical data, Weber saw that many complex connections obtained in social and economic relations, and he did not think they were reducible to laws; in his view, that would have been to simplify the subject.

As a philosopher, Weber was deeply influenced by Friedrich Nietzsche others have included Martin Heidegger, Karl Jaspers, Martin Buber and Michel Foucault, to name but a few. He was an assiduous researcher and gatherer of empirical data. Nietzsche's theory of the social sciences argued that all judgements from data were necessarily from a perspective, and so they were not objective in a scientific sense. Weber was sensitive to this position, but his method – to the extent that he can be said to have had one – was to analyze data, explore it in the context of multiple perspectives that may relate to it, and, after taking on board those perspectives, return to give a judgement that is objective, but enriched by an understanding of perspectivism.

The Protestant Ethic and the Spirit of Capitalism

In *The Protestant Ethic and the Spirit of Capitalism* Weber developed the concept of *elective affinity* to describe the fact that the worldview of Protestantism had an inbuilt sympathy with the aims of capitalism, so facilitating their joint ascendancy. The *rationalization* resulting from this affinity leads to man being imprisoned in what Weber called the 'iron cage' of ends-means efficiency. While Weber was critical of capitalism, he disagreed with Marx that socialism would free man from his chains; by replacing capitalism, he argued, socialism would not solve social ills, but rather compound them because it would need to create an even larger bureaucratic machine, leading to yet another rationalization and iron cage, and to constraints on freedom.

Social action and power

By social action, Weber meant 'all human behaviour when and in so far as the acting individual attaches a subjective meaning to it'. This definition laid out for Weber a research agenda that would lead to a consideration of social, economic and political factors as they impinged on man's happiness, which he increasingly saw as being threatened by the process of rationalization in which modern bureaucracies turned human beings into cogs in a machine. Rationalization is the process whereby social actions designed for economic efficiency became increasingly predominant in capitalist societies. These social actions replaced ones that had previously guided the development of societies (for instance, traditions, communal interest, morality, etc.).

Weber was a student of the mechanisms of power, and among the first to define it as a subject for serious study, the beginning of a tradition that would reach maturity in the work of Michel Foucault. In 'Politics as a Vocation' (1919) Weber identified the state as 'the sole source of the "right" to use violence. Hence, "politics" for us means striving to share power or striving to influence the distribution of power, either among states or among groups within a state.' In his essay 'Class, Status, Party' (1922) Weber defined power as 'the chance of a man or of a number of men to realize their own will in a communal action even against the resistance of others who are participating in the action'. He recognized three types of power: traditional (long-established by custom; for instance, monarchy), charismatic (authority deriving from the appeal of an individual leader) and legal-rational (authority that derives, for instance, from a constitution). Weber explored the conflict that arose between the arrival of a charismatic leader and a legal-rational bureaucracy. Weber favoured an equilibrium whereby the legal-rational authority could be balanced by a parliament and free elections of political leaders by plebiscite.

Weber greatly influenced the work of Jürgen Habermas, whose concept of the 'public sphere' and analyses of capitalism, democracy and law owe much to him. Karl Jaspers, one of the founders of existentialism, learned a lot from Weber's social analysis, which underpinned Jaspers' theories of intersubjectivity. Weber's influence can also be seen operating quietly in the background of Hannah Arendt's work (even though they disagreed on the subject of political violence). Weber's concept of the iron cage described precisely how Adolf Eichmann came to accommodate himself to the administration of transportation of Jews to Nazi death camps.

Weber's chief philosophical concern was the same as Kant's: the situation of man's freedom in a world in which the pace of change was beginning to quicken. Weber's concern for freedom arose at the moment when capitalism was on the rise, and the speed of technological growth and social change was quickening in ways never seen before, and with unseen consequences. Weber sought to identify the problems facing human freedom in an increasingly rationalized society. He did it in an unprogrammatic way; and his uniquely *un*methodological method continues to provide a practical way of understanding the situation of the individual in society and identifying the circumstances that reinforce or threaten freedom.

The idea of the *obligation* of man to the possessions entrusted to him, to which he subordinates himself as servant and steward or even as 'moneymaking machine', lies on life with its chill weight. *If* he will only persevere on the ascetic path, then the more possessions he acquires, the heavier becomes the feeling of responsibility to preserve them undiminished to God's glory and to increase them through tireless labour. Some of the roots of this style of life go right back to the Middle Ages, like so many elements of the capitalist spirit, but it was only in the ethics of ascetic Protestantism that it found a consistent ethical foundation. Its significance for the development of capitalism is obvious . . . it breaks the fetters on the striving for gain by not only legalizing it, but (in the sense described) seeing it as directly willed by God.

Max Weber, *The Protestant Ethic and the Spirit of Capitalism* (1905) (trans. Peter Baehr)

Max Weber is widely regarded as the greatest figure in the history of the social sciences, and like Karl Marx or Adam Smith, who might be regarded as rivals to this title, Weber was much more than a disciplinary scholar . . . Unlike Smith and Marx, there is no 'ideological Weber': no one has turned Weber's thought directly into a political worldview and set of policy recipes for the consumption of the general public. But there is a very important 'political Weber' whose account of the morality of political life has influenced many politicians and political thinkers and remains central to questions about the nature of political responsibility.

Stephen P. Turner, 'Introduction',
The Cambridge Companion to Weber (2000)
(trans. peter Baehr, 2002)

24

G. E. Moore

4 November 1873 – 24 October 1958

British philosopher who moved from early idealism to become a founder of analytic philosophy and who defended common sense as a philosophical stance.

G. E. Moore, along with Bertrand Russell and Ludwig Wittgenstein, was among the most influential British philosophers of the first half of the twentieth century. His output was not as voluminous as Russell's, but what he published was highly influential. His article 'The Refutation of Idealism' (1903) was published in the leading British philosophical journal *Mind*, which Moore would go on to edit from 1921 to 1947. 'The Refutation of Idealism' became a founding document of analytic philosophy and Moore's *Principia Ethica* (1903) became one of its principal texts. His later essays 'A Defence of Common Sense' (1925) and 'A Proof of the External World' (1939) solidified Moore's position as an apostle of clear thinking in a highly accessible and engaging prose style.

Moore was the quintessential Cambridge don. He read Classics and moral sciences at Trinity College, becoming a fellow there and then a professor, holding the chair in Mental Philosophy and Logic from 1925 to 1939. His entire working life was spent at Cambridge, while his colleagues Russell and Wittgenstein enjoyed more peripatetic careers. Like most British philosophers of the time, Moore began life as an idealist. As an undergraduate he studied under J. M. E. McTaggart (1866–1925), who was then a fellow at Trinity. At the same time Moore fell under the spell of the most influential of British idealists, the Oxford philosopher F. H. Bradley. After graduating in 1896, however, Moore became increasingly disenchanted with idealism, taking against it with a vengeance. In 'The Refutation of Idealism' he began by saying that 'Modern Idealism, if it asserts any general conclusion about the universe at all, asserts that it is spiritual.' Moore began to think that this assertion led to a number of assumptions – too many – that required proof for idealism to hold. And that, 'If I can refute a single proposition which is a necessary and essential step in all Idealistic arguments then no matter how good the rest of these arguments may be, I shall have proved that Idealists have no reason whatever for their conclusion.' This was the beginning of analytic philosophy: the attempt to reduce philosophical inquiry to a few facts that can be proven through logic. Moore's essay had a profound effect on his colleague Bertrand Russell, who was then an idealist. The effect of Moore's essay was to spell the end of British idealism.

Principia Ethica and the intuition of goodness

Moore's *Principia Ethica* set out to refute ethical naturalism by identifying what he called the *naturalistic fallacy*: the idea that 'goodness' can be defined in terms of natural properties such as 'pleasant', 'desired' or 'evolved'. Moore believed that goodness is not analyzable, but is only to be discovered through intuition. Good is 'one of those innu-

merable objects of thought which are themselves incapable of definition, because they are the ultimate terms by reference to which whatever is capable of definition must be defined'. He advanced a
consequentialist argument which holds that the chief concept of ethics
is the good, and whatever actions maximize the good are right actions.
Moore's consequentialism eschewed the hedonism inherent in the utilitarianism of Jeremy Bentham (1748–1832) and John Stuart Mill. Moore
thought that, ultimately, the good resided in love and friendship, and
the contemplation of beauty and art. *Principia Ethica* became a hand-
book of the Bloomsbury Group, which included other influential
Cambridge graduates like the political theorist and publisher Leonard
Woolf (1880–1969), the economist J. M. Keynes (1883–1946) and the
biographer Lytton Strachey (1880–1932).

A philosophy of common sense

While Russell's work in mathematical logic is mind-breakingly
difficult for non-mathematicians, and Wittgenstein's aphoristic style
can be hard to interpret because it is so incredibly compressed and
dense, Moore's appeal to common sense is bewitching in its apparent
simplicity. He used ordinary language and homely arguments to
demonstrate proofs. For instance, in a 1939 lecture he summarized his
refutation of idealism and scepticism about the real world by holding
up one hand, waving it about, and saying, 'Here is a hand.' He then
waved his other hand about, and said, 'Here is another hand.' Moore's
conclusion: *things exist.* They are real. They are not products of perception or any projection of a mind on the outside world. For Moore,
idealism is refuted because his hands are demonstrably real, however
Idealists could reply that in a debate with Kant Moore would have to

try harder. Some of the arguments and proofs one encounters in Russell's or Frege's logic are difficult to master, but no complex proof needs to be understood to follow Moore's arguments. As a consequence, his prose style differs greatly from that of Russell, who is anxious to find a mathematical or logical proof for each atom of knowledge. Moore, on the other hand, is content to make grand claims about what is. For instance, the central claim about ethics in *Principia Ethica* is that 'the fundamental principles of ethics must be self-evident'. In other words, they are what they are. The fundamental truths of ethics are regarded by Moore to be irreducible, and he would give no further reason why this was true.

Moore's Paradox

Wittgenstein coined the phrase 'Moore's paradox' in response to a problem Moore raised in a lecture. The question Moore was considering was the nature of problematic meanings; he proposed, and then began to analyse this statement: 'It's raining, but I don't believe it is.' The sentence is absurd, but it is the nature of the absurdity that Moore wanted to understand. The first part ('It's raining') simply describes a state of affairs. The second part ('but I don't believe it is') may be seen as a truthful first-person expression of a state of mind. The nature of the paradox involved here is beguiling, since the statement, as just described, can be true, logically consistent and not obviously contradictory. The paradox arises in the attempt to analyze why the sentence is absurd or lacking in meaning. It may seem a small problem, but its nature is still discussed by philosophers. In 2007 Mitchell Green and John N. Williams published *Moore's Paradox: New Essays on Belief, Rationality and the First Person*, a substantial collection of essays which explore issues of knowledge, belief and consciousness arising from Moore's apparently simple discovery.

Moore's belief in friendship and art as the foundations of ethics also informed his personal life. He was a popular colleague at Cambridge, a member of the Bloomsbury Group, entertained his friends by singing German *lieder* at the piano, and enjoyed a happy relationship with his wife Dorothy, who affectionately (if rather oddly) called him 'Bill'. By contrast, his colleague and co-founder of analytic philosophy Bertrand Russell was married four times and was often curmudgeonly and downright rude, so that Moore eventually declined invitations to social gatherings which he knew Russell would attend. They represent two different styles of analytic thinking; and two very different views on the relationship between philosophy and everyday life, and how we live our everyday lives. Russell was a great philosopher; Moore was a good philosopher, and a great teacher and friend.

The question requiring to be asked about material things is thus not: What reason have we for supposing that anything exists corresponding to our sensations? but: What reason have we for supposing that material things do not exist, since their existence has precisely the same evidence as that of our sensations? That either exist may be false; but if it is a reason for doubting the existence of matter, that it is an inseparable aspect of our experience, the same reasoning will prove conclusively that our experience does not exist either, since that must also be an inseparable aspect of our experience of it.

G. E. Moore, 'The Refutation of Idealism' (1903).

25

Bertrand Russell

18 May 1872 – 2 February 1970

*British logician and philosopher, influential thinker in mathematical
logic and a developer of the analytic school of philosophy.*

Few British philosophers of the twentieth century wrote as much
as Bertrand Russell; fewer still published as much. Some of his work
ranks with the best of their kind. His *Principia Mathematica* (1910–13),
co-authored with Alfred North Whitehead (1861–1947), is a bold and
monumental attempt to reduce mathematics to a few logical principles.
By universal agreement it is one of three seminal texts in logic – the
other two being the *Organon* of Aristotle (384–322 BC) and Gottlob
Frege's *The Foundations of Arithmetic* (1893, 1903). Furthermore,
Russell's essay 'On Denoting' (1905) is a founding document of analytic
philosophy, introducing the concept of the 'denoting phrase' and
Russell's theory of descriptions.

Russell is often regarded as one of the greatest British philosophers
after David Hume (1711–76) and John Locke (1632–1704), but he also
wrote a lot of popular philosophy, some of it uneven. His most finan-
cially successful work, *A History of Western Philosophy* (1945), was
dismissed by the critic and philosopher of language George Steiner

(*b.* 1929) as 'vulgar', while the American philosopher George Boas (1891–1980) once observed that Russell 'never seems to be able to make up his mind whether he is writing history or polemic'.

Russell's reputation rests on his brilliant early career as a logician and mathematician (he once noted that no philosopher has more than ten years of good work in him, and his own later work may be seen as proof of this). However, Russell did use his early and enduring reputation to carve for himself a unique place as a public intellectual who spoke out against the nuclear arms race and the Vietnam War.

Education of a mathematical genius

Many philosophers could be described as 'well-born', but Russell is more deserving of the epithet than most. His lineage was aristocratic not just in the sense of belonging to the peerage, but also in its philosophical antecedents. His godfather was John Stuart Mill, while his grandfather Lord John Russell (1792–1878) was a wealthy landowner and twice prime minister. Russell had an unfortunate sad childhood: when he was two years old his mother and his sister died, followed by his father when he was only four. Orphaned, Russell was raised by his grandmother, Lady Russell, and his aunts.

He was educated at home, where he learned the Classics, along with French and German language and literature. His facility for languages opened up the work of continental European thinkers and readied him for his career as a philosopher whose influence would extend far beyond the boundaries of his native England. In the closing years of the nineteenth century Russell built a reputation in Europe by engaging in a debate with the French mathematician Henri Poincaré (1854–1912) on the foundations of geometry and the nature of space; and by giving a paper in 1900 at the International Congress of Philosophy in Paris at the invitation of the French logician Louis Couturat (1868–1914). At this time Russell became acquainted with the work of the Italian mathematician and philosopher Giuseppe Peano (1858–1932), upon whose foundations he would begin to develop his own ideas of mathematical logic and set theory. In 1902 began reading the then obscure logician Gottlob Frege and through Frege he would be introduced to Ludwig Wittgenstein, his most famous pupil and harshest critic.

From idealism to analytic philosophy

Russell's early development was peculiar. Like Wittgenstein he often contemplated suicide as a child, but overcame this when he began to express himself sexually (a step that was more problematical for Wittgenstein). Russell's brother Frank taught him Euclidean geometry and from that moment on Russell was hooked on mathematics. He entered Trinity College, Cambridge, in 1890, taking a First in mathematics in 1893. There he became friends with the Hegelian J. M. E. McTaggart (1866–1925), whose idealism, along with that of F. H. Bradley was the dominant current in British philosophy. After meeting G. E. Moore, however, Russell lost his early admiration for metaphysics.

While Moore originally tried to ground ethics in a form of post-Kantian idealism, he changed course in 1903 with his landmark paper 'The Refutation of Idealism' (1903), which signalled a move away from the idealist tradition in Britain that had descended from George Berkeley (1685–1753) and was an early effort to ground ethics in analytic philosophy. Moore was doing for ethics what Russell was doing for logic. Together they laid the foundations for the approach to language that would be taken up by Wittgenstein and all who followed in the analytic tradition. Two further texts published in 1903 confirmed the ascendancy of analytic philosophy over idealism in Britain: Russell's *The Principles of Mathematics* and G. E. Moore's *Principia Ethica*.

Russell's Paradox

In 1901, while composing *The Principles of Mathematics* (in which he argued that logic and mathematics are one and the same), Russell discovered a flaw in Gottlob Frege's logic. He wrote to Frege just when the second volume of Frege's groundbreaking work *The Foundations of Arithmetic* had gone to press. Both philosophers were pursuing similar projects: to avoid psychologism and Kantian synthetic *a priorism*, while reducing the laws of arithmetic to a set of *a priori*, analytically determined rules of logic.

The flaw that Russell exposed in Frege is known as Russell's Paradox and it involves the concept of the set of all sets that are not members of themselves. If such a set existed, it would be a member of itself only if it were not a member of itself. Russell found a solution to the paradox by developing the theory of types, which allowed for the segregation of properties, relations and sets. Frege's error, Russell argued – and it was a fatal one – was to assume that classes and their members conformed to a single, homogeneous type instead of a number of types that conformed to a hierarchy.

Principia Mathematica

Written in partnership with the British philosopher A. N. Whitehead and published in three volumes in 1910, 1912 and 1913, *Principia Mathematica* (*Principles of Mathematics*) is an attempt to reduce the truths of mathematics to logic. Enormously influential, not only in mathematics but in philosophy, the way it broke down philosophical problems into logical units set the agenda for the analytic approach that dominated Anglophone philosophy in the twentieth century. It also influenced the logical positivism of Rudolf Carnap (1891–1970) and the Vienna Circle.

Early forays into politics philosophy of mind

Perhaps because Russell's work in mathematics and logic is so advanced, and only really open to a small group of specialists, he is perhaps better known for his political activism, which swung from an intensely nationalistic stance in favour of the Second Boer War (1899–1902) to becoming a conscientious objector during the First World War, and finally a supporter of the Argentinian Che Guevara (1928–67), a comrade of Fidel Castro (*b*. 1926), the leader of the Cuban Revolution (1953–9). Russell's anti-government views temporarily denied him a passport, caused him to be sacked from his lectureship at Trinity College, Cambridge, and landed him a six-month sentence in Brixton Prison. However, his experience of prison life differed from most inmates. Russell was given a large cell in which he could have whatever books he wished, along with writing materials and a desk; fresh, cut flowers were sent from his mistress Ottoline Morrell's famous garden at Garsington; he did not eat with the other prisoners but had catered meals delivered to his cell; he also employed a fellow prisoner to clean his cell and act as his factotum.

After the First World War Russell published two significant philosophical works: *The Analysis of Mind* (1921) and *The Analysis of Matter* (1927). In his introduction to the former he described his project as trying to reconcile what he saw as the materialist tendency of (behaviourist) psychology with the anti-materialist tendency of physics; his analyses of mind and matter were therefore an attempt to develop the American philosopher William James's idea that 'the "stuff" of the world is neither mental nor material, but a "neutral stuff" out of which both are constructed.'

Russell also visited Russia and lived for a year in China (1920–1). In *The Problem of China* (1922) he predicted that 'all the world will be vitally affected by the development of Chinese affairs, which may well prove a decisive factor, for good or evil, during the next two centuries.' In private, Russell often made overtly racist and anti-Semitic remarks well beyond the casual prejudices of British society at the time.

Popular works and public intellectual

Russell, who was married four times and had many affairs, wrote some of his popular works in defence of his lifestyle: *What I Believe* (1925), *Why I Am Not a Christian* (1927) and *Marriage and Morals* (1929). In Britain his sexual incontinence, atheism and political views caused only a minor stir, but this was not the case in the United States, where Russell repeatedly sought employment. After a brief spell at the University of California at Los Angeles, he was appointed to the philosophy faculty at the City College of New York in 1940. However, his appointment was revoked following a complaint from a parent and a court judgement found Russell 'morally unfit' to teach there. The plaintiff's attorney told the court that Russell was 'lecherous, libidinous, lustful, venerous, erotomaniac, aphrodisiac, irreverent, narrow-minded, untruthful, and bereft of moral-fibre'. After the City College debacle Russell got work at the Barnes Foundation in Merion, Pennsylvania, which had been established by the medical doctor and philanthropist Albert C. Barnes who advocated education and advancement of the arts for all. Russell gave a series of lectures there that formed the basis of his *History of Western Philosophy* (he managed to get himself sacked from the job, but later proved unfair dismissal).

The *History of Western Philosophy* appeared in 1945 and Russell was awarded the Nobel Prize for Literature in 1950. The *History of Western Philosophy* is a highly opinionated essay in which Russell presents the tradition according to his own narrow, analytical views. One can argue that all essays on the history of philosophy – this one included – are marked by the perspective of the writer. It is one thing to be critical of a philosophical tradition; but another thing altogether to proceed from the view that all metaphysics is nonsense, and to treat the works of greater minds across two and a half millennia with sneering contempt, as was noted by several reviewers.

Russell as political activist: nuclear disarmament and the Vietnam War

In 1960 Russell led the British Campaign For Nuclear Disarmament's Committee of 100, which was set up to organize non-violent direct action in the tradition of Mohandas Gandhi (1869–1948) and Martin Luther King (1929–68). In February 1961 Russell led 4,000 demonstrators in a sit-down protest outside the British Ministry of Defence in Whitehall. A demonstration in September of that year resulted in 1,300 arrests in Trafalgar Square, among them Russell (who was 89 at the time).

Russell's activism led to one of the most unlikely philosophical pairings in history, as the grandfather of analytic philosophy teamed up with the most famous of existentialists, Jean-Paul Sartre. From 1966 to 1967 the two philosophers teamed up to head the International War Crimes Tribunal (popularly called the Russell-Sartre Tribunal) to investigate the United States' role in the Vietnam War. The tribunal was based on Russell's 1966 book *War Crimes in Vietnam*, and was a wholly private affair with no official standing. It concluded (among other things) that the 'United States committed acts of aggression against Vietnam under the terms of international law' and was also guilty of the 'bombardment of purely civilian targets . . . hospitals, schools, medical establishments, dams'. It also found the United States guilty of 'repeated violations of the sovereignty, neutrality and territorial integrity of Cambodia' and 'attacks against the civilian population of a certain number of Cambodian towns and villages.' Old age only increased Russell's radicalism. At the time of his death in 1970 he supported Che Guevara's call for a worldwide revolution against US imperialism.

Russell's place in the history of philosophy as a pre-eminent logician and mathematician is assured. It is also the case that his strenuous efforts against idealism and for atomism helped change the course of philosophy in the twentieth century. As analytic philosophy exhausts itself, Russell's influence on philosophy may wane; but his contributions to mathematics now live on in a graphic novel *Logicomix: An Epic Search for Truth*.

Modern Philosophy begins with Descartes, whose fundamental certainty is the existence of himself and his thoughts, from which the external world is to be inferred. This was only the first stage in a development through Berkeley and Kant, to Fichte, for whom everything is only an emanation of the ego. This was insanity,

---

and, from this extreme, philosophy has been attempting, ever since, to escape into the world of everyday common sense.

Bertrand Russell, *A History of Western Philosophy* (1945)

My own view on religion is that of Lucretius. I regard it as a disease born of fear and as a source of untold misery to the human race. I cannot, however, deny that it has made some contributions to civilization.

Bertrand Russell, 'Has Religion Made Useful Contributions to Civilization?' (1930)

It is difficult to overestimate the extent to which Russell's thought dominated twentieth-century analytic philosophy: virtually every strand in its development either originated with him or was transformed by being transmitted through him. Analytic philosophy itself owes its existence more to Russell than to any other philosopher.

Nicholas Griffin, 'Introduction', *The Cambridge Companion to Bertrand Russell* (2001)

26
Martin Buber

8 February 1878 – 13 June 1965

Austrian Jewish thinker who developed a philosophy of dialogue based on the I-Thou relationship; a Zionist who wanted a bi-national state for Palestine.

Martin Buber was among the first of the religious existentialists, and the first Jewish one. In his philosophy and politics he promoted the value of dialogue between individuals, groups and nations. His most important work is *I and Thou* (1923), which achieved a wide readership in English translation during the 1960s and 1970s. Buber was a religious man who struggled with Jewish orthodoxy. He turned to philosophy, reading Kant, Kierkegaard, Feuerbach and Nietzsche. He was particularly drawn to Nietzsche's *The Birth of Tragedy* (1872) for its exploration of Apollonian and Dionysian modes of being or expression, which can be understood as the tension that exists between 'opposed' pairs such as thinking and feeling, or the plastic arts and music.

I-Thou relations

What Buber captures in *I and Thou* is a moment in the understanding of what it is to be a human being, between Kant's idealism and the existentialism of Heidegger and Sartre. Using an aphoristic style that owed much to Nietzsche, Buber was concerned to situate human existence in a realm that took account of man's subjectivity, while ensuring that the world of objects – constituted by the 'It' – retained an adequate place. I-It relations can translate roughly as those obtaining between a person and objects, or a person who approaches another person as an object (as in the Sartrean concept of the Other). I-Thou relations refer to those in which a person relates to another person in his or her fully human being, as another subject, rather than the means to an end – a concept adumbrated by the German philosopher Ludwig Andreas von Feuerbach (1804–72). In developing the dialogic principle of I and Thou Buber thought he had revealed an underlying structure of being that lay before or beyond language.

In the Jewish theological tradition, the name of God is traditionally not spoken (in the Torah God is referred to as Yahweh, translated in the King James Bible as 'I am that I am', and in others as 'I am who I am'). However, Buber not only speaks God's name in his work, but he also meets him: Buber argued that in I-Thou relations one actually encounters God. One does not necessarily find God by looking for Him through the traditional routes of prayer or meditation, Buber argued. Rather, God finds us, unexpectedly, in the process of human dialogue. God appears in this moment of fully interactive human inter-subjectivity.

Conciliation and communitarianism

Buber resigned his teaching position at the University of Frankfurt am Main in 1933 in protest at Hitler's rise to power. Like the German-American political philosopher Hannah Arendt, Buber was a cultural Zionist. His response to Nazism was to devote himself to Jewish adult education. He immersed himself in the Hasidic tradition, in which he found an authentic way of being through religious belief and practice. With the philosopher and theologian Franz Rosenzweig (1886–1929) he translated the Bible into German.

Buber had two defining moments of loss. One was being forced to leave Germany for Palestine in 1938. Buber loved German philosophy and literature, and was a master of the German language, his mother tongue. An earlier moment of loss occurred when Buber was three years old. His parents divorced and he never saw his mother again. This kind of trauma often triggers a negative reaction in a child, perhaps a broken sense of self or resentment towards others or difficulties with close relationships, but Buber's reaction was entirely different. He made it his life's mission to promote dialogue and to find ways to restore communication where it has broken down. So when he fled Nazi Germany in 1938 and settled in Palestine he argued for the creation of a bi-national state to include Jews and Arabs. One could say that he practised his I-Thou philosophy religiously, excluding no others from its purview.

After the founding of Israel Buber taught at the Hebrew University of Jerusalem. His book *Paths in Utopia* (1946) showed him to be an early proponent of communitarianism (an ethically reasoned approach to social organization and political action). His communitarianism is defined by his belief that relationships and joint effort, rather than individual action, are more positives forces in the building of societies.

As the twenty-first century proceeds, Buber's work is likely be 'rediscovered', and to occupy a more prominent position in the canon of ontology and philosophical theology, if only because, in common with his fellow religious existentialist Gabriel Marcel (1889–1973), his elaboration of being and the phenomenon of intersubjectivity is attractive to students of all faiths or none.

If *Thou* is said, the *I* of the combination *I-Thou* is said along with it.
If *It* is said, the *I* of the combination *I-It* is said along with it.
The primary word *I-Thou* can only be spoken with the whole being.
The primary word *I-It* can never be spoken with the whole being.

Martin Buber, *I and Thou* (1923)
(trans. Ronald Gregor Smith, 1958)

27

Albert Einstein

14 March 1879 – 18 April 1955

German physicist who propounded theories of relativity and was the first superstar of science.

Einstein – his name is synonymous with genius – made a fundamental break with Newtonian physics by offering new theories to explain the nature of space, time and gravity. More than any other scientist in history, the implications of Einstein's work are known to most people. Nearly everyone has heard of his famous mathematical equation $E=mc^2$, which demonstrates the interconvertibility of mass and energy. We know it because it is the breakthrough that made the atomic bomb and subsequent nuclear weapons possible. No scientific discovery in the history of humankind has ever had greater import. It is essential to an understanding of the creation of the universe and the composition of the physical world, as well as containing the knowledge required to destroy our world.

Einstein's path to success in science was not conventional by twenty-first century standards. He was born to a non-observant Jewish family in Ulm, Germany. Together with his uncle, Einstein's father founded a company that made electrical equipment based on direct current (DC).

The business failed because the American inventor Thomas Edison (1847–1931), a champion of alternating current (AC), eventually won the 'war of currents' (AC proving much cheaper to produce).

The young Einstein was naturally gifted in mathematics, and as a child he absorbed *Euclid's Elements* (*c.* 300 BC), the first textbook on geometry; and, as a young man, Kant's (1724–1804) *Critique of Pure Reason* (1781). Einstein was a student at the Luitpold Gymnasium in Munich, but he did not do well (he objected to the school's rote-learning method of teaching). When the family business collapsed, the Einsteins moved to Italy, and at sixteen young Albert failed the entrance examination for the Swiss Federal Polytechnic in Zurich, although he did well in mathematics and physics. After a year of remedial work, Einstein entered the Zurich polytechnic and earned a four-year teaching diploma in mathematics and physics.

Upon graduation, and after two years of searching, Einstein could not find a teaching post. He went to work at the federal patent office in Bern from 1902 to 1909, as an assistant examiner whose job was to evaluate patent applications involving electromagnetic devices. While it may seem an odd incubator for the greatest mind in physics, Einstein's tenure at the patent office gave him the opportunity to look at inventions that often raised fundamental problems in physics. It was the contemplation of these that gave rise to the famous scientific papers of 1905, which has been termed his *annus mirabilis*. The papers include 'On a Heuristic Viewpoint Concerning the Production and Transformation of Light' (photoelectric effect); 'On the Motion – Required by the Molecular Kinetic Theory of Heat – of Small Particles Suspended in a Stationary Liquid' (Brownian motion); 'On the Electrodynamics of Moving Bodies' (special relativity); and 'Does the Inertia of a Body Depend upon Its Energy Content?' (mass-energy equivalence).

1905: Einstein's *annus mirabilis*

The four papers Einstein published in 1905 laid down much of the theoretical groundwork for modern physics. 'On a Heuristic Viewpoint Concerning the Production and Transformation of Light' established the concept of energy quanta – the idea that light is transmitted (and absorbed) in discrete 'packets' or quanta. This discovery overturned the conventional electromagnetic theory of James Clerk Maxwell (1831–79) and the longstanding view that energy is infinitely divisible – Max Planck (1858–1947) demonstrated that there is a minimum time interval in which light can travel in a vacuum, known as Planck's constant. Einstein's discovery in this paper is known as the photo-electric effect, and it is the work primarily cited in his Nobel Prize award in 1921.

Einstein's second groundbreaking article of 1905, 'On the Motion of Small Particles Suspended in a Stationary Liquid, as Required by the Molecular Kinetic Theory of Heat', proved the existence of atoms. The concept of the atom as a small building block of matter was first posed by Leucippus (5th century BC) and then by Democritus (*c*. 460–*c*. 370 BC). Until Einstein, the existence of atoms was unproven. The way he demonstrated their existence was to use the concept of Brownian motion, which had been developed by Robert Brown (1773–1858) to account for the apparently random movement of particles suspended in a liquid or gas. In fact, the development of Einstein's idea – particle theory – refers directly to this early understanding provided by Brown.

Einstein's third 1905 article, 'On the Electrodynamics of Moving Bodies', unveils his special theory of relativity. Einstein's theory is built on two assumptions. The first is that *all inertial frameworks are equivalent when describing all physical phenomena*; the second is that *the speed of light is constant for all observers, irrespective of the speed at which the observer may be travelling or the source from which light is emitted*. An inertial frame (or a Newtonian frame or reference) refers to a device by which measurements may be taken, and one in which a body subject to no net forces moves in a rectilinear path with constant velocity. The speed of light (299,792,458 metres per second) is fixed, does not change, irrespective of the speed of the observer. Consequently, no matter how fast an observer travels, he cannot overtake a ray of light. The closer the observer comes to approaching the speed of light, however, measurements of space, time and light become relative to the observer. As a result, clocks slow down, lengths contract, and mass gains in density – these effects becoming greater the closer the observer approaches the speed of light. Events measured as simultaneous from an inertial frame will not appear as simultaneous with those measured from a different inertial frame. A significant consequence of this is that space and time cease to be separate and exist as one unity known as space-time – the three dimensions of space, with time added – a concept mathematically developed by Hermann Minkowski (1864–1909). The most significant practical consequence of Einstein's special theory of relativity was its conclusion that energy and mass are equivalent.

The equation $E=mc^2$, dates from Einstein's fourth *annus mirabilis* paper of 1905, which explores the major consequence of the special theory of relativity: 'Does the Inertia of a Body Depend Upon Its Energy Content?'. The equation parses like this: the energy of a body at rest (E) equals its mass (m) times the speed of light (c) squared: $E=mc^2$. In this equation it is not *mass* that is converted to energy, but *matter* (of which mass is a measurement). In 1919 Einstein described mass-energy equivalence as 'the most important upshot of the special theory of relativity' ('What is the Theory of Relativity?', 1919). It is a core idea of modern physics and it was essential to understanding the secrets of the atom that led to nuclear fission and fusion, and to the development of nuclear weapons. Einstein's equation demonstrated how accelerated particles could achieve great mass and therefore could release tremendous amounts of energy in a nuclear explosion.

General theory of relativity and quantum physics

While Einstein's special theory of relativity dealt with *inertial* frameworks, his general theory (1916) considers what happens in *non-inertial* systems – systems accelerating relative to one another. The general theory overturns the old Newtonian model of gravity, which is now understood as a metrical property of space-time that is curved in relation to matter. Einstein's new description of the atomic building blocks of the universe and how gravity works led to the prediction and understanding of many physical phenomena that (despite their complexity) have entered the public consciousness: for instance, black holes – the sites of dying stars, regions of space where gravity is so dense that even light cannot escape.

In his 1905 paper on the photoelectric effect Einstein proposed that light is composed of 'packets' of energy called *quanta*. In its interaction with matter, Einstein showed, light is absorbed – and emitted – in quanta. This understanding of the nature of light would be essential to the development of particle physics. The atom would be shown to have at its core a nucleus surrounded by negatively charged electrons, positively charged protons and electrically neutral neutrons. But Einstein posited a fourth elementary particle, the *photon*, the quantum of light and electromagnetic radiation, which carries electromagnetic force. Physicists were slow to accept Einstein's photon, but after fifteen years of experiments that confirmed its existence, Neils Bohr (1885–

1962), perhaps the most prominent of the anti-photon physicists, finally accepted Einstein's discovery.

Einstein and the philosophers

In addition to opening new worlds for science, Einstein also opened a can of worms for philosophers. In the third century BC Euclid of Alexander established the principles of geometry from a few axiomatic proofs. Euclidean geometry had prevailed for twenty-three centuries, but it wasn't called 'Euclidean' until Einstein's general theory of relativity came along, because before that it was the only geometry that existed. One of the consequences of Einstein's theory was the creation of a non-Euclidean geometry to explain the curvature of space and time (space-time) due to the strong gravitational pull of bodies.

One part of Immanuel Kant's worldview – which had, perhaps, underpinned the entire modern period, since philosophers either had to develop his ideas or respond to them with new ones – was seriously challenged by Einstein. Kant's transcendental idealism rested on his belief in the synthetic *a priori* truth of Euclidean geometry. Does Kant's whole system crumble because of Einstein's discovery that when space-time bends triangles do not add up to 180 degrees? Does it matter that space-time is curved and not flat? The problem is solved if one acknowledges that while Kant did rely on an argument from geometry to the transcendental ideality of space, and that it is 'intimately connected with his views on geometry', Kant's doctrine of the ideality of space is not, in the end, dependent upon it – see Allison, *Kant's Transcendental Idealism* (1983). Einstein's theorizing and style of doing science-philosophy was not unlike that of his hero Kant, who conceived the nebular hypothesis nearly 300 years ago to describe the birth of our solar system (the only scientific tools he had were pen, paper and his own mind). It is, with variations, the explanation that holds good today. In this sense, Einstein, though primarily a scientist, may be seen as an inheritor of Kant.

The consequences of Einstein's discoveries like relativity and the concept of wave-particle duality (light behaves either as a wave or a particle, depending upon the location, the point of view, of an observer) were enormous, not just for science, but for all fields of inquiry. His emphasis on perspective has been problematic for science, but has also brought to it to a more mature understanding of the concept of objectivity (and, by implication, of subjectivity).

Legacy beyond science

Einstein was born in Germany, but he eventually took Swiss citizenship and then, like so many European Jewish intellectuals of the period, emigrated to the United States in 1933 to avoid Hitler's Final Solution. Although his discoveries did most to unleash the destructive power of the atom, Einstein was a pacifist. Underlying his scientific thinking was a deep ethical commitment in the Kantian tradition. He viewed science as a 'powerful instrument' for good or ill, comparing it to a knife – a useful tool, which can also be used to kill. Einstein's thinking was equally composed of instinct and intellect: 'My pacifism is an instinctive feeling, a feeling that possesses me because the murder of men is abhorrent. My attitude is not derived from intellectual theory, but is based on my deepest antipathy to every kind of cruelty and hatred.'

The general theory of relativity owes its origin to the attempt to explain a fact known since Galileo's and Newton's time but hitherto eluding all theoretical interpretation: the inertia and the weight of a body, in themselves two entirely distinct things, are measured by one and the same constant, the mass. From this correspondence follows that it is impossible to discover by experiment whether a given system of coordinates is accelerated, or whether its motion is straight and uniform and the observed effects are due to a gravitational field (this is the equivalence principle of the general relativity theory). It shatters the concepts of the inertial system, as soon as gravitation enters in.

Albert Einstein, 'The Fundaments of Theoretical Physics'
(1940)

As long as I have any choice, I will only stay in a country where political liberty, toleration, and equality of all citizens before the law are the rule . . . These conditions do not obtain in Germany at the present time.

Albert Einstein, 'Manifesto' (1933)

A journalist once asked Albert Einstein, the greatest scientific genius since Isaac Newton, to explain his formula for success. The great thinker thought for a second and then replied, 'If A is success, I should say the formula is A = X + Y + Z. X being work and Y being play.'
And what is Z? asked the journalist.
'Keeping your mouth shut,' he replied.

Michio Kaku, *Einstein's Cosmos* (2004)

28

José Ortega y Gasset

9 May 1883 – 18 October 1955

Modernized Spanish philosophy, which had been labouring under the yoke of Scholasticism.

José Ortega y Gasset was largely responsible for the creation of twentieth-century Spanish philosophy. Spain had remained under the influence of the Catholic Church longer than any other European country and, as a consequence, medievalism endured and Enlightenment ideas were slow to take hold there. Ortega's mission was to popularize philosophy without oversimplifying it, and his *What is Philosophy?* (1957) is a landmark in Spanish thought. He introduced Husserl's phenomenology to a Spanish audience in a series of newspaper articles (his father was the director of the newspaper *El Imparcial*, which his mother's family owned). Under a repressive regime, Ortega utilized the power of wealth and privilege to spread modern ideas. He founded numerous journals in which such ideas could flourish: *Faro* (1908), *España* (1915–23), *El sol* (1917) and *Revista de la Occidente* (1923–36). His public lectures on the history of philosophy were a model of clarity and drew large audiences. Ortega's skill as a popularizer was akin to that of the German philosopher Christian Wolff

(1679–1754), the Frenchman Henri Bergson and the American William James.

Razón vital

A key concept of Bergson's philosophy is *élan vital*, which he used to describe the evolution of man in terms other than the reductive ones of Charles Darwin; he also used it to describe man's creative impulse. The key concept behind Ortega's thought is *razón vital* or vital reason, which matured into the idea of *razón histórica*, historical reason. Ortega summed up his idea of vital reason in the phrase *yo soy yo y mi circumstancia* (I am myself and my circumstance). Rather like Jean-Paul Sartre's existential treatment of man in the context of his *situation*, Ortega's philosophy centres on man's interaction with the world, which contains possibilities that can be indentified by reason, which is intuitive. Ortega's concept of reason is influenced by Husserl and refers to sensible intuition in which consciousness actively constitutes a 'state of affairs', which is constantly changing.

What is unusual about Ortega's philosophy is that it is infused not only with an interest in man's historical context, but also with a prescriptive idea of what Spain as a nation should be. Ortega was influenced by the German philosopher Wilhelm Dilthey's (1833–1911) scientific concept of history, which also influenced Martin Heidegger, whom Ortega met in 1951. For Ortega, the dictum *I am myself and my circumstance* refers particularly to the circumstance of Spain at the historical moment of his writing.

If Spain was still labouring under the effects of medieval Church teaching in the early twentieth century, its situation was further complicated by its politics. In 1923 the Spanish king recognized the dictatorship of General Miguel Primo de Rivera (1870–1930), who ruled until 1930. The Spanish Civil War, which pitted Republicans against right-wing Nationalists, tore Spain apart from 1936 to 1939 and left the country under the dictatorship of General Francisco Franco (1892– 1975) until his death. The situation for philosophy was grave. The fascist Nationalists were no more supportive of open inquiry and debate than the Catholic Church.

Miguel de Unamuno y Jugo

The philosopher Miguel de Unamuno y Jugo (1864–1936) tried to forge a philosophy in which reason had its place alongside Christian belief. He expressed his ideas in poetry and novels as well as philosophy; his most famous work is *The Tragic Sense of Life* (1911, 1912). But Unamuno was a victim of the political mayhem that gripped Spain. He was dismissed from his post as rector of the University of Salamanca in 1914, and during the Rivera dictatorship he was exiled to France. He reassumed his post at Salamanca in 1931, but in 1936 he was arrested for criticizing Franco. During a heated public exchange at the University of Salamanca, when the fascist José Millán-Astray y Terreros (1879– 1954) shouted 'Death to the intelligentsia!' Unamuno responded: 'This is the temple of intelligence, and I am its high priest. You are profaning its sacred domain. You will win, because you have enough brute force. But you will not convince. In order to convince it is necessary to persuade, and to persuade you will need something that you lack: reason and right in the struggle.'

Unamuno's learning was prodigious, and he brought the philosophies of the proto-existentialist Kierkegaard and the pragmatist William James to the attention of the Spanish public. Ortega had greater success in communicating his philosophical ideas to a popular audience, partly because he had access to the media, and partly because he was such an accomplished lecturer. But Unamuno was also a clear and concise prose stylist who endeavoured to make his works accessible.

Phenomenology and literature

Unusually, there was a pragmatic bent to Ortega's use of Husserl's phenomenological method in *Meditations on Quixote* (1914). Taking a phenomenological approach in a critical reading of the great novel by Miguel de Cervantes (1547–1616), Ortega does two strikingly original things. He is one of the first to show how phenomenology could be incorporated in critical theory (the appropriation by literary critics of continental philosophy to open new roads in textual analysis). Ortega's second achievement in *Meditations on Quixote* is that he used a seventeenth-century text that remained popular in Spain's conservative culture to make observations on the current state of Spain and where it should be headed. Ortega's aesthetics is bound up with an ethics and political philosophy that explores the relationship between the individual and the masses – the group, the state. In *Meditations* he proclaims: 'All that is recognized today as truth, as perfect beauty, as highly valuable, was once born in the inner spirit of an individual, mixed with his whims and humours.'

Ortega saw totalitarianism as the enemy of philosophy, but he was also critical of mass movements. In *The Revolt of the Masses* (1930) he argues for political leadership by a minority of educated citizens as opposed to rule by despots who appeal to the masses. He prizes effort over inertia – inertia among the masses being a precondition for totalitarianism. Ortega wanted leadership to come from 'superior minorities', a sort of new intellectual aristocracy. Ortega was unceasing in his efforts to create a Spain that not only *had* philosophy, but was *governed* by it. In *The Revolt of the Masses* he declared: 'The day when a genuine philosophy once more holds sway in Europe – it is the one thing that can save her – that day she will once again realize that man, whether he like it or no, is a being forced by his nature to seek some higher authority. If he succeeds in finding it of himself, he is a superior man; if not, he is a mass-man and must receive it from his superiors.'

So far as ideas are concerned, meditation on any theme, if positive and honest, inevitably separates him who does the meditating from the opinion prevailing around him, from that which, for reasons more serious than you might now suppose, can be called 'public' or 'popular' opinion. Every intellectual effort sets us apart from the commonplace, and leads us by hidden and difficult paths to secluded spots where we find ourselves amid unaccustomed thoughts. These are the results of our meditation.

José Ortega y Gasset, *What is Philosophy?* (1957)

There is one fact which, whether for good or ill, is of utmost importance in the public life of Europe at the present moment. This fact is the accession of the masses to complete social power.

José Ortega y Gasset, *The Revolt of The Masses* (1930)

29

Karl Jaspers

23 February 1883 –26 February 1969

German psychiatrist-turned-philosopher who stood up to the Nazis and founded humanist existentialism.

Karl Jaspers and Martin Heidegger were the founding fathers of existentialism. Before them, Kierkegaard heralded the essential themes of existentialism, including the concerns of subjectivity and anxiety in the face of death. After them, Jean-Paul Sartre elaborated existentialism's themes in novels, plays and philosophical works throughout the period of its dominance in France from the end of the Second World War to the 1960s. But of the two founding fathers Heidegger was politically and morally compromised by his membership of the Nazi Party. Later, Sartre would support Stalin and Mao (1893–1976) for longer than most. Of these modern existentialists only Jaspers advocated liberal democracy, developing a philosophy of existence that understood the subjective angst of living, while also incorporating science and religion as essential components. His courageous adherence to a middle path during the most tumultuous period in modern history makes him the sole founder of humanist existentialism. Jaspers main philosophical works are the three-volume *Philosophy* (1932) and *Von der Wahrheit* (1947), the English translation of which might be *Of Truth*. An enormous work of more than a thousand pages, *Von der Wahrheit* is the mature expression of Jaspers' philosophy and guarantees his future rediscovery and reappraisal.

Jaspers's 'pre-philosophical' period

Jaspers studied law, then took PhDs in both medicine and psychology at Heidelberg, where he eventually became Professor of Philosophy. His early influences were Kant, Nietzsche and Kierkegaard. This philosophical bent caused Jaspers to question the prevailing method of psychiatric diagnosis; looking beyond diagnostic labels, he studied the biographies of patients. His method, then revolutionary, is now an everyday part of psychiatric practice. His two-volume work *General Psychopathology* (1913) became a standard text. In 1919 he published *Psychologie der Weltanschauungen* (*Psychology of Worldviews*). This work remains untranslated in English, but its title gives a sense of how Jaspers's thought had developed, and where it was heading, incorporating his reading of Wilhelm Dilthey and Friedrich von Schelling and adapting their hermeneutics for a new age. During this 'pre-philosophical' period Jaspers developed a strong belief in the importance of science. At the same time he also valued religion and faith (he was influenced by Kierkegaard's concept of the 'leap of faith'). However, Jaspers' respect for both science and religion came with serious caveats: he did not believe in a personal God or in the objectivity of science. He was pre-eminently sceptical on the subject of certainty.

Jaspers's mature philosophy

Jaspers was open to a broad range of conversations as his philosophy developed. He spent time with the sociologists Max Weber and Georg Simmel (1858–1918) and the Marxist literary theorist György Lukács (1885–1971). Jaspers' work was also deeply influenced by the phenomenology of Edmund Husserl. One of Jaspers's accomplishments was to incorporate the phenomenological attitude into his treatment of psychiatric patients. This clinical experience gave rise to his concept of the *limit-situation* – moments when the human subject faces extremes of guilt or anxiety. In these moments the human being's potential for undetermined freedom manifests itself as the possibility for transcendence. Science and experience of the self – *Existenz* – are both the subjects of (and methods toward) the ultimate goal of transcendence, which is irreducible.

Jaspers's goal was to derive from Kant's transcendental idealism a way to describe human freedom and the inner life of the subject in a manner that was informed by new discoveries in the social sciences and his own experience as a psychiatrist. The subject *is itself a method* because, in Jaspers' view, philosophy is always an activity, never merely an item on a curriculum or the history that resides in libraries. In his focus on limit-situations Jaspers borrows from Kierkegaard's concern with the personal, but moves philosophy's attention beyond the subject's experience to his *communication* of it. In this he prefigures the hermeneutics of Paul Ricoeur (1913–2005) and the communicative rationality of Jürgen Habermas. After the Second World War, in post-Nazi Germany, Jaspers devoted most of his efforts to promoting liberal democracy.

Heidegger and the Nazis

In 1910 Jaspers married Gertrud Mayer. The fact that his wife was Jewish would determine the course of his career, and was instrumental in separating him from his friend and sometime collaborator Martin Heidegger. Jaspers's fundamental decency and courage in the face of the Third Reich contrasts strongly with Heidegger's currying of favour with the Nazis. Jaspers even took on Hannah Arendt as a doctoral student after Heidegger, who had been having an affair with her, dropped her – she was Jewish, and her thesis was on St Augustine's (354–430) concept of love. The two men could not have been more different. Jaspers, a physician and a humanist, used his broad learning to craft a philosophy that promoted intersubjectivity, whereas Heidegger, a self-serving genius, situated *Dasein* or human being in the temporal condition of a being-towards-death.

Loving struggle

At the heart of Jaspers' philosophy is the concept of *loving struggle*, which refers to the manner in which each human being or *Existenz* confronts the other (not the reified Other of Sartre). Loving struggle is Jaspers's gloss on Hegel's concept of *death struggle*, the battle for supremacy when subjectivities confront each other without recognizing the consciousness of the other (the key concept behind Hegel's master/slave dialectic). After the Nazis stripped him of his chair at Heidelberg in 1937, Jaspers gave a series of lectures in Frankfurt that would later be published as *The Philosophy of Existence* (1956). In these he set out an existential ontology, describing a situation in which, 'In *Existenz*, the man who is himself present speaks. He speaks to another *Existenz* as one irreplaceable individual to another.'

In Heidegger's Germany individuals were not irreplaceable, they were disposable. Jaspers's account of loving struggle is the complete opposite of the struggle of one group to dominate or eliminate another; it is the arena in which 'communication takes place in a loving struggle – not for power but for openness – in which all weapons are surrendered but all modes of the encompassing appear'. Jaspers used 'the encompassing' to describe the indefinite horizon beyond our own perspective, '*being* itself, which always seems to *recede* from us, in the very manifestation of all the appearances we encounter'. It is 'not the horizon of our knowledge at any particular moment. Rather it is the source from which all new horizons emerge, without itself ever being visible even as a horizon.' During the post-war denazification process Heidegger begged Jaspers to intervene for him; Jaspers refused.

Jaspers devoted much of his work after 1945 to political reflections on subjects such as German guilt, nuclear weapons and the future of liberal democracy. These works are, of necessity, sober and 'unexciting'. Because they were his last works, and widely translated, they give an unfortunately incomplete impression of the scope of Jaspers's thought. As he is reassessed by new readers in the twenty-first century, the full extent of his achievement should become more apparent. A neglected philosopher, Jaspers deserves to be rediscovered.

We always live, as it were, within a horizon of our knowledge. We strive to get beyond every horizon which still surrounds us and obstructs our view. But we never attain a standpoint where the limiting horizon disappears, and from where we could survey the whole . . .

Karl Jaspers, *The Philosophy of Existence* (1956)

30

Martin Heidegger

26 September 1889 – 26 May 1976

German philosopher who developed an ontology of being that situated man in a temporal context, demanding that meaning be found in the context of being-towards-death.

Martin Heidegger is the most controversial European philosopher post-Hegel. Most continental philosophers see his work as a breakthrough in the history of thinking; most analytic philosophers reject it as total nonsense. His main contribution to European thought is an ontology in which he situates *Dasein* or man's being in the stream of time and moving towards the nothingness of death. Man defines himself in this context, where he confronts the opportunity for authentic being.

In 1933 Heidegger fell under the spell of Adolf Hitler and joined the Nazi Party, although after 1934 he was sidelined by the Nazis as unreliable. After Germany's defeat in the Second World War, the Allied denazification tribunal banned Heidegger from teaching until 1950; Heidegger never apologized for his actions.

The influence of Catholicism

Heidegger was born into a Roman Catholic family of modest means in south-western Germany. His father was a church sexton, and from childhood Heidegger was set on a career path towards the priesthood. In parallel with his Catholic vocation, Heidegger cultivated an interest in philosophy which, in the beginning, informed his understanding of Roman Catholicism, but ultimately clashed with it. Heidegger left the Church (though he always acknowledged its importance, and he had a Catholic funeral).

Like his mentor Edmund Husserl, Heidegger was influenced by the work of Franz Brentano (1838–1917), the German philosopher who became a Jesuit priest. The young Heidegger was deeply influenced by Brentano's essay 'On the Several Senses of Being in Aristotle' (1862). He also read (and re-read several times) Husserl's *Logical Investigations* (1900–1901). Husserl was deeply influenced by the work of Saint Thomas Aquinas (*c.* 1225–74), especially the Thomist concept of intentionality, which he made the central concept of his own phenomenological philosophy. Thus Heidegger from a young age developed the three influences that would combine to inform his own philosophy: a belief that only the Greeks — and Aristotle in particular — had captured the sense of wonder and astonishment that is the beginning of any philo-sophical investigation; a Thomist turn of mind in understanding how we constitute the world; and Husserl's phenomenology, which provided a starting point and a method for his own ontological investigations.

Heidegger was a novitiate in the Jesuit order, but he dropped out, citing a recurring 'heart condition' as the cause; his biographer Rüdiger Safranski suggests that perhaps Heidegger's heart wasn't in it. After studying theology for two years at Freiburg, Heidegger switched to philosophy, taking his doctorate in 1913. His thesis was on 'The Doctrine of Judgement in Psychologism' (1914). Heidegger had his sights set on the chair of Catholic philosophy at Freiburg and he politicked his way into position, qualifying himself for the post with a dissertation on 'Duns Scotus' Doctrine of Categories and Meaning' (1916). He was bitterly disappointed when a better-qualified rival got the job. Disgruntled, Heidegger remained a lecturer at Freiburg. However, his luck turned for the better in 1916 when Edmund Husserl joined the faculty. The impact of the First World War delayed the start of Heidegger's personal relationship with Husserl. During the war, Heidegger served as a weatherman – an important job in planning poison gas attacks against American troops (it would spell disaster for the Germans if the wind were blowing the wrong way).

Assistant to Husserl

After the war, Heidegger made two radical changes to his life. The first was his formal rejection of Roman Catholicism. In doing so he broke his vow to raise his children in the Catholic faith, which was a condition of his marriage to his Protestant fiancée Elfriede Petri. Elfriede had been a student of Heidegger's; she was a vicious anti-Semite who expressed her views publicly and loudly.

Heidegger's second life-changing action was to become Edmund Husserl's assistant, succeeding Edith Stein (1891–1942). Working for Husserl was demanding, but it also provided Heidegger with a small, much needed stipend (his Freiburg lectureship was unsalaried). Heidegger's financial position had always been precarious. He had used Catholic Church funding to pay for his university education, and now his work for Husserl contributed to the family coffers. By then

Heidegger was married with two sons (the first of whom was the result of an affair his wife Elfriede had with the family doctor).

Husserl was a tireless writer and reviser of his work. He composed in shorthand and would often jump from one topic to another, leaving his assistant to make sense of jumbles of paper. Part of Heidegger's task was to put the thoughts of The Master (as his students called him) in order. As a result, Heidegger was privileged to have an up-close view of how this great mind worked. Observing at first hand how Husserl elaborated his phenomenological method would be fundamental to Heidegger's formation as a philosopher.

Heidegger was drawn to Husserl's early 'scientific' phenomenology, which had as its mantra a call to 'the things themselves'. It was this early phenomenological method of investigating *things* that interested Heidegger. In the things themselves, he experienced a shimmering presence that was astonishing; he perceived the existence of things in a way that was so powerful it could be terrifying. He did not believe like Kant or the mature Husserl that human beings assigned meaning to the things. The things already had being. Man could manipulate the significance of things, but they were already there, being themselves, prior to and after man. In his desire to avoid neo-Kantianism, Heidegger largely rejected the German idealist tradition and returned to Aristotle for his starting point.

Being and Time

Eventually, the attraction of assisting Husserl waned and Heidegger longed for the promotion he thought befitted a philosopher of his calibre. Chairs were open at Marburg and Göttingen. Heidegger had not published while working for Husserl, and in pursuit of the Marburg chair he quickly wrote the essay 'Phenomenological Interpretation of Aristotle (Demonstration of the Hermeneutical Situation)', given as a series of lecture at Freiburg from 1921 to 1922 (but not published until 1985). Heidegger was appointed professor and set about the task of changing philosophy in Germany. He began to develop the themes that would result in his masterwork, *Being and Time* (1927), which defined Heidegger's views on being in all its manifestations: the being of objects and the nature of human existence. Man is always proceeding from his past, existing in a present that is forever changing into the past as he moves into the future. The future contains death.

In the face of impending death man encounters anxiety or dread. Here Heidegger shows the influence of the Danish philosopher Søren Kierkegaard, whose *Fear and Trembling* (1843), *The Concept of Anxiety* (1844) and *The Sickness Unto Death* (1849) were the first works to explore man's position faced with death from what would later be termed an existentialist perspective. The other important influence on Heidegger's thinking as he composed *Being and Time* was Friedrich Nietzsche. Nietzsche had proclaimed the 'death of God'; Heidegger was one of the first to describe what man's position was in this new situation, and how he should proceed. *Dasein*, as Heidegger calls man's existence, occurs in a river of time. As *Dasein* rushes into the future, towards nothing, it achieves authenticity by a recognition of this facticity (*Faktizität*) or thrownness (*Geworfenheit*), as Heidegger called it, from which it proceeds.

Heidegger and Arendt

At Marburg, Heidegger would teach two of his most famous students: Hans-Georg Gadamer and Hannah Arendt. Gadamer would develop the philosophical hermeneutics of the late Heidegger into a branch of philosophy in its own right. Arendt would develop Heidegger's phenomenological method in several important works, including *The Human Condition* (1958) and *The Origins of Totalitarianism* (1951). The latter book has triple significance because, as a Jew, Arendt fled Germany for her life in 1933 at the same time that Heidegger joined the Nazi Party after dropping her as his secret lover.

From the moment he met her in 1924 Heidegger had been overwhelmed by Arendt and she had reciprocated. Their love affair lasted several years, even after Arendt left Marburg to study with Karl Jaspers (1883–1969). Jaspers and Heidegger had been friends, but Jaspers's marriage to a Jew and Heidegger's support for the Nazis strained their relationship. After the war, Arendt forgave Heidegger for his membership of the Nazi Party. Heidegger craved Arendt's forgiveness, just as he sought 'rehabilitation' from his students, colleagues and his disciples – Jaspers and Sartre declined.

Heidegger, Dilthey and German destiny

The most that can be said in mitigation of Heidegger's Nazism is that he was not a Nazi philosopher in the mould of Alfred Rosenberg (1893–1946), who promoted the superiority of the Aryan race and the inferiority of the Jews. What Heidegger saw in Hitler was a renewal of the German spirit and the opportunity for himself to be the philosopher who would lead and define German thought as its historical moment arrived (as if German philosophy hadn't dominated the field since Kant!). Heidegger was far too grand a philosopher to concern himself with the twin tendencies of socialism and fascism that dominated the political landscape of the 1930s in Europe. His concern was with a much broader sweep of destiny, which, in his view, led directly from Aristotle to himself. Apart from Aristotle, Aquinas and Husserl, the philosopher who is key to Heidegger's grasp of 'his' historical moment is Wilhelm Dilthey.

Dilthey (1833–1911) was the grandfather of a modern hermeneutics that would develop through Heidegger to Gadamer, and he provided Heidegger with the bold understanding that meaning originates in man and his history. While he shunned post-Kantian German romanticism, Heidegger subscribed to the kitschy version of it known as *Volkstum*, as evidenced by his sporting of specially designed peasant smocks and turning up for lectures with a pair of skis on his shoulder. After joining the Nazi Party he ran a 'scholarship camp', part-Hitler Youth, part-traditional summer camp, in which mountain air, philosophical discussion and German purity were experienced around a campfire to the accompaniment of guitar music.

After proclaiming his view that Hitler would be the saviour of Germany, Heidegger schemed and positioned his way – successfully on this occasion – to his appointment as rector of Freiburg University. He blocked the progress of Jewish colleagues and declined to take on Jewish graduate students. He gave the Nazi salute with a triple *Seig Heil*. He showed contempt for his master Husserl, who, along with his wife, was of Jewish descent, though a believer in Christianity. Heidegger did not attend Husserl's funeral in 1938 and when a new edition of *Being and Time* was published in 1941, Heidegger succumbed to the Nazi censor's demand that he remove the dedication to his teacher that had graced the first edition.

After the Second World War Heidegger was briefly barred from teaching in German universities. His old friend Karl Jaspers was not as forgiving of Heidegger's Nazism as Hannah Arendt had been. In August

1945 Jaspers stated to the Freiburg University senate, which was considering the case of Heidegger: 'Heidegger's mode of thinking, which seems to me to be fundamentally unfree, dictatorial and uncommunicative, would have a very damaging effect on students at the present time.'

Judging Heidegger

In one way, Heidegger's case is not unique, as nearly half of the philosophers in Germany joined the Nazi Party after 1933. But Heidegger continues to trouble philosophy into the twenty-first century, because he is probably the greatest thinker of the age and because his example is so execrable. Supporters of the 'greatest thinker' camp include George Steiner (*b*. 1929) and Hannah Arendt. Steiner only survived the Holocaust because his father moved the family from France weeks before the German occupation in 1940; Arendt fled Germany in 1933 and then France, shortly after the occupation. For Steiner, Heidegger is a philosopher whose greatness lies in his unique way of posing questions about being, and his focus on the role of language in thought. For Arendt, Heidegger is simply one of the greatest philosophers of all time.

The British philosopher Gilbert Ryle (1900–76) is among those who dismiss Heidegger because of his behaviour. Although he praised *Being and Time* in a 1930 review in *Mind*, Ryle is later reported to have remarked that Heidegger could not have been a good philosopher because he was a bad man. Others have argued that Heidegger's philosophy is 'bad', foremost among them Rudolf Carnap (1891–1970), the father of logical positivism. He rejected Heidegger's work as outright nonsense. A. J. Ayer (1910–89) seconded this view in his best-selling *Language, Truth and Logic* (1936). Bertrand Russell (1872–1970) omitted to even mention Heidegger in his popular *History of Western Philosophy* (1945), as does Anthony Kenny (b. 1931) in his *An Illustrated Brief History of Western Philosophy* (2006).

Perhaps the dilemma of Heidegger is best reflected in the view of Emmanuel Levinas (1906–95), the Lithuanian-born French Jewish Talmudic scholar and philosopher who was a student of Husserl and Heidegger. Levinas found much to appreciate in Heidegger, but felt that Heidegger failed to address the question of ethics that lay beyond pure inquiries into Being. Levinas once remarked that while it was possible to forgive many Germans after the Second World War, it was not possible to forgive Heidegger.

Enduring themes

Heidegger was always critical of the subject. He rejected Husserl's turn towards the transcendental ego, preferring to stay with 'the things themselves'; thus his metaphysics developed in a very different direction from Husserl. Heidegger further defined himself against Husserl through his concern with language. His later philosophy further explored the role of language in a way that helped to usher in the era of the decentred subject that defines post-structuralist thinking (language speaking through man, the death of the author, etc.). Michel Foucault, Jacques Derrida, Jacques Lacan, Julia Kristeva and anyone working in the post-structuralist milieu entered through a door opened by Heidegger.

Heidegger was critical of technology because he believed it dislocated man in relation to time. He saw Europe as squeezed between the pincers of a twin evil: the 'dreary technological frenzy' of the United States and the Soviet Union. In *An Introduction to Metaphysics* (1935) he spoke of how technology led to the 'unrestricted organization of the average man'. Technology provides tools of exploitation, turning the earth to profit. Technology leads to a speeding up of men and information, causing time to be distorted into mere 'velocity, instantaneousness and simultaneity'. As a result, 'time as history has vanished from the lives of all peoples'. Some find in Heidegger's work early seeds of the Green movement. However, Heidegger's mistrust of technology was matched by a romantic belief in 'blood and soil', which played into Nazi ideology about the Fatherland. In a lecture given in Bremen in 1949, Heidegger managed to combine his thoughts about technology and the earth with his only recorded mention of the Holocaust. He said: 'Agriculture is now a motorized food industry, the same thing in its essence as the production of corpses in the gas chambers and the extermination camps, the same thing as blockades and the reduction of countries to famine, the same thing as the manufacture of hydrogen bombs.'

We assert now that *being is the proper and sole theme of philosophy*. This is not our own invention; it is a way of putting the theme which comes to life at the beginning of philosophy in antiquity, and it assumes its most grandiose form in Hegel's logic. At present we are merely asserting that being is the proper and sole theme of philosophy.

Martin Heidegger, 'The Basic Problems
of Phenomenology' (1927)

What characterizes metaphysical thinking that grounds the ground for beings is the fact that metaphysical thinking, starting from what is present, represents it in its presence and thus exhibits it as grounded by its ground.

Martin Heidegger, 'The End of Philosophy and the Task of Thinking' (1969)

To Heidegger the meaning of Being is Time: passing and happening. To him there is no Being's ideal of permanency; indeed he holds that the task of thinking is to make man sensitive to the passage of time.

Rüdiger Safranski, *Martin Heidegger: Between Good and Evil* (1998)

31

Gabriel Marcel

7 December 1889 – 8 October 1973

French playwright, philosopher and Christian existentialist.

Gabriel Marcel coined the term 'existentialism' in the mid-1940s, but distanced himself from it once Jean-Paul Sartre used it in his defining lecture *Existentialism is a Humanism* (1946). Sartre divided existentialists into two camps: Christians such as Gabriel Marcel and Karl Jaspers; and atheists like himself, Simone de Beauvoir and Albert Camus (1913–60). After 1946 Marcel rejected the term 'existentialism' as applied his work. He preferred the term 'philosophy of existence' and he often referred to himself as a neo-Socratic. A fierce critic of the influence of Cartesianism, he argued that man suffers from the reductive and dehumanizing effects of science and technology, which, presaging Hannah Arendt, he saw as threats to human subjectivity. He eschewed philosophical jargon in favour of plain language, and developed a phenomenology independent of Edmund Husserl's to describe what he called 'the ontological mystery'. His best-known works include *Being and Having* (1935) and *The Mystery of Being* (1951).

The Broken World and the functionalized person

From a twenty-first-century perspective Marcel is regarded principally as a philosopher; but more of his contemporaries knew him primarily as a playwright, music critic and composer. Marcel regarded the stage as the most effective venue for the spread of his philosophical ideas. He wrote nearly thirty plays, his most successful being *The Broken World* (1932), in which he outlined a critical view of modernity, to which he would refer in his later philosophical work. Marcel thought the world was 'broken' because man had become 'functionalized' due to a prevailing mechanistic view of the world that denied man's transcendence – his ability to reach spiritually beyond his immediate situation.

Marcel uses the image of the ticket-taker to illustrate the functionalized person, someone whose life is reduced to a repetitive, machine-like function. His natural yearning for transcendence – what Marcel calls his *ontological exigence* – is lost in the daily repetition of a machine-like existence. Eventually, the power of the mechanized world is such that it destroys the functionalized person's natural sense that something is amiss – that, indeed, the world is broken. The feeling of displacement, the worrying sense of the brokenness of the world, is eventually eroded by the repetition of functionality, and the functionalized person loses his desire for transcendence, laying the foundations for despair

In the period before the First World War Marcel hosted a salon in Paris that included important French philosophers like Jean Wahl, Paul Ricoeur, Emmanuel Levinas and Sartre, who would meet to discuss philosophical ideas of mutual interest. Marcel remained an agnostic until his conversion to Roman Catholicism at the age of thirty-nine, after which he broke with Sartre.

Marcel's style of phenomenology

Marcel's focus was on giving a phenomenological description of man's subjectivity and the possibility of intersubjectivity – themes that were also central to Martin Buber and Karl Jaspers. Marcel outlined his version of phenomenological method in *The Mystery of Being*, where he assigns subjects of investigation to one of two categories: *problems* or *mysteries*. Marcel asks: what type of thinking is specific to each type of problem? The answer is that problems require a detached, technical approach. Mysteries, on the other hand, are to be explored in a way that involves the subject's whole being. Marcel identifies these two radically different approaches as *primary reflection* and *secondary reflection*. Primary reflection is analytic; secondary reflection is synthetic. Primary reflection breaks the object of inquiry into its constituent parts; it is a technical approach. Secondary reflection does not attempt to reduce a mystery to its component parts; it is what Marcel refers to as a 'recuperative' act, which attempts to restore and realize the unity of experience.

As an existentialist and a phenomenologist Marcel was concerned more with method than with system. He could be described as a thematic philosopher, as opposed to a systematic one. He did not attempt to present a full account of the world, but rather to introduce methodological tools with which one could make sense of the world. His analysis yielded key themes that included the distinction between *being* and *having*; the idea of *availability/unavailability* towards others and the possibilities for *intersubjectivity* through *reciprocity*.

Being and Having

In *Being and Having* Marcel drew an important ontological distinction: I may have a bicycle, but I don't *have* anger or love or belief – I *am* anger or love or belief; I am *being* those feelings. The most challenging use of the being and having distinction is in considering our bodies – our selves, as embodied human subjects. We both *have* our bodies and *are* our bodies. Neither having nor being alone adequately accounts for what our experience of our bodies is; it is a unique amalgam of both being and having.

Marcel's distinction between *availability* and *unavailability* is central to his theme of intersubjectivity. In order to create a shared world with others, one has to be available to them. The failure or absence of availability is a bar to intersubjective relations. Pride – the mistaken belief that one is self-sufficient, for example – is an impediment to intersubjectivity. To be in a state of unavailability means to be alienated from others, to regard them as objects rather than subjects. In this Marcel covers ground similar to Martin Buber, and his definition of intersubjectivity being based on an I–Thou relationship, rather than I–It. For the available subject to achieve intersubjectivity with another, the condition of *reciprocity* must be met.

What distinguishes Marcel from the Sartrean existentialists is his ultimate optimism, his focus on intersubjectivity. In his lifetime, Marcel was eclipsed by Sartre, both as a philosopher and as a playwright, but his work is laden with significant ideas which will provide much opportunity for development by future philosophers and theologians.

There is an order where the subject finds himself in the presence of something entirely beyond his grasp. I would add that if the word 'transcendent' has any meaning it is here – it designates the absolute, unbridgeable chasm yawning between the subject and being, insofar as being evades every attempt to pin it down.

Gabriel Marcel, *Tragic Wisdom and Beyond* (1973)

The reader who is looking for a 'system' of thought with clear lines of demarcation and connection can be certain of disappointment. And those readers not troubled by a lack of system may find the easy conversational style of Marcel misleading, for the lack of system does not mean a lack of order. There are an order and direction, as well as an underlying rigour, which permeate all of Marcel's work.

Clyde Pax, *An Existential Approach to God:*
A Study of Gabriel Marcel (1972)

32

Ludwig Wittgenstein

(26 April 1889 – 29 April 1951)

Austrian philosopher of language and logic who set the agenda
for British and American analytic philosophy.

English-speaking commentators often refer to Wittgenstein as the greatest philosopher of the twentieth century. It might be more accurate to say that he was the most influential philosopher in the Anglo-American tradition of analytic philosophy, just as Edmund Husserl was the most influential in the continental tradition.

Wittgenstein achieved this by publishing only one book in his lifetime, the exceptionally dense and aphoristic *Tractatus Logico Philosophicus* (1921). In it Wittgenstein developed two theories: *logical atomism* and the *picture theory of meaning* (or language). Logical atomism was first put forward by Bertrand Russell in his 1918 paper 'The Philosophy of Logical Atomism', and it holds that philosophical problems may be solved by breaking them down into atoms of meaning. Wholly original to Wittgenstein was the picture theory of meaning, in which a sentence shares a pictorial form with a state of affairs. After the Second World War (1939–45) Wittgenstein would abandon his picture theory as too rigid an underlying structure, and developed the notion of *language games* to account for language as it is actually used.

Despite his being pigeonholed as an analytic philosopher in the British tradition, Wittgenstein's interests intersected with those of numerous continental philosophers – including Kant, Kierkegaard, Schopenhauer, Nietzsche and Heidegger – and this fact alone sets him apart from his British colleagues. Wherever one 'places' him, Wittgenstein remains a thinker of rare intensity and originality, whose aphoristic writing style and mystical depth mark him as a unique thinker.

A tortured life

While Wittgenstein never published an autobiography, he often considered doing so because he believed it was the moral duty of a man to give an account of himself. Despite being born into one of the wealthiest families in Europe, Wittgenstein chose to make his life hard, signing his fortune away to his sisters and pursuing an ascetic, contemplative lifestyle. A homosexual, he was tortured by physical urges that conflicted with his striving for purity. He was a religious man whose struggles with faith were worthy of Kierkegaard. Wittgenstein's father's family were Jews who had converted to Lutheranism and were assimilated; his mother was a Roman Catholic. In his interwar diaries, Wittgenstein went through an intense period of anti-Semitism. Three of his four brothers killed themselves and Wittgenstein himself was frequently on the verge of suicide from his youth until his naturalization as a British citizen in 1939.

Logical atomism and the *Tractatus*

Wittgenstein had originally intended to become an aircraft engineer, having studied mechanical engineering at Berlin's Technische

Hochschule. But he was obsessed by philosophical problems, particularly those to do with the foundations of mathematics. In 1911, in an effort to discover whether or not he would be a suitable candidate for philosophical study, Wittgenstein visited Gottlob Frege at the University of Jena. Frege did not think Wittgenstein particularly talented, but he gave him an introduction to Bertrand Russell. Russell recognized Wittgenstein's genius and took him on as his pupil at Cambridge.

The First World War separated Wittgenstein from his Cambridge colleagues. He volunteered for the Austro-Hungarian army and carried early drafts of the *Tractatus* with him in his rucksack. During the war years he struggled with Christian religious belief, thoughts of suicide and the demands of his wholly original philosophy. The *Tractatus* – like all of Wittgenstein's writing – went through an unusually painful process of draft and revision. The work was finally completed and served as his PhD thesis at Cambridge under the supervision of G. E. Moore. Russell contributed an introduction, ensuring that the *Tractatus* and its author would be widely noticed.

The *Tractatus Logico-Philosophicus* (1921) argues that philosophical analysis can reduce language to 'atoms' of meaning, which relate to states of affairs or facts. Thus, Russell wrote in his introduction to the *Tractatus*, 'The essential business of language is to assert or deny facts.' Wittgenstein opened the *Tractatus*, more intriguingly, with the first of seven propositions:

1   The world is all that is the case.
1.1 The world is the totality of facts, not of things.
1.11 The world is determined by the facts, and by their being all the facts.

The other six propositions that form the structure of the *Tractatus* are:

2   The world is everything that is the case.

3   What is the case (a fact) is the existence of states of affairs.

4   A logical picture of facts is a thought.

5   A thought is a proposition with a sense. (An elementary proposition is a truth-function of itself.)

6   A proposition is a truth-function of elementary propositions. The general form of a proposition is the general form of a truth function, which is: $[\bar{p}, \bar{\xi}, N(\bar{\xi})]$. This is the general form of a proposition.

7   Whereof one cannot speak, thereof one must be silent.

The *Tractatus* moves beyond logical atomism to make the original contribution (later renounced by Wittgenstein) of the picture theory of meaning. Along with Russell and others analytics, Wittgenstein originally held that metaphysics is nonsense. That is because 'Most of the propositions and questions of philosophers arise from our failure to understand the logic of our language . . . And it is not surprising that the deepest problems are in fact *not* problems at all.' (*Tractatus*, 4.003) When language is properly understood and used, problems are dissolved. In the picture theory of meaning, a sentence shares a pictorial form with a state of affairs. To illustrate his point Wittgenstein likens language to musical notation, which he describes as the pictorial form of the state of affairs that is the musical composition.

But Wittgenstein did not fully believe that linguistic philosophy or logic really 'dissolves' all philosophical problems, because he struggled with existential and religious questions to which analytic philosophy held no answers. He wrote in the *Tractatus* that 'There are, indeed, things that cannot be put into words. They *make themselves manifest*. There are what is mystical.' (6.522). Sounding more Nietzschean than like an analytical philosopher, Wittgenstein ends the *Tractatus* with these words: 'Whereof one cannot speak, thereof one must be silent.'

After his First World War service Wittgenstein trained as a teacher and deliberately asked to be posted to a rural district. He befriended boys from poorer families whom he thought showed promise, but he was overly liberal in the use of corporal punishment when students did not answer questions correctly. He would routinely 'box the ears' of students or pull their hair so hard that clumps of it came out. He finally had to leave teaching after he hit a boy so hard that he knocked him unconscious.

Relations with Russell, Moore and British academia

While Russell considered Wittgenstein to be a genius, Wittgenstein found Russell obtuse and immoral: obtuse because Russell asked for repeated and annoying explanations of what Wittgenstein had meant in parts of the *Tractatus*, and immoral because Wittgenstein fiercely disapproved of Russell's licentiousness. In correspondence, Wittgenstein would explode at Russell, saying that he'd already explained a point once and he wasn't going to waste time writing it down for him again. Wittgenstein also considered G. E. Moore a good example of 'how far a man can go who has absolutely no intelligence whatsoever'. However, it was Moore who arranged for Wittgenstein to receive a Cambridge PhD for the *Tractatus* in 1929, even though Wittgenstein had not, strictly speaking, fulfilled all of the requirements for the degree. Wittgenstein's Cambridge connection also saved his life. As the son of a Jew he was destined for the gas chambers in the Second World War, but because he had taught at Trinity College, Cambridge, the economist John Maynard Keynes (1883–1946) was able to use his influence to fast-track Wittgenstein's British naturalization.

As a university lecturer at Cambridge, Wittgenstein's pure philosophical temperament did not allow for the niceties of academic convention. He would talk without notes, extemporaneously, often lapsing into long silences in front of a class. He favoured students from less privileged backgrounds, and advised them not to take up philosophy as a profession, but to do something useful in the real world (carpentry or medicine, in the cases of two students who followed his advice). As a teacher and a thinker, Wittgenstein eschewed theory, although he was fascinated by the work of Sigmund Freud. He didn't regard Freud's explanations of the workings of the human mind as scientific in the sense that one can regard Darwin's theory of evolution as scientific, but he found psychoanalysis compelling, having often sought to understand the dreams he recorded in his diary. Wittgenstein was increasingly interested in those things 'Whereof one cannot speak', the things about which 'one must be silent'.

Language games

During the interwar years Wittgenstein came to reject the logical atomism of the *Tractatus*, and in his thinking and in his lectures at Cambridge he rejected the assumption that the meaning of a word is the thing that it stands for. He abandoned the notion of language and meaning as a cut-and-dried business, and that the role of a proposition is to describe a state of affairs. He no longer thought that meaningful sentences depended upon a hidden logical structure that corresponded to a similar logical structure underlying the facts being pictured by those sentences. He came to think that language could only be understood by paying attention to how words were actually used in everyday life. To this end he developed the concept of language games, which came to him as a result of his school teaching experience and from reflecting upon how children acquire and use language.

A full account of Wittgenstein's theory of language games only appeared after his death. In *Philosophical Investigations* (1953) he attempted to clarify problems of philosophy that he believed were caused by language. It is one of the key texts of what would come to be called the *ordinary language* school of philosophy at Oxford, whose proponents included Gilbert Ryle and J. L. Austin (1911–60). Wittgenstein's theory of language games tries to show how meaning arises in everyday use of language. Language doesn't have fixed meanings – this can be demonstrated by any word e.g. 'hold' that can be used as different parts of speech, i.e. a verb and a noun. As a verb I can hold an object in my hand, the shop assistant can hold an item for me until I can pay for it, I can hold you up when you are about to fall and the police could hold me in a cell. As a noun, 'hold' could be a controlling force (she's really got a hold on me), a wrestling hold (he's got me in the Polish hammer), it could be fortified place (a fort) or the cell in which the police are holding me. Wittgenstein developed the view that while language has rules, they cannot be definitively nailed down. Language is a social activity, not a collection of fixed definitions employed according to a rigid set of rules. The meaning of language resides in the use to which it is put.

In *Philosophical Investigations* Wittgenstein introduces the hypothetical problem of *private languages*. 'The words of this language are to refer to what can be known only to the speaker,' he wrote in *Philosophical Investigations*, 'to his immediate, private, sensations. So another cannot understand the language.' A private language would be understood only by the individual who invented it. One of the key philosophical uses of the idea of a private language is to challenge the idea of fixed meanings. Wittgenstein argues that philosophers make mistakes when they consider problems such as numbers or sensations that force upon us fixed rules for how we name them. Wittgenstein argues the notion of a private language is an unacknowledged presupposition of much epistemology, metaphysics and twentieth-century representational theory of mind.

The problem of belief versus knowledge

As Wittgenstein neared the end of his life he spent much time contemplating religious belief. While he could not be a Christian in a doctrinaire way, during his service in the First World War he frequently prayed to Jesus. He believed in the concept of salvation and, indeed, it could be argued that this kept him from committing suicide. Although he published only one book in his lifetime, Wittgenstein was prolific. He filled notebooks with observations on mathematics, ethics, a theory of colour and more. But the last words he wrote, in the hours when he was facing death, were a refutation of doubt and scepticism. They were published in 1969 under the title *On Certainty*. He had a Roman Catholic funeral.

Now think of the following use of language: I send someone shopping. I give him a slip marked 'five red apples'. He takes the slip to the shopkeeper, who opens the drawer marked 'apples', then he looks up the word 'red' in a table and finds a colour sample opposite it; then he says the series of cardinal numbers – I assume that he knows them by heart – up to the word 'five' and for each number he takes an apple of the same colour as the sample out of the drawer.

– It is in this and similar ways that one operates with words. – 'But how does he know where and how he is to look up the word "red" and what he is to do with the word "five"?' – Well, I assume that he 'acts' as I have described. Explanations come to an end some-where. – But what is the meaning of the word 'five'? – No such thing was in question here, only how the word 'five' is used.

Ludwig Wittgenstein, *Philosophical Investigations* (1953)

I believe that every human being has two human parents; but Catholics believe that Jesus had only a human mother. And other people might believe that there are human beings with no parents, and give no credence to all the contrary evidence. Catholics believe as well that in certain circumstances a wafer completely changes its nature, and at the same time that all evidence proves the contrary. And so if Moore said 'I know that this is wine and not blood', Catholics would contradict him.

Ludwig Wittgenstein, *On Certainty* (1969)

Wittgenstein occupies a unique place in twentieth-century philos-ophy and he is for that reason difficult to subsume under the usual philosophical categories . . . The difficulty is magnified because he came to philosophy under complex conditions which make it plausible for some interpreters to connect him with Frege, Russell and Moore, with the Vienna Circle, Oxford Language Philosophy and the analytic tradition in philosophy as a whole, while others bring him together with Schopenhauer or Kierkegaard, with Derrida, Zen Buddhism or avant-garde art.

Hans Sluga, 'Ludwig Wittgenstein: Life and Work, An Introduction' (1996)

33

Herbert Marcuse

19 July 1898 – 29 July 1979

German-American philosopher and father of the New Left who coined the term 'repressive tolerance'; his philosophy envisaged liberation through a revolutionary reading of Freud and Marx.

Herbert Marcuse represents the high point of a humanistic Marxism, which aimed to transform society by ending restrictions on freedom (which Marcuse located in sexuality) and thereby eliminating alienation. In *Eros and Civilization* (1955) he used categories devised by Sigmund Freud (1856–1939) to examine how the mechanisms of repression in the individual also held true for the state; and, for Marcuse, the Marxist revolution would include the liberation of sexuality. This idea appealed to the counter-culture movement of the 1960s, when the propitious timing of radical politics and the sexual revolution created a climate in which Marcuse's work flourished. For a while he was the most widely read left-wing thinker in the United States.

Marcuse's intellectual path – like that of his fellow Jewish émigré Hannah Arendt – begins with Martin Heidegger. After serving in the German army in the First World War, Marcuse took a PhD in German Literature. For six years he was a bookseller in Berlin, before returning in Freiburg in 1928 to study with Heidegger, who had just published *Being and Time*. Unlike Heidegger, who would join the Nazi Party, Marcuse came to his philosophical studies as a committed student of Karl Marx (1818–83), though not an uncritical one. Marcuse was looking for a way to combine Marxist revolutionary ideals with a concern for the individual. In this he predated by nearly a generation similar attempts by the French existentialists Jean-Paul Sartre and Maurice Merleau-Ponty (1907–61).

Marcuse and the Frankfurt School

After presenting a thesis on *Hegel's Ontology and Theory of Historicity* (1932) Marcuse moved to Frankfurt to join the Institute for Social Research – more popularly known as the Frankfurt School, which is also a catch-all term to encompass the Marxist critical theory for which it became famous through the work of Max Horkheimer (1895–1973), Theodor Adorno (1903–69) and Erich Fromm (1900–80). Here he wrote against the rising tide of fascism, locating its source in free-market liberalism – which he saw as repressive rather than 'free'.

'The turn from the liberalist to the total-authoritarian state occurs with the framework of a single social order,' Marcuse argued in his thesis. 'With regard to the unity of this economic base, we can say that it is liberalism that "produces" the total-authoritarian state out of itself, as its own consummation at a more advanced stage of development.'

In 1934 Marcuse left Germany for New York, and a year afterwards the entire Frankfurt School relocated to Columbia University. It would not return to Germany until 1953. In 1940 Marcuse became a US citizen and decided to remain in his adopted country.

A Marxist intellectual in post-war America

During the Second World War Marcuse advised the US Office of Strategic Services (forerunner of the CIA) on fascism and communism: fascism he had witnessed at first hand and he was a leading theorist of communism. His post-war work for the US State Department's denazification programme brought Marcuse back in contact with his old professor, Heidegger, whom he visited in 1947 in a vain attempt to persuade him to recant his Nazi past. In his penultimate letter to Heidegger, Marcuse wrote: 'I – and very many others – have admired you as a philosopher; from you we have learned an infinite amount. But we cannot make the separation between Heidegger the philosopher and Heidegger the man, for it contradicts your own philosophy' (28 August 1947). No less painful was Marcuse's growing realization that Joseph Stalin's Soviet Union was not a Marxist utopia, and in 1958 he published *Soviet Marxism: A Critical Analysis*.

That year also marked the beginning of his teaching at Brandeis University in Massachusetts, where he remained until 1965, when the university declined to renew his contract (the University of California at La Jolla welcomed him, however, and he stayed there until his retirement). Marcuse's Brandeis years were among his most productive and, for the authorities, unsettling, as American tolerance of left-wing thought began to recede. In 1964 he published *One Dimensional Man: Studies in the Ideology of Advanced Industrial Society*. It is a bitingly concise description of the consequences of industrialization and economic liberalism. 'Freedom of enterprise was from the beginning not altogether a blessing,' Marcuse claims. 'As the liberty to work or to starve, it spelled toil, insecurity and fear for the vast majority of the population.' He argues that once human rights and freedoms become institutionalized, 'these rights and liberties shared the fate of the society of which they had become an integral part. The achievement cancels the premises.'

In *Repressive Tolerance* (1965) Marcuse identified the mechanism that governs unfreedom as the 'ideology of tolerance, which, in reality, favours and fortifies the conservation of the status quo of inequality and discrimination'. Marcuse's Marxist analysis enables him to pin-point aspects of what Michel Foucault (1926–84) would identify as the discourses of power that govern our daily life. For Marcuse, analysis demands action on the part of the intellectual, whose role in the advanced industrial period is 'to recall and preserve historical possibilities which seem to have become utopian possibilities – that it is his task to break the concreteness of oppression in order to open the mental space in which this society can be recognized as what it is and does'. Marcuse was embraced by a broad range of New Left groups, including violent ones like the Baader-Meinhof gang. In 'The Problem of Violence' (1967) Marcuse described his stance thus: 'Perhaps instead of invoking the "right of resistance" we should say that we are sacrificing lower-level laws in order to defend constitutional law. Furthermore, the theo-retical reasons against the principle of nonviolence contradict the humanitarian reasons for it.'

By 1978 Marcuse no longer believed that the utopian revolution he dreamed of was possible in the United States. He turned his focus on art and the role it plays in developing a revolutionary consciousness. In *The Aesthetic Dimension: Toward A Critique of Marxist Aesthetics* (1978) Marcuse insisted upon the relevance of art and art criticism not only for Marxist thought, but in its wider social function. Marcuse was impatient with the left-wing attitude which held that art was frivolous and a diversion from political action. While acknowledging that 'In a situation where the miserable reality can be changed only through radical political praxis, the concern with aesthetics demands justification,' Marcuse shows that works of art are products that spring from specific social, economic and political circumstances, and therefore have much to tell us about their origins, which are the ultimate subject of Marxist analysis. 'It seems,' says Marcuse, 'that art as art expresses a truth, an experience, a necessity which, although not in the domain of radical praxis, are nevertheless essential components of revolution.'

The Nixon period and the collapse of the American Left

Marcuse belonged to an era in which the politics of Left and Right in the United States collided in a mighty battle of contesting ideologies – not only in the carnage of the First World War, but also as a philosophical response to the Cold War. He represents a vital gauge of United States realpolitik in the period between its entry into the Second World War in 1941 and the 1968 election of Richard Nixon as president. In 1941 the mood in Washington was such that a lifelong Marxist revolutionary émigré like Marcuse could be employed by the key national security organization, the Office of Strategic Services, and, after the war, by the US Department of State as head of its Central European section, a post from which Marcuse retired in 1951. By contrast, the years following Nixon's election marked a turn to the Right in American politics that was reinforced rather than ameliorated by the demise of the Soviet Union in 1991. In the 1990s the influence of Marxism in American life had all but disappeared; more significantly, it had also waned to the point of near-extinction in American universities. In the post-9/11 period, what started as a conservative drift would turn into a right-wing tide against any thinking that questioned the legitimacy of capitalism and its values, or even attempted to understand its workings using the critical tools of Marxist analysis.

Marcuse's influence has not fared well in the early years of the twenty-first century. He is overshadowed by Frankfurt School successors like Jürgen Habermas (*b.* 1929) and by contemporaries like Adorno, who have remained fashionable with French post-structuralists, whose prevailing discourse is at odds with Marcuse's. The post-structuralist and deconstructionist project concerns itself with language and the problematic of meaning and the self. Marcuse, on the other hand, pursued what the post-structuralists would call a 'grand narrative', a theoretical explanation that would account for history by 'totalizing' it. In plain language, he used Marxist analysis to analyze the world in which he lived, in order to propose a better one, full of meaning. As capitalism lurches from crisis to crisis in the early twenty-first century, with consequent social and political turmoil, political philosophers are likely to revisit Marcuse, whose critique of capitalist social organization may enjoy a newfound relevance.

Economic freedom would mean freedom *from* the economy – from being controlled by economic forces and relationships; freedom from the daily struggle for existence, from earning a living. Political freedom would mean liberation of the individuals *from* politics over which they have no effective control. Similarly, intellectual freedom would mean the restoration of individual thought now absorbed by mass communication and indoctrination, abolition of 'public opinion' together with its makers. The unrealistic sound of these propositions is indicative, not of their utopian character, but of the strength of the forces which prevent their realization.

Herbert Marcuse, *One-Dimensional Man* (1964)

> The Fascist organization of society requires a change in the entire setting of culture. The culture with which German idealism was linked, and which lived on until the Fascist era, accented private liberties and rights, so that the individual, at least as a private person, could feel safe in the state and in society.
>
> Herbert Marcuse, *Reason and Revolution* (1941)

> Because he was so concretely and immediately involved in opposing German fascism, he was also able and willing to indentify fascist tendencies in the United States.
>
> Kellner, Douglas, 'Radical Politics, Marcuse, and the New Left' (2001)

34

Gilbert Ryle

(19 August 1900 – 6 October 1976)

British philosopher who coined the term 'ghost in the machine'
to describe Cartesian dualism, which he refuted.

Gilbert Ryle was the most prominent of the so-called ordinary language philosophers who gathered at Oxford between the First and the Second World Wars, including J. L. Austin (1911–60) and Peter Strawson (1919–2006). Ryle wrote in his 1970 essay 'Autobiographical' that, for him, philosophy consisted of asking 'What constitutes a philosophical problem; and what is the way to solve it?' Ryle's unvarnished presentation of his project conceals more than it reveals. Some of his rivals at Cambridge dismissed him as a rather simple and derivative thinker – but in reality Ryle was anything but. He is the author of one of the enduring texts of modern British philosophy, *The Concept of Mind* (1949), which identifies Cartesian dualism as a problem that has bedevilled philosophy since the Enlightenment. Referring to the Cartesian mind-body split as the problem of a 'ghost in the machine', Ryle develops a theory of language based on what he calls 'category mistakes'. The *Concept of Mind* is generally thought of as 'behaviourist', in that it describes dispositions to behaviour that a person might have. Ryle himself called it 'a sustained essay in phenomenology, if you are at home with that label' ('Phenomenology Versus "The Concept of Mind"', *Collected Papers Vol. 1*, 1971); a provocative statement, since British philosophers were generally very much not at home with that label.

Ryle and the phenomenologists

More than any other analytic philosopher Ryle made a close study of the father of phenomenology Edmund Husserl and his predecessors Alexius Meinong (1853–1920) and Franz Brentano (1838–1917). Ryle visited Husserl in Germany in 1929 and his first publication was a review of *Essentiale Fragen* by Husserl's pupil Roman Ingarden (1893–1970). Returning to Oxford he offered lectures on Husserl, Brentano and Meinong that no one attended. Self-taught in German, Ryle was one of the first in any language to tackle Heidegger's *Being and Time* (he reviewed it in *Mind*, vol. xxxviii, 1928). However, while he recognized the value of phenomenology, Ryle eventually rejected it as a fatally flawed and jargon-ridden enterprise. He did not believe that Husserl's phenomenology was a truly presuppositionless inquiry, and thought it put doctrine before description. In his surprisingly positive review of *Being and Time* he remarked: 'It is my personal opinion that qua First Philosophy Phenomenology is at present heading for bankruptcy and disaster and will end either in self-ruinous Subjectivism or in a windy Mysticism.'

Ryle and the mind-body problem

Cartesian dualism – what Ryle calls the 'official doctrine' of Western thought – is, he contends, based on 'one big mistake and a mistake of a special kind': a category mistake. A category mistake 'represents the facts of mental life as if they belonged to one logical type or category . . . when they actually belong to another'. His famous example is that of an overseas visitor being shown around the Universities of Oxford or Cambridge. The visitor might see what appears to be a disparate collection of individual college buildings, libraries, playing fields, administrative offices – not a single, easily identifiable campus. The visitor might ask 'Where is the university?' The visitor's error is in not understanding that the university *is* the things he has just seen. Category mistakes, says Ryle, lead to absurdity. 'When two terms belong to the same category, it is proper to construct conjunctive propositions embodying them. Thus a purchaser may say that he bought a left-hand glove and a right-hand glove, but not that he bought a left-hand glove and a right-hand glove and a pair of gloves.' So conjoining terms of different types leads to absurdity. Ryle offers as an example Charles Dickens's humorous solecism in *The Pickwick Papers* (1836–7): 'Miss Bolo came home in a flood of tears and a sedan-chair.' The point being, Ryle argues, that 'It would have been equally ridiculous to construct the disjunction "She came home either in a flood of tears or else in a sedan-chair".'

In Ryle's view Cartesian mind-body dualism makes precisely this category mistake, because by positing a 'ghost in the machine' it creates an absurd conjunction. Ryle uses this example of absurdity to discount Cartesian dualism's claim that there are both bodies and minds, physical processes and mental ones. The sedan-chair remark from Dickens is an example of the figure of speech that linguists and grammarians call zeugma (from a Greek word meaning 'yoke') in which a single adjective or verb is employed to modify two or more nouns, even when this is inappropriate or illogical. It is this kind of appeal to the rules

of grammar that gives Ryle's ordinary language philosophy much of
its force.

The Concept of Mind

Ryle saw the work of the philosopher as resembling that of a gram-
marian and a cartographer. In outlining his theory of mind, he noticed
that 'Many people can talk sense with concepts but cannot talk sense
about them.' They know how to employ concepts, but 'they cannot
state the logical regulations governing their use'. Ryle compares these
people (other philosophers?) as being 'like people who know their way
about their own parish, but cannot construct or read a map of it, much
less a map of the region or continent in which their parish lies'. Moving
beyond Cartesian dualism, Ryle addresses problems of knowledge, will,
emotion, self-knowledge and imagination. One of the enduring distinc-
tions that he makes in *The Concept of Mind* is between knowing *how*
and knowing *that*; for instance, I know *how* to play chess; by contrast,
I know *that* my name is Stephen.

Ryle's prose style is one of the best arguments in favour of ordinary language philosophy, and he had the rare gift of making philosophical prose charming, witty and pithy ('Only a person who is at
least a partial master of the Russian tongue can make the wrong sense
of a Russian expression. Mistakes are exercises of competences'). He
was a leading British philosopher at a time when the influence of Russell
and Moore had waned and the stars of his fellow ordinary language
philosophers – J. L. Austin, Gilbert Ryle, H. L. A. Hart, Peter Strawson
and later Ludwig Wittgenstein – were on the rise. Russell was profoundly
irritated by Ryle and one cannot imagine two more different person-
alities: Russell was aggressive and socially disagreeable; Ryle was affable

and liked cricket, gardening and playing bridge. Russell condemned ordinary language philosophy in his article 'The Cult of "Common Usage"' (1953) as 'a trivial and uninteresting pursuit. To discuss endlessly what silly people mean when they say silly things may be amusing but can hardly be important.' Later, in 'Some Replies to Criticism' (1959) Russell grumpily noted that 'it is not an altogether pleasant experience to find oneself regarded as antiquated after having been, for a time, in the fashion. It is difficult to accept this experience gracefully.'

Ryle further solidified this change in British philosophy by succeeding G. E. Moore as editor of the main British philosophy journal *Mind*, a position he held from 1947 to 1972. The editorship gave him great control over who and what got published (and whose book got reviewed by whom). As the professionalization of philosophy that began with T. H. Green continued apace, Ryle wielded enormous influence over who got what job and where.

> There is a doctrine about the nature and place of minds which is so prevalent among theorists and even among laymen that it deserves to be described as the official theory. Most philosophers, psychologists and religious teachers subscribe, with minor reservations, to its main articles and, although they admit certain theoretical difficulties in it, they tend to assume that these can be overcome without serious modifications being made to the architecture of the theory. It will be argued here that the central principles of the doctrine are unsound and conflict with the whole body of what we know about minds when we are not speculating about them.
>
> Gilbert Ryle, *The Concept of Mind* (1949)

35

Hans-Georg Gadamer

(11 February 1900 – 13 March 2002)

German creator of modern hermeneutics, which he showed to have relevance that extended beyond aesthetics and philosophy to politics and the law.

One of the twentieth century's most prolific philosophers, Gadamer took the German idea of hermeneutics (the study of the meaning of texts, usually biblical ones) and developed it into a sophisticated tool for the interpretation of 'texts', understood more broadly to include – in the aftermath of structuralism and post-structuralism – any thing or phenomenon the investigator wishes to investigate. Beyond the text, Gadamer viewed the hermeneutical stance as a decisively philosophical one; for him, hermeneutics *is* philosophy. His key work is *Truth and Method* (1960), which continues to appeal to students today, particularly because it looks beyond philosophy as a single academic discipline to address the whole of experience.

In order to appreciate the work of Gadamer we need to be acquainted with Wilhelm Dilthey (1833–1911), a philosopher who provides a vital link between Kant and present-day hermeneutics, as well as the work of Friedrich Schleiermacher (1768–1834). Dilthey was instrumental in transforming hermeneutics from its historical roots in biblical exegesis to a method for reading texts in the social and historical context in which they are created. He is most famous for the concept of the hermeneutic circle, an interpretive process that takes account of the relationship between the parts and the whole of a text, with the one always referring back to the other in a circular movement. Schleiermacher's contribution to modern hermeneutics was to regard works of art and literature as legitimate subjects of philosophical study. Biblical exegesis was only one use of hermeneutics; Schleiermacher regarded hermeneutics as an interpretive tool that could be applied to all texts. In this, he established a precedent that led the way not only to Dilthey but also to Heidegger and post-structuralists like Foucault and Derrida.

The authorial 'I'

Unlike the post-structuralists who emerged a century later, Dilthey 'believed' in the author (post-structuralists would downplay the role of the author, viewings texts as the result of social, historical, linguistic and political conventions). Dilthey included in the hermeneutical circle the author's biography, the circumstances of his life – birth, education, profession, life experiences in general – as well as the text itself, regarded from a number of viewpoints. All of these parts combined to make a whole that would reveal further layers of meaning as time passed and the circumstances of the text – including the reader – changed. Dilthey saw life as a continuum, and the hermeneutical circle as a living, pulsating force in history, reinterpreting itself as it moves forward in time.

Dilthey's view of historical flux and change influenced Heidegger and his ontology of *Dasein* or human being. Dilthey's key historical work is *The Formation of the Historical World in the Human Sciences* (1910), in which he brings to history the structural analysis he developed in his psychology of how human beings organize themselves. Dilthey moves beyond the concern of the individual and groups to address universal historical understanding, taking into account parts as small as the individual 'biography' and as large as a nation. The parts, large and small, inform each other in an ever more complete understanding of the whole. The behaviour of individuals and the groups they formed was important for Dilthey because he sought to find there a definition of objectivity for the human sciences. In 'The Rise of Hermeneutics' Dilthey wrote: 'Action everywhere presupposes the understanding of other persons; much of our happiness as human beings derives from being able to feel the states of mind of others; the entire science of philology and of history is based on the presupposition that such reunderstanding of what is singular can be raised to objectivity.' Dilthey brought into greater currency the concept of the 'worldview' – that is, the attempt by science or philosophy to posit a unified outlook on life. He viewed philosophies as having special relevance for their times.

Gadamer and the war years

Gadamer's career began under testing circumstances. He was one of Martin Heidegger's most illustrious students. Unlike fellow Heidegger students Herbert Marcuse and Hannah Arendt, he was not Jewish, and so was not forced to flee Nazi Germany; but, unlike his mentor Heidegger, Gadamer did not join the Nazi Party. However, his signature appeared along with those of other academics on a 1933 document supporting Hitler and his leadership. Gadamer later claimed that he was a 'political innocent' and did not know what he was signing. However, given that his work is rooted in close analysis of language and meaning, this excuse seems less than convincing. For Gadamer, to exist is to use language, to *be* in language. He was appointed professor at Leipzig in 1938 and he was appointed rector after the Second World War. Under Communist rule Gadamer organized the reconstruction of the university. In 1947 he returned to West Germany, to Frankfurt University. In 1949 he succeeded Karl Jaspers as professor at Heidelberg.

Finitude

Influenced by Husserl's phenomenological method of proceeding without preconceptions, and regarding hermeneutics as a descriptive rather than a prescriptive enterprise, Gadamer nevertheless knows that we cannot *entirely* bracket out our prejudices, that we always, because of our history, bring with us some pre-judgements. Here, the French hermeneutical theorist Paul Ricoeur, who shares with Gadamer the intellectual lineage descending from Husserl through Heidegger and Jaspers (1883–1969), marks the starting point of inquiry as 'a humble one of acknowledging the historical conditions to which all human understanding is subsumed in the region of finitude' (*Hermeneutics and the Human Sciences*, 1981). It is not only the investigator who is 'subsumed in the region of finitude'; the text, also, brings with it a history: made by so-and-so at such-and-such a place in such-and-such a time.

Hermeneutics, history and meaning

Classical hermeneutics as practised by Schleiermacher and (with modifications) by Dilthey proceeded on the basis that there can be a 'right' or 'objective' interpretation of texts. The limits that Gadamer and Ricoeur (1913–2005) place on epistemology – the acknowledgment of prejudice and the understanding that there can be no final knowledge – are, in fact, liberating. They show that all human understanding occurs in an historical context, and that temporal context affects the ontology of the interpreter and the text. This temporal aspect of hermeneutical understanding comes obviously from the Heidegger of *Being and Time* (1927) and, to a lesser degree, from Heraclitus (*c.* 535– *c.* 475 BC): 'All things come out of the One and the One out of all things . . . I see nothing but Becoming. Be not deceived! It is the fault of your limited outlook and not the fault of the essence of things if you believe that you see firm land anywhere in the ocean of Becoming and Passing. You need names for things, just as if they had a rigid permanence, but the very river in which you bathe a second time is no longer the same one which you entered before.' (*Fragment 41*).

Gadamer's understanding of history and meaning is expressed in the concept of the 'fusion of horizons' in which 'old and new are always combining into something of living value'. The fusion of horizons gives Gadamer's hermeneutics its perpetually fresh quality, as meanings are revised with each investigation. His view of history opposes historicism, which would fix the text as immutable fact; instead, Gadamer uses history to create a 'historically effected' consciousness. 'Our need to become conscious of effective history is urgent,' he writes in *Truth and Method*, 'because it is necessary for scientific consciousness.' Historically effected consciousness is central to hermeneutics, because 'it is an element in the act of understanding itself'; its practical use is to help in '*finding the right questions to ask*' (Gadamer's emphasis).

The value of intersubjectivity

Gadamer, like the French psychoanalyst Jacques Lacan, identifies the subject as 'decentred'. We find ourselves 'outside of' ourselves in a world of significance generated by language; but since all subjects find themselves in this position, our experience and our knowledge is inter-subjective. The author gives birth to a text through the medium of language, but, once published, the text is no longer defined by autho-rial intention. It now belongs to time, to history – to interpretation. This does not mean, however, that the text and its meaning are lost in a fog of relativism. While Gadamer argues that there is no one 'right' reading, he makes it clear that there is not an unlimited number of right readings.

Even if one accepted, in the study of a 'non practical' discipline such as poetry, the kind of aesthetic relativism which Gadamer abjured, one could never accept it in law or jurisprudence, where the law must be recognized for what it is and upheld judiciously. That is, for Gadamer, interpretations of texts become meaningful when they are reasonable and coherent and have an *intersubjective* value. One cannot imagine the legal code of Germany being subjected to arbitrary and subjective inter-pretation; along with any other legal code or binding set of rules it depends upon the agreement of members of a community. Gadamer's method for finding truths to which we could all subscribe is the dialogue. Following Plato (*c*.428/7–*c*.348/7 BC), he promotes a version of Socratic dialogue which encourages the free exchange and develop-ment of views in order to find adequate interpretations of texts through a hermeneutical process that results in self-understanding and self-trans-formation, and the discovery of the intersubjective truths of a shared world.

> The understanding and the interpretation of texts is not merely a concern of science, but obviously belongs to human experience of the world in general.
>
> Hans-Georg Gadamer, *Truth and Method* (1960)

[Gadamer] has for so long exemplified both in his person and in his writings the moral dimensions of the hermeneutic project. He has been for much of our time the *phronemos* [practical wisdom] of hermeneutics, the exemplary practitioner of the hermeneutic virtues, both intellectual and moral. It may be that in the future others will be able to advance the hermeneutic enterprise further, but, if so, it will only be because they have first been able to learn what Gadamer has taught.

Alasdair MacIntrye, 'On Not Having the Last Word:
Thoughts On Our Debts to Gadamer' (2002)

Hermeneutics is the theory of the operations of understanding in their relation to the interpretation of texts.

Paul Ricoeur, *Hermeneutics and the Human Sciences* (1981)

36

Jacques Lacan

(13 April 1901 – 9 September 1981)

French psychoanalyst and philosopher who argued that the uncon-
scious is structured like a language.

Jacques Lacan's work marries a deep reading of the history of the
Western philosophical canon with a practical and theoretical knowledge of psychoanalysis that results in a highly original way of defining
the human subject, and of addressing problems arising from the fact
of existence. Lacan's theorizing draws from a wide range of sources,
including medicine, mathematics, biology, myth and literature, with
the consequence that his thought, in turn, cross-pollinates many
disciplines. In this sense he may be regarded as a 'founder' of interdisciplinary studies.

Lacan's reinterpretation of Freudian psychoanalysis focuses on the
role of language in analysis, and also on the creation of the subject
and his world. In this he was influenced by the work of Ferdinand de
Saussure. The effect of Saussure's theory of the arbitrary nature of
the sign in what is signified by language, combined with a critical view
of the subject outlined by Martin Heidegger, and further developed in
the hermeneutics of Hans-Georg Gadamer and the deconstructionism

of Jacques Derrida, was to create a *decentred subject*. No longer the confidently acting subject who features in the philosophy of Immanuel Kant, the subject is now defined 'outside' of himself by language. The concept of the decentred subject is at the heart of Lacan's most famous contribution to psychoanalysis, the *mirror stage*. In the mirror stage the child sees a reflection from which he derives a sense of himself, but as 'other', as an object. It is from this experience that the rest of Lacanian thinking follows.

A Freudian and a maverick

Lacan was the bad boy of the French psychoanalytic establishment. From his perspective, psychoanalysis had become too comfortable, rooted in a dogma repetitively applied in a routine therapeutic encounter. He argued that psychoanalysis (in common with any other body of thought) was a constantly changing and dynamic assemblage, and that the rules governing it must accommodate this fact. The French establishment was outraged at Lacan's introduction of the variable length session – Freud had fixed the length of a psychoanalytic 'hour' at fifty minutes. Lacan and his followers quit the Société Parisienne de Psychanalyse in protest and created the Société Française de Psychanalyse. Psychoanalysts, like socialists, are almost pathologically schismatic.

The Lacanian seminar: philosophy as theatre

Lacan spurned the tradition of academic publishing, preferring his work to 'appear' in the form of regular seminars held at various Parisian venues, including the École Normale Supérieure and then the Sorbonne.

The seminars ran from 1953 to 1980 and selections from them are published in English under the title *Écrits* (a series running from 1977). In this spoken format, Lacan built idea upon idea, while at the same time demolishing his structure behind him as he proceeded.

His seminars drew crowds of the brilliant, the fashionable and the curious; not since Henri Bergson had philosophy been such a public spectacle. What Bergson and Lacan had in common was a large audience; what separated them was intelligibility. Bergson's philosophy was presented in exquisite prose which made his thought accessible to a wide audience; Lacan's philosophy is couched in neologisms and obscure references piled so deep as to elude all but the most learned. He draws heavily upon the history of philosophy after Aristotle (384–322 BC): there are those from whom he takes bricks for the building of his own edifice – Karl Jaspers, Heidegger, Hegel – and those whom he rejects, defining himself against them – J. S. Mill and Jeremy Bentham (1748–1832), for instance.

Jouissance

A good example of the philosophical density of Lacan's thinking is his use of the word *jouissance*. A dictionary translation of the word yields 'enjoyment' (but English translations of Lacan generally leave the word untranslated, because English equivalents do not carry the sexual charge of the French original). Lacan uses it to mean a kind of orgasmic pleasure that exceeds phallogocentrism – Jacques Derrida's term for male-dominated discourse. *Jouissance* is a kind of maverick, outlaw, bliss-seeking, tendency, an *id* left unsupervised by the male parent, free to do as it wishes without interference from ego or superego. On one occasion Lacan defines *jouissance* as 'no more than a negative instance';

a definition that he supplements with the explanation that it 'is what serves no purpose' (*On Feminine Sexuality: The Limits of Love and Knowledge*, 1999).

On another day, he offers *jouissance* as the key to the question, 'What am *I*?' (*Écrits*, Lacan's emphasis). He answers this rhetorical question as if it had been posed as '*Where* am I?' as opposed to '*What* am *I*?' '*I*,' says Lacan, 'am in the place from which "the universe is a flaw in the purity of Non-Being" is vociferated.' Umberto Eco (*b.* 1932) would take this up in *Kant and the Platypus* (1999), noticing that here we find ourselves confronted with the great metaphysical question 'Why is there being rather than nothing?', and its answer, '*Because there is*' (Eco's emphasis). Returning to Lacan's siting of 'I' in its location as 'the place from which "the universe is a flaw in the purity of Non-Being" is vociferated', he comments: 'And not without reason for, by protecting itself, this place makes Being itself languish. This place is called *Jouissance*, and it is *Jouissance* whose absence would render the universe vain.' And so on . . . It is by this incremental method that Lacan builds his concepts, looking at them afresh each time he revisits them. They are informed not only by the change they undergo as soon as they are uttered in public, but also by the new life they acquire by virtue of having been understood (or not) by others; and also by Lacan's continuing programme of study.

Lacanian thinking: methodology and style

Perhaps students of critical studies take so naturally to Lacan because of his method of incorporating texts from philosophy, literature and the social sciences in his work to find in them fresh and methodologically useful meanings. In some cases Lacan's reading of a text forms the basis for a central plank in his theory. For instance, he takes events from Edgar Allan Poe's short story 'The Purloined Letter' to form his concept of 'repetition automatism', which he uses to describe the 'compulsive repetition or reproduction of an internalized social structure which the subject repeatedly and compulsively re-enacts' (*Encyclopedia of Lacanian Analysis*).

The density of Lacan's thinking – and its economy – can be illustrated by a passage in *Écrits* in which he describes an aspect of the mirror phase. He writes: 'Regardless of what covers the image, nevertheless, the latter merely centres a power that is deceptive insofar as it diverts alienation – which already situates desire in the Other's field – toward the totalitarian rivalry which prevails due to the fact that the semblance exercises a dyadic fascination on him: that "one or the other" is the depressive return of the second phase in Melanie Klein's work; it is the figure of Hegelian murder.' Here it is as if Lacan is having an intimate conversation with a fellow thinker who (a) has mastered Freud; (b) is familiar with the nature of reification by which the Other materializes via alienation in Karl Marx and subsequent treatments in France, first by Simone de Beauvoir and then by Jean-Paul Sartre; (c) has mastered the work of Freud's disciple Melanie Klein (1882–1960); is familiar with the novel *The Stranger* (1942) by Albert Camus, and Lacan's view of the murder that occurs in it as evidence of 'the idea that the self is always in conflict with the other, always seeks the other's death' (translator's notes, *Écrits*). The above quotation is a good example of why Lacan's critics call him unintelligible, a charlatan and a purveyor of gibberish; but it is also an example of how, in seventy-two words, he constructs an extremely condensed, compacted thought.

Lacan's act of thinking has the irrepressible power of a locomotive pulling behind it the entire train of European thought it as it wends its way into the future. His legacy is assured partly because his analyses of feminine sexuality helped rescue psychoanalysis from its fate as a phallogocentric discourse, and partly because of the influence of his student Julia Kristeva, whose work influences a wide range of disciplines.

> The man who is born into existence deals first with language; this is a given. He is even caught in it before his birth.
>
> Jacques Lacan, 'Les Clefs de la Psychanalyse' (1957)

> I am not playing at being paradoxical by claiming that science need know nothing about truth. But I am not forgetting that truth is a value that (cor)responds to the uncertainty with which man's lived experience is phenomenologically marked or that the search for truth historically motivates, under the heading of the spiritual, the mystic's flights and the moralist's rules, the ascetic's progress and the mystagogue's finds alike.
>
> This search, by imposing on an entire culture the pre-eminence of truth in testimony, created a moral attitude that was and remains for science a condition of its existence. But truth in its specific value remains foreign to the order of science: science can be proud of its alliances with truth; it can adopt the phenomenon and value of truth as its object; but it cannot in any way identify truth as its own end.
>
> Jacques Lacan, 'Beyond the "Reality Principle"' in *Écrits* (2002)
> (trans. Bruce Fink).

> I keep trying to read him and failing, and reading books about him and not getting the point.
>
> Richard Rorty, interview with Josefina Ayerza in *Flash Art* (1993).

37

Karl Popper

(28 July 1902 – 17 September 1994)

Austrian-born thinker who made the philosophy of science into an established discipline and outlined the origins of totalitarianism in Plato, Hegel and Marx.

Like several Austrian philosophers of note, Karl Popper was a Jew who fled the Nazis – first to New Zealand, and then to the United Kingdom, where he established his reputation as the most significant philosopher of science of his generation. Unusually, he made major contributions to philosophy in two separate (though he would argue related) fields.

First, he was concerned to explain how it is that scientific theories come into existence and why successful ones thrive. These questions are addressed in his first book, *The Logic of Scientific Discovery* (1934), and in a series of lectures published as *Conjectures and Refutations* (1963). Second, he argued against historicism, identifying it as an essential ingredient of totalitarian thought. His early work on that subject is *The Poverty of Historicism* (1936), followed by his two-volume study *The Open Society and Its Enemies* (1945). Popper was a passionate defender of liberal democracy.

Popper was born into a family of Viennese Jews who converted to

Lutheranism. His father was a prominent lawyer, his mother a musician, and the house was filled with books, which he was encouraged to read. The year 1919 – Popper was seventeen years old – would prove decisive for him for three reasons. First, he embarked upon a passionate flirtation with Marxism. He joined the Association of Socialist School Students, but it didn't take long for him to reject its doctrinaire attitudes. Second, he developed an interest in psychoanalysis. He was introduced to Freudian theory by Alfred Adler, who arranged for Popper briefly to get a job as a social worker with disadvantaged children. The third and most important experience that Popper had in 1919 was to hear Albert Einstein lecture on his theory of relativity in Vienna. This event was crucial in Popper's intellectual development. It made him come down forcefully on the side of science. Popper recognized right away that Einstein's theory was a model of scientific thinking: its hypotheses were testable and verifiable. He would come to believe that the ideas of Marx, Darwin and Freud were not. And so, in the space of single year, Popper acquainted himself with, and made life-defining philosophical choices about, the four great trendsetters of twentieth-century Western thought.

Popper obtained a primary school teaching diploma in 1925, took a PhD in philosophy in 1928, and qualified to teach mathematics and physics in secondary school, which he did from 1930 to 1936. He published *The Logic of Scientific Discovery* in 1934, while still a school-teacher. Here he laid out his theory that potential falsifiability is the criterion to be used in distinguishing science from non-science. In 1937, seeing the Nazi threat for what it was, Popper emigrated to New Zealand, where he worked as a lecturer in philosophy at Canterbury University College in Christchurch.

Popper's philosophy of science

Popper rejected the logical positivism of the Vienna Circle led by Moritz Schlick (1882–1936), in particular its focus on the verifiability of statements as a test of their meaning. Instead, he argued that *falsifiability* should be the criterion for scientific work. He said that hypotheses should actually be designed to attract attempts to falsify them. Genuine scientific theories are in search of a counter-instance that will cause the theory to fail. Popper called his approach *critical rationalism*, styling himself as the inheritor of David Hume and Immanuel Kant.

For Popper, the crucial question in the philosophy of science is the *problem of demarcation* – the business of identifying the differences between science and non-science. In essence, Popper takes a position radically opposed to the logical positivists, who claim that their work is 'scientific'. Their empirical approach to philosophy leads them to *induce* conclusions from empirical premises that entail something beyond their content as probable or likely. For Popper – and for that other critic of Viennese positivism, W. V. Quine – 'simple' empirical observation is never simple; it is always selective in the sense that it occurs from a perspective; and that perspective is always coloured by the theoretical bent that drives the inquiry. Popper upsets the empiricists' apple cart by arguing that science cannot be reduced to some specific methodology like induction. He sees science as a problem-solving endeavour and one that is uniquely human.

Popper's political philosophy evolves directly from his thinking about science. Following on from his rules of verification Popper analyzes the most popular theories of the late nineteenth and early twentieth centuries – those of Marx, Freud and Darwin – to judge their claims to legitimacy as science. Marx and Freud fail the test, Popper concludes, and only Darwin is a scientist. Popper's criteria here have to do with the way science proceeds. Darwin's theory of evolution is scientific because parts of it are falsifiable; others aren't, and corrections are made by future generations of scientists, so that the Darwinist account of the origins of life is seen to be broadly accurate, with the details requiring constant tweaking. Marx and Freud, on the other hand, are unscientific 'totalizers'; instead of using objections to invalidate their theories they make them go away by incorporating them into their theory.

Popper's political philosophy

Popper came to see Marx's historicism – or any historicism for that matter – as having disastrous consequences for humankind. Volume one of *The Open Society and Its Enemies* focuses on Plato – it is subtitled *The Spell of Plato* – as the first in a long line of historicists that descends through Hegel and Marx, the subjects of volume two (subtitled *The High Tide of Prophecy*). For nearly 2,500 years Plato enjoyed the reputation of a benign father of modern philosophy, faithful student of Socrates and wise in most things. In contrast, Popper's reading of Plato's *Republic* highlights the totalitarian nature of the Platonic state. He identifies four ingredients of Platonic totalitarianism: (1) 'strict division of classes . . . herdsmen and watch-dogs must be strictly separated from the human cattle'; (2) the fate of the state is to be identified with the ruling class, with 'rigid rules for breeding' – an early eugenics programme; (3) the ruling class is a military class, but excluded from economic activities; (4) censorship of all activities of the ruling class.

In the second volume Popper takes on Marx. The problem with Marxism, he argues, is that it misuses science. Marx and all historicists

(Hegel included) mistakenly believe that human history can be predicted according to 'scientific' principles; this is impossible, in Popper's view, since the knowledge that societies acquire in the course of their development affects that history in ways that cannot be predicted. At root, freedom is unpredictability.

Popper, Polanyi and Kuhn: the history of science as a discipline

Popper brought the philosophy of science to the forefront of the discipline of philosophy, and created an environment in which it could flourish. His researches necessarily had an historical element, and from the 1960s the history of science began to develop as a discipline its own right, informed by and informing the philosophy of science. The central figures in exploring both of those areas are the Hungarian-British philosopher Michael Polanyi (1891–1976) and the American physicist T. S. Kuhn (1922–96). Polanyi's *Personal Knowledge: Towards a Post-Critical Philosophy* (1958) explored issues raised by the subjectivity of the scientific observer. Kuhn was a practising physicist who turned to the history of science, having been influenced by Polanyi's work.

Kuhn's book *The Structure of Scientific Revolutions* (1962) had a tremendous effect on how scientific progress is viewed. Previously, scientific knowledge was thought to accumulate in an orderly, linear way, one discovery leading the to the next, and so on, in a kind of steady, evolutionary progress. Kuhn exploded this idea with the thesis that each scientific age is governed by a paradigm – a worldview, a way of seeing the world and doing things in it – that is upended in a violent epistemic rupture, leading to a new paradigm in place of the old one. That is the structure of the scientific revolution.

Most scientific work is what Kuhn calls 'normal' science – lab work and experimentation that is done in support of the new ruling paradigm. It is not the task of 'normal' science to challenge the new paradigm. For instance, Einstein's theory of relativity necessitated a paradigm shift. Einstein challenged the order of the universe as established in the physics of Isaac Newton (1643–1727); as a result, the work of scientists post-Einstein is to solve the many questions posed by quantum mechanics and the new way of conceiving the universe that upset the Newtonian paradigm.

> I hoped to direct attention . . . to the conspiracy theory of ignorance which interprets ignorance not as a mere lack of knowledge but as the work of some sinister power, the source of impure and evil influences which pervert and poison our minds and instil in us the habit of resistance to knowledge.
>
> Karl Popper, *Conjectures and Refutations* (1963)

> The prophetic element in Marx's creed was dominant in the minds of his followers. It swept everything else aside, banishing the power of cool and critical judgement and destroying the belief that by the use of reason we may change the world. All that remained of Marx's teaching was the oracular philosophy of Hegel, which in its Marxist trappings threatens to paralyse the struggle for the open society.
>
> Karl Popper, *The Open Society and Its Enemies, Vol. 2: Hegel, Marx, and the Aftermath* (1962)

38

Jean-Paul Sartre

(21 June 1905 – 15 April 1980)

French philosopher, playwright and novelist who popularized exis-
tentialism. He defined the role of the public intellectual for the
twentieth century.

Possibly the best-known philosopher of modern times, Jean-Paul
Sartre defined the role of the politically engaged public intellectual in
a uniquely French way. In a culture that places a high value on its
educational institutions and their qualifications, Sartre never was a
university professor. While he came first in the examination for the
philosophy *agrégation* at the École Normale Supérieure in 1927, his
academic career after that amounted to teaching for several years in
various lycées. His position was earned solely on the basis of his published
works – the most important of which is *Being and Nothingness* (1943)
– and the force of his public arguments in plays, novels, essays and
philosophical works was so great that an entire nation was in awe of
it. Some idea of the regard in which Sartre was held in France can be
measured by the fact that – despite his unpopular pro-Soviet and pro-
Maoist sympathies long after the full horrors of those totalitarian regimes
were made public – Sartre's funeral procession attracted a crowd of

50,000 people who followed his coffin. In pardoning Sartre after his arrest during the events of May 1968, French president Charles de Gaulle remarked, 'You don't arrest Voltaire.'

In 1936 Sartre burst on the scene with two books: *The Imagination*, a survey of pre-Husserlian philosophical theories of the imagination; and *The Transcendence of the Ego*, which argues against Husserl's view of the transcendental ego, defining it as a construct created by others. Sartre went on to reject Freud's view of the unconscious in *Sketch For a Theory of the Emotions* (1939). But it was his novel *Nausea* (1939) that brought Sartre his first fame and the world a first taste of his existentialism. The novel's main character, Roquentin, is literally made nauseous by the fact of his existence in the world; by his realization of the 'thingness' of objects and the lack of meaning to be found in the world outside himself. Sartre's concept of *facticity* refers to the situation in which the subject finds himself: his gender, parentage, nationality, abilities, etc. It is in the context of this situation that the subject confronts his freedom, which is limited by facticity. For Sartre, man is condemned to be free. This situation gave rise to the concept of the 'absurd'.

Albert Camus and the absurd

One of the most coherent expressions of the absurd can be found in the novels and essays of Sartre's friend and rival Albert Camus (1913–60). Camus was an Algerian *pied noir* (French-speaking colonist) who was raised in poverty and went on to win the Nobel Prize for Literature in 1957. His novel *The Stranger* (1942) tells the story of a murder committed seemingly without reason by the principal character, Meursault, who is apparently indifferent to his actions and to his fate.

In Camus's atheistic universe, all human behaviour is permitted. But the consequences of this unlimited freedom must also be accepted; Meursault must accept his punishment for a senseless murder: he is condemned to death. In his essay *The Myth of Sisyphus* (1942) Camus uses the story from Greek mythology of a king condemned to roll a great boulder up a hill, only for it to roll back again once the task is completed – an action he is condemned to repeat for eternity – to explore the dilemma of modern man in a godless world. The task is pointless; but by embracing it, man defines himself.

Contrasting fortunes of war

Camus was a communist. Excluded from service in the French army because he suffered from tuberculosis, during the Nazi occupation of France Camus edited the resistance paper *Combat*, often at great personal risk. Sartre's war was different. He served in the French army weather corps, before his capture during the fall of France in May 1940, after which he spent nearly a year at a German prisoner-of-war camp called Stalag XIID near Trier. During that time he continued studying *Being and Time* (1927) by Heideggee, which he had started in Berlin in 1933. Sartre passed the time teaching Husserl's phenomenology to the priests who were his fellow prisoners, and at Christmas in 1940 he wrote and produced a play for his fellow captives. *Bariona or The Son of Thunder* was, he assured his lover Simone de Beauvoir (1908–86) in a letter, a nativity play that did not rely upon Christian belief for its enjoyment. While a prisoner Sartre also started his most important philosophical work, *Being and Nothingness*. With the help of a priest, he obtained false medical papers and was liberated from German captivity in 1941. Sartre returned to Paris to live with Beauvoir and their coterie of friends and lovers, and he taught at the Lycées Pasteur and Condorcet while finishing *Being and Nothingness*.

During the Occupation Sartre also wrote and produced two successful plays that were passed by the Nazi censors. *The Flies* (1943) is an existentialist take on the Electra story from Greek mythology, while *No Exit* (1944) featured four characters in a room without doors or windows, and concludes with the famous line 'hell is other people'.

The nature of Sartrean existentialism

Existentialism is a refutation of essentialism, the doctrine which holds that things or persons have intrinsic essences. Sartre's famous dictum is that 'existence precedes essence'. For him, existence has two modes: being and nothingness. Being has two categories: 'in-itself' and the 'for-itself'. The in-itself is being as a non-conscious object. The for-itself is conscious being, but it is not an object: it is no-thing. The in-itself and for-itself are distinct and cannot be combined. To combine them would constitute an 'unrealizable totality'. That ideal, Sartre claimed, would constitute God.

Other people are problematic for Sartre because they give rise to a confrontation in which subjectivity reduces other subjectivities to what Beauvoir called 'the Other'. Borrowing from Hegel, Sartre views relations with others in terms of a master/slave dialectic. In brief, we alienate each other. The ethical component of Sartre's ontology consists in what he calls 'bad faith'. Bad faith is essentially lying to oneself. He gives three famous examples: the waiter who exaggerates the gestures of service, while telling himself he's only 'playing' the role of a waiter; the woman who extends her hand to a man, denying the sexual provocation that is implicit in the gesture; and that of a pederast who denies that he is 'essentially' or 'by nature' a pederast, but simply someone who has sex with boys.

Sartre and Merleau-Ponty

In 1945 Sartre and Beauvoir invited their friend Maurice Merleau-Ponty (1908–61) to launch the literary and philosophical review *Les Temps Modernes*. Merleau-Ponty's work was also influenced by Husserl and Heidegger, but while Sartre focused on problems of ontology, Merleau-Ponty was concerned with perception: how does the subject apprehend the world? His *Phenomenology of Perception* (1945) is one of the key works in what might be loosely termed 'French existentialism'. Merleau-Ponty argues for the role of human embodiment and its role in understanding how it is that humans perceive. For Merleau-Ponty it is the embodied subject who encounters the world, actively engaging with it and creating meaning in it. Like Gabriel Marcel, Merleau-Ponty rejects Cartesian dualism. He moves beyond Husserl's phenomenological reduction to establish the key category of his philosophy: *being-in-the-world*. Being-in-the-world is prior to 'objectivity' and 'subjectivity', and is what gives them significance. An understanding of time as subjectively constituted completes Merleau-Ponty's phenomenology of perception.

In 1945 Sartre and Merleau-Ponty were in broad agreement in their left-wing political views. In *Humanism and Terror* (1947) Merleau-Ponty looked at the Marxist experiment from the October Revolution up to the end of the Second World War and asked the question: was Stalin's terror justified? He answered in the negative. But he also argued that the Soviet Union had to be given time, that Marxism had to work, because its failure would be mankind's failure. In his thinking about the Soviet Union Merleau-Ponty has been compared to Kant and his consideration of the French Revolution. While Kant could not forgive regicide, the idea of government based on the principles of reason was attractive to him. However, Merleau-Ponty disagreed with Sartre over the Korean War (1950–53), which he viewed as an exercise in Soviet imperialist power. The two friends split acrimoniously over the issue and in 1948 Merleau-Ponty gave up the editorship of *Les Temps modernes*.

Critique of Dialectical Reason

Sartre began to revise his existentialist philosophy to take account of Marxism in *Search For a Method* (1957), which was later incorporated into a long and unfinished work, *Critique of Dialectical Reason* (vol. 1, 1960; vol. 2, 1985). Sartre belongs to the ranks of those philosophers whose work is exceptionally challenging to read. *Being and Nothingness* is a book more purchased than read, and more read than understood, one suspects. This is partly because of the inherent difficulty of Sartre's thought (he enjoyed taunting Camus, whom he judged not clever enough to understand his ideas), and partly because his terminology is borrowed from the even more complex German technical language employed by Husserl and Heidegger. Sartre's *Critique* is even more difficult to read than *Being and Nothingness*, and it would not be uncharitable to attribute that in part to his lifelong addiction to amphetamines and alcohol. He would write in long binges, thousands of words per day, with more emphasis on quantity than quality. Nevertheless, Sartre's effort to reconcile the freedom of existentialism with the determinism of Marxism is a remarkable feat of philosophical analysis. While working on the *Critique* (from the post-war period to the end of his life) Sartre also laboured at another massive, unfinished project: his five-volume biography of the novelist Gustave Flaubert (1821–1880) entitled *The Family Idiot* (1971–2).

Existentialism gives way to structuralism

Sartre remains a towering figure in post-war twentieth-century philosophy; but existentialism's influence began to wane with the rise of structuralism, as practised by Claude Lévi-Strauss and then Roland Barthes. The post-structuralist movement finished the job structuralism had started, with its focus on texts rather than authors (the 'de-centred self'). It is a measure of the sheer speed of developments and the rapidly shifting landscape in continental philosophy that such a powerful body of work as Sartre's should have been supplanted so quickly. In the United States interest in Sartre has suffered as a result of the decline of Marxist philosophy, following a general shift to the right in political opinion after the collapse of the Soviet Union in 1991. Philosophers, like clothing and cars, are not immune to the vagaries of changing taste and fashion. There is no doubt, however, that Sartre's work will be read and reassessed by future generations of scholars who are interested in the uses to which he put the phenomenological method of Husserl and the existential analyses of Heidegger.

> Man is all the time outside of himself: it is in projecting and losing himself beyond himself that he makes man to exist; and, on the other hand, it is by pursuing transcendent aims that he himself is able to exist. Since man is thus self-surpassing, and can grasp objects only in relation to his self-surpassing, he is himself the heart and centre of his transcendence.
>
> Jean-Paul Sartre, *Existentialism is a Humanism* (1946)
> (trans. Philip Mairet, 1956)

I'm in the park. I drop onto a bench between great black tree-trunks, between the black, knotty hands reaching towards the sky. A tree scrapes at the earth under my feet with a black nail. I would so like to let myself go, forget myself, sleep. But I can't, I'm suffocating: existence penetrates me everywhere, through the eyes, the nose, the mouth . . .

Jean-Paul Sartre, *Nausea* (1938)

(trans. Lloyd Alexander, 1964)

Central to all of Sartre's activities was his attempt to describe the salient features of human existence: freedom, responsibility, the emotions, relations with others, work, embodiment, perception, imagination, death, and so forth. In this way he attempted to bring clarity and rigour to the murky realm of the subjective, limiting his focus neither to the purely intellectual side of life (the world of reasoning, or, more broadly, of thinking), nor to those objective features of human life that permit of study from the 'outside'. Thus, his work addressed, in a fundamental way, and primarily from the 'inside' (where Sartre's skills as a novelist and dramatist served him well) the question of how an individual is related to everything that comprises his or her situation: the physical world, other individuals, complex social collectives, and the cultural world of artefacts and institutions.

David Detmer, *Sartre Explained: From Bad Faith to Authenticity* (2008)

39

Hannah Arendt

14 October 1906 – 4 December 1975

German-Jewish political philosopher who emigrated to the US and analyzed totalitarianism, coining the term 'banality of evil' to describe the actions of Nazis in the Holocaust.

Hannah Arendt helped to define and defend the ethical centre of philosophy during the period of Hitler and Stalin's totalitarian rule. Her enduring achievement is the successful application of phenomenological method to political philosophy. A towering achievement is her study of – and, for the first time ever, useful definition of – totalitarianism in *The Origins of Totalitarianism* (1951). In *The Human Condition* (1958) she developed a post-Marxist analysis of the individual in society, and in *Eichmann in Jerusalem: A Report on the Banality of Evil* (1963) she offered a highly controversial, but also honest and searching account of Adolf Eichmann's journey from Nazi party functionary to enabler of the Holocaust.

Arendt grew up in Königsberg, the birthplace of Immanuel Kant, in a secular Jewish family. She enrolled at the University of Marburg to study the New Testament with Rudolf Bultmann (1884–1976) and philosophy with Martin Heidegger. Heidegger encouraged her passion for

Greek philosophy, and she often returned to Plato and Aristotle for the grounding concepts of her work. She was deeply influenced by the phenomenological method of Edmund Husserl, whose student she became upon moving to Heidelberg. At Heidelberg she formed a close and enduring friendship with her thesis supervisor, the psychiatrist-turned-philosopher Karl Jaspers. Her thesis was on the question of love in the work of Saint Augustine *Love and Saint Augustine*, 1929.

From Heidegger to Heidelberg; from Paris to Portugal

Of all her philosophical interests, it was the ontology developed by Heidegger in his lectures on Aristotle and then in *Being and Time* (1927) that truly fired Arendt's philosophical imagination. There are many who regard Heidegger as the greatest philosopher of the twentieth century, and Arendt was decidedly of that view. She was energized by his exploration of human existence or *Dasein*, as he called it. From Heidegger she developed a sense that human existence demands reflection. This urgent business is to be conducted in the stream of time by a subject whose existence is bracketed by death. Like Nietzsche, Heidegger searched for the meaning of human existence after the 'death of God'. For Heidegger, *Dasein* is defined by its movement towards death. It is in the context of time and the fact of death that man finds authentic being.

Arendt was – in all senses of the word – seduced by Heidegger. While at Marburg she became his secret lover (he was married with two sons), and their affair lasted until Heidegger joined the Nazi Party in 1933. By then, Arendt had moved to Heidelberg and Heidegger no longer accepted Jewish graduate students. Arendt was married to Günther Anders (1902–92) from 1929 to 1937, and then,

in 1940, she married Heinrich Blücher. Arendt was arrested and inter-
rogated for several days by the Gestapo, after which she fled Nazi
Germany. She eventually made her way to Paris, where she became
part of a group of intellectuals that included the German expatriate
philosopher and critic Walter Benjamin and the French philosopher
Raymond Aron.

Soon after the German occupation of France Arendt and Blücher
moved to the so-called Unoccupied Zone in the south of France
controlled by the Vichy government. However, Arendt was caught in
a police round-up and sent to an internment camp at Gurs. Anticipating
the fate of stateless Jews in her situation, she escaped. Arendt and
Blücher obtained exit visas for the United States and, staying one step
ahead of the French police, cycled to Portugal. They sailed from Lisbon
to New York – and freedom from persecution – in 1941.

Natality and plurality: Arendt's phenomenological method

In New York Arendt began to develop a philosophical position that
owed much to Heidegger, while also going beyond and before him.
Arendt agreed with Heidegger that human existence might ultimately
be towards death, but she argued that it also proceeds *from* natality.
Natality – the fact of individual human beings born into existence in
a state of freedom and facing a plenitude of choice – is at the centre
of Arendt's thinking. It infuses her philosophy with an attitude of positivity that stands in stark contrast to the less optimistic perspectives of
Heidegger and his follower Sartre.

Like Husserl, Arendt was concerned to describe philosophical begin-
nings. In any investigation, she was careful to mark out its starting
points and identify the method she would employ. Natality was

Arendt's starting point. Proceeding from the moment of birth and noting the possibilities inherent in life, Arendt developed a phenomenological method that sought to describe the way we experience our existence. For Arendt, human existence is to be understood as a phenomenon that occurs both individually and in concert with others. She departs from Heidegger in her development of the idea of plurality to describe a world of interacting subjects who ultimately are able to participate in group activity, the most important of which is political action. This does not mean that Arendt has nothing to say about individual existence and its manifestations and concerns. Ultimately, she identifies love as a defining feature of individual existence. In this she is joined by other philosophers of a phenomenological or existential bent, such as Jaspers, Edith Stein, Max Scheler and Gabriel Marcel.

Totalitarianism and anti-Semitism

Arendt honed her phenomenological skills in her first book, *The Origins of Totalitarianism*. Writing in English, a language she had only recently acquired after being forced to exchange her beloved German for French, Arendt provides a comprehensive critical survey of the history of anti-Semitism in Europe, identifying the conditions that allowed fascism to take root in Germany, and Soviet communism in Russia. Both the Nazi Holocaust and Stalin's wholesale liquidation of 'enemies of the state' relied on a mechanism of terror that was integral to the totalitarian state's aim of creating permanent states of terror. Large-scale murder and genocide were the result of ideologies that prescribed the historical inevitability of their desired outcomes. For the communists, this outcome was the dictatorship of the proletariat; for the Nazis, it was a racially pure and militarily dominant nation. Totalitarianism is, of course, a kind of action, but it is not the kind of authentic action that Arendt saw as arising from a true plurality. By plurality, Arendt means a situation in which individual subjects exist in their uniqueness, in a condition of freedom, while choosing to come together in political action. She notes that one of the most fertile soils for totalitarian ideas to take root is the class of persons in a democracy that chooses not to vote.

The Human Condition: labour, work and action

In *The Human Condition* Arendt is concerned to reclaim action (*vita activa*) as the highest form of human activity. Since Plato, she argues, the *vita activa* had been toppled by an obsessive celebration of thinking (*vita contemplativa*). In placing action above thinking, Arendt directly contradicts Heidegger. In one of the most sustained meditations in the history of phenomenology, Arendt identifies three human activities: labour, work and action. Labour is the production of consumables necessary for human survival. Arendt describes labour as a state of slavery, in contradiction to Marx who characterizes it as the highest human activity. Work as distinct from labour produces durable things (both objects and institutions) that enable man to separate himself from nature and to establish a world that is uniquely human. However, it is in action that human being finds its freedom. Labour is an animal-like activity, work creates the enduring things that establish man against nature, and action is the sphere in which man realizes his existence through the exercise of freedom.

Forgiving Heidegger

After the Second World War Arendt returned to Europe numerous times in connection with war reparation work. There she re-established her relationship with Heidegger, and also with Jaspers. Heidegger never apologized for his Nazi Party membership, his activities or the views he expressed; and while he never advocated the extreme side of Nazi racial politics, he blocked the advancement of Jewish colleagues at Freiburg. How, then, did Arendt come to forgive Heidegger? One answer is found in a chapter of *The Human Condition* entitled 'Irreversibility and the Power to Forgive'. In this work Arendt is more Heideggerian than Heidegger himself: it is as if she is his good twin, taking from him concepts such as the 'location' of human activity, the 'thing-character of the world', 'instrumentality' in connection with human activity and 'disclosure' of the self in language and action. Arendt takes these concepts and develops them in the context of a world understood as a plurality of individuals with a capacity to act freely in an ethical way. In the chapter 'Irreversibility and the Power to Forgive' Arendt reflects that human acts, once committed, can have unimagined consequences, or ones very different from the intention of the actor. Actions are unpredictable; they, and their consequences, are the ultimate expression of human freedom. They can result in good and they can result in harm. Where harm is done and recognized, what is to be done about it, since actions are irreversible?

Forgiveness, Arendt argues, is the action by which we are 'released from the consequences of what we have done'. Why is this necessary? Without forgiveness, she says, we would be condemned to exist only inside the bad deed and its consequences. Without forgiveness, the bad deed would lead to if not a metaphorical death sentence for human freedom, at least a term of life imprisonment and a negating of the future. Arendt says that 'forgiveness is the exact opposite of vengeance'. Vengeance is natural, but it leads to a never-ending cycle of offence and reoffence. It is a circle of determined unfreedom. Forgiveness, on the other hand, is a powerful act of release that opens up the future and offers a way out of the impasses of hatred and vengeance. The act of forgiving finds human existence at its most Heideggerian: in the stream of time, it is an action that is unpredictable in its occurrence, with potential outcomes that are themselves unpredictable. It is the giving of a new beginning to another; it is a metaphorical rebirth, the possibility for which follows from natality. Arendt's 'forgiveness' is not restricted to Heidegger; it is available to everyone who is cognizant of – and a jealous guardian of – freedom. Heidegger was the fortunate recipient of the largesse of a mind which, if not as acute and deep-digging as his own, was infinitely more far-seeing. He was the bene-ficiary of a largesse of spirit the depths of which he was probably incapable of imagining.

The banality of evil

In 1963 Arendt was commissioned by the *New Yorker* magazine to cover the trial in Jerusalem of the Nazi Adolf Eichmann (1906–62), the man responsible for the mass transportation of Jews to extermination camps during the Second World War. In observing Eichmann, and in drawing on her own experience as a Jew who had fled Nazi Germany in 1933, Arendt coined the term 'the banality of evil' to describe Eichmann and those like him. She observed that Eichmann had no raging hatred of Jews, nor was he motivated by extreme political views. He was a func-tionary of below average intellectual ability who did what he was told.

There were (and are) many who find Arendt's description wanting, because they feel it somehow devalues the horror of the Holocaust. The terrible truth of Arendt's analysis is that it makes the Holocaust *more* awful to contemplate.

In the case of Eichmann, Arendt could not argue for forgiveness, and she approved of the death sentence that was meted out. Arendt's lifelong project was to study what she considered the three most important human activities: thinking, acting and judging. She sensed that the post-war world was moving against the faculty of judgement; that a creeping relativism was leading to an obsession with false equalities and a tendency to be 'non-judgmental' about individuals, groups, nations and their actions. But her study of philosophy, from the ancient Greeks up to the Enlightenment, taught her that there are 'long forgotten propositions' which tell us that great crimes against nature exist, and cry out for vengeance. The Holocaust was such a crime. In *Eichmann in Jerusalem* she notes, 'I think it is undeniable that it was precisely on the ground of these long-forgotten propositions that Eichmann was brought to justice to begin with, and that they were, in fact, the supreme justification for the death penalty.' Heidegger's offence was forgivable for Arendt; Eichmann's wasn't, and as a consequence she judged him no longer fit to live among the community of men.

In living through the years of the Weimar Republic, experiencing the rise of the Nazi Party first hand, and commenting on those events as they related to the present in which she found herself (and the future she anticipated), Arendt conducted philosophical investigations that described in terrible detail the landscape of totalitarianism and offered tools for future human organization in pursuit of real freedom. She regarded the United States as the greatest chance for freedom and democracy in the post-war world. Of the two great revolutions sparked by the Enlightenment – the French Revolution and the American Revolution (1775–83) – the American one was superior because of its written constitution with its guarantee of civil liberties.

Forgiving . . . is the only reaction which does not merely re-act but acts anew and unexpectedly, unconditioned by the act which provoked it and therefore freeing from its consequences both the one who forgives and the one who is forgiven.

Hannah Arendt, *The Human Condition* (1958)

Arendt, who escaped the Holocaust, in *The Human Condition* develops the grand outlines of a philosophy of being able to begin. And this philosophy in particular bears a trace of her love for Heidegger. When he used to climb up to her attic in Marburg, he was working on his philosophy of gaining authenticity through 'anticipation of death'. She, having escaped death, replies, in the complementary manner of lovers, with a philosophy of being able to begin.

Rüdiger Safranski, *Martin Heidegger: Between Good and Evil* (1998)

40

Simone de Beauvoir

9January 1908 – 14 April 1986

French philosopher and novelist working in the phenomenolog-ical-existentialist tradition, whose The Second Sex *was the founding text of second-wave feminism.*

Simone de Beauvoir set the agenda for the feminist movement of the 1960s and 1970s with *The Second Sex* (1949, English trans. 1963), in which she argued that 'One is not born a woman, one becomes one.' In other words, woman is a social construct. She belongs to a class of reified Others, deprived of subjectivity and existing, literally, at the pleasure of men. But Beauvoir was not just a revolutionary chronicler of woman's place in the world. She was a philosopher in her own right, whose contributions were only valued by a male-dominated profession after her death. (And only, one might add, because of the developing influence of women in academia which resulted from the publication of *The Second Sex*.)

In *Pyrrhus et Cinéas* (1944) and *The Ethics of Ambiguity* (1947) Beauvoir developed original existentialist themes that have been regarded as tangled up with those of her life partner Jean-Paul Sartre. Although Sartre is widely credited with disseminating the ideas of Martin Heidegger to a broader European and American audience, he privately acknowledged to Beauvoir her deeper and clearer grasp of Heideggerian thought. In her novels, particularly *She Came to Stay* (1943) and *All Men Are Mortal* (1946), Beauvoir explored existentialist themes in the context of lives lived by her colleagues, friends and lovers. In 1945 she co-founded, along with Sartre and Maurice Merleau-Ponty (1908–61), the philosophical and literary journal *Les Temps Modernes*.

Beauvoir was born into a solid bourgeois family in Paris that had fallen on hard times. Her father encouraged her to read, and her devoutly Catholic mother sent Simone to a convent school. Indeed, Beauvoir was deeply devout and wanted to be a nun until, aged fourteen, she abandoned religion and became an atheist. Her life and work cannot be understood outside the context of her shared existence with Sartre, with whom she formed a lifelong relationship based on their 'necessary' love for each other, with an agreement that each could take 'contingent' lovers. As students together at the École Normale Supérieure they finished first and second in the philosophy agrégation in 1927 (the agrégation is a civil service examination that qualifies successful candidates to teach in lycées as *professeurs agrégés*). While Sartre finished top, Beauvoir, at twenty-one, earned the distinction of being the youngest *professeur agrégé* in French history.

Sartre, Beauvoir and Heidegger

Together Beauvoir and Sartre read Søren Kierkegaard, Edmund Husserl and Heidegger's *Being and Time* (1927). Heidegger's influence on Sartre is well-known, and *Being and Nothingness* (1943) is partly an account of Sartre coming to terms with the main themes of *Being and Time*. But Beauvoir also absorbed Heidegger, and she went on to explore his idea of 'disclosure' in *The Ethics of Ambiguity*. By disclosure Heidegger meant the authentic moment of *Dasein*'s self-revelation. *Dasein*, which means 'existence' in ordinary German usage, is employed by Heidegger to refer to the human condition of being. The self-revelation that *Dasein* experiences in disclosure is the opening up of all human possibilities, including death. Indeed, it is death that gives urgency and authenticity to *Dasein* through disclosure. In *Being and Nothingness* Sartre had characterized man as a 'useless passion'. Beauvoir found in the Heideggerian notion of disclosure a recognition of oneself and the Other as free and now able to experience the 'joy of existence'. Her existentialism is thus more optimistic than Sartre's, and her thoughts on this basic tenet of existentialism are elaborated in *Pyrrhus et Cinéas*.

Throughout their shared life, Beauvoir would be Sartre's helpmate, more than once writing articles that were published under his name when he was unable to make a deadline due to incapacity from alcohol or drugs. Throughout the Nazi occupation of Paris it was Beauvoir who would find food, cook it and feed the extended family of mutual lovers and friends that lived uncomfortably at the Hôtel Mistral in Montparnasse. Despite her early rejection of Roman Catholicism and bourgeois values, Beauvoir's knowledge that woman was not born but made as a social construct, and her radical belief that one could make one's own world by choice – despite all of this – Beauvoir still found herself in a state of Otherness that did not apply to the powerful men with whom she associated. This reduced state applied to her and to all women.

The Second Sex and its influence

In *The Second Sex* Beauvoir combined her mastery of Husserl's phenomenological method and Heidegger's understanding of *Dasein* to create an historical and philosophical account of woman. She was taken by the statement of her friend Maurice Merleau-Ponty in his

Phenomenology of Perception (1945) that 'man is a historical idea'. Among the theoretical tools she used were the concept of the master/slave dialectic developed by Hegel and an analysis based on her reading of the early Karl Marx, which led her to conclude that, by virtue of their reproductive capacity and their exclusion from production and the economy, and because of their role as mothers and housewives, women were reduced to a state of absolute Otherness.

In France *The Second Sex* was greeted with revulsion and Beauvoir was castigated as a destroyer of the social fabric, because she rejected marriage and motherhood and argued that women were free to choose their lives (including the right to abortions). She was the subject of hate mail and threats, the violence of which surprised her. But when it was translated into English in 1963 *The Second Sex* became the inspirational text of second-wave feminism, particularly in the United States, where *The Feminine Mystique* (1963) by Betty Friedan (1921–2006) would take aim at the plight of the suburban housewife, whose position Beauvoir found so appalling on her first trip to the States in 1947.

Two other important texts of second-wave feminism that owed much to *The Second Sex* were *Sexual Politics* (1970) by Kate Millett (*b*. 1934) and *The Female Eunuch* (1970) by Germaine Greer (*b*. 1939). *Sexual Politics* examines the history of patriarchy and role of women as portrayed in literature, particularly in the work of D. H. Lawrence (1885–1930), Henry Miller (1891–1980) and Norman Mailer (1923–2007). In *The Female Eunuch* Greer, like Friedan, focuses on the suburban, nuclear family. She concludes that its organization is repressive, turning women into 'eunuchs'. Later, third-wave feminists such as bell hooks (*b*. 1952) and Maxine Hong Kingston (*b*. 1940) would argue that the upper middle-class perspective of second-wave feminists ignored women of colour and issues of diversity.

European feminism after Beauvoir tended to have a Marxist aspect that was absent from the American movement. In France Beauvoir is revered by contemporary feminists, even though the existentialism of which she was a key exponent along with Sartre and Merleau-Ponty gave way after the 1970s to structuralism and post-structuralism as the ruling discourses of intellectual life. Nonetheless, post-structuralist feminists like Julie Kristeva, Luce Irigaray and Hélène Cixous acknowledge a debt to Beauvoir.

The novel as philosophy

Beauvoir was a prolific novelist, but it can be argued that her novels are works of philosophy populated by characters, as much as they are works of literature. Her first novel, *She Came to Stay*, created thinly veiled characters to explore a real event: the effect upon the relationship of Beauvoir and Sartre when they were joined in a ménage à trois (really, a ménage à quatre) by Beauvoir's young student Olga Kosakiewicz and, eventually, Olga's sister Wanda. In this novel Beauvoir developed the concept of the 'Look' and the 'Other', to define the subject in relation to other subjects: two themes that would be crucial to Sartre's *Being and Nothingness*. Beauvoir won the Prix Goncourt in 1954 for another roman à clef, *The Mandarins*. It was dedicated to the American novelist Nelson Algren, with whom she had an affair.

Questions of authenticity

Beauvoir published five volumes of autobiography, beginning with *Memoirs of a Dutiful Daughter* (1958), as well as a memoir of Sartre, *Adieu: Farewell to Sartre* (1981), all of which were hailed as works of honest self-examination. But evidence began to surface after her death that Beauvoir's public commitment to authenticity masked private actions and behaviour that could be judged inauthentic. She has been criticized for giving in to Vichy government demands that all school teachers sign a certificate declaring they were neither Jews nor Freemasons, and that she accepted work from the Nazi-controlled Radiodiffusion Nationale as a producer of radio programmes (a post Sartre obtained for her through the intervention of the collaborationist René Delange, who edited the *Comoedia*, a paper for which Sartre wrote that was published with the support of the German Institute in Paris).

With the money they earned Beauvoir and Sartre were able to move to larger quarters at the Hôtel La Louisiane in Saint-Germain-des-Prés. It is difficult from a distance of seventy years – and without personal experience of enemy occupation – to judge the fine lines of collaboration and resistance, or to fully grasp the realities of survival under those conditions. The question arises: as writers, should Beauvoir and Sartre have kept silent? Or were they justified in their actions, because they 'used' the Nazi-controlled organs of publishing (book and newspaper publishers), the theatre and radio for their own 'authentic' purposes?

Whatever the answers to those questions, one issue that contemporary readers find difficult to accept is the revelation that Beauvoir engaged in sexual relations with several of her teenage female pupils. One girl, Nathalie Sorokine, was seduced by Beauvoir and then by Sartre and his friend Jacques-Laurent Bost (who was also one of Beauvoir's lovers). Sorokine's mother brought charges against Beauvoir, which were dismissed after a hearing at which Bost and Sartre denied their affairs with Sorokine, or that Beauvoir engaged in sexual activities with women. In a wider context, Beauvoir is criticized for joining

Sartre in his continuing support of the Soviet Union, even when they both knew about Stalin's purges and the gulags.

A man would never set out to write a book on the peculiar situation of the human male. But if I wish to define myself, I must first of all say: 'I am a woman'; on this truth must be based all further discussion.

Simone de Beauvoir, *The Second Sex* (1949)

There has been one undoubted success in my life: my relationship with Sartre. In more than thirty years, we have only once gone to sleep at night disunited.

Simone de Beauvoir, *Hard Times* (1963)

The strength of her [Beauvoir's] theory of alienation as constitutive of sexual difference is not only that it manages to suggest – albeit somewhat imperfectly – that patriarchal power structures are at work in the very construction of female subjectivity, but also that it attempts to show exactly *how* this process works. There is an admirable effort here to develop a fully *social* understanding of subjectivity. The major flaw of her analysis remains the absence of any real discussion of the relationship between the anatomical and the social.

Toril Moi, Simone de Beauvoir:
The Making of an Intellectual Woman (2008)

41

Ferdinand de Saussure

26 November 1857 – 22 February 1913

Swiss linguist who was the father of structuralism and showed language to be a system rather than a set of words and definitions.

Ferdinand de Saussure was a retiring Swiss professor of linguistics who changed our understanding of language and meaning. His apparently simple discovery – that language is not a set of fixed words with largely unambiguous meanings, but is rather a system of signs in which the connection between the signifier and the signified is always arbitrary – gave birth to the discipline of structuralism. His radical ideas were published posthumously in the *Course in General Linguistics* (1916), which the Frenchman Charles Bally (1865–1974) and his Swiss colleague Albert Sechehaye (1870–1946) edited from lecture notes taken by Saussure's students.

The erosion of the certainty of fixed meaning in language led to a re-examination of conventionally held assumptions in epistemology and ontology. Structuralism also proved to be an exceptionally useful tool in language-dependent activities such as psychoanalysis and literary theory; but extrapolation of Saussure's method meant that the metaphor of *a language* could be applied to virtually any investigation, thus giving us concepts such as the *'grammar* of film' to talk about the operation of narratives in that medium. Saussure's conception of language as a system provided a model for two important innovators: the anthropologist Claude Lévi-Strauss and Roland Barthes, a structuralist who regarded the whole world as a 'text'.

From comparative linguistics to internal reconstruction

aussure was born in Geneva, and his academic training was in Sanskrit and comparative linguistics. He studied at the universities of Geneva, Paris, Berlin and Leipzig – the latter being the centre of the Neogrammarian movement, which focused on how changes in the sound of language affect all other words around it. (Saussure's example is the French word *nu*, meaning 'naked', which also sounds like *nous*, meaning 'we'.) At Leipzig Saussure was mentored by the German linguist Karl Brugmann (1849–1919) and by the Danish linguist Karl Verner (1846–96). Saussure taught for eleven years in France at the École Pratique des Hautes Études, before accepting a professorship at the University of Geneva in 1891. His main area of teaching was Sanskrit and Indo-European languages, and in his lifetime Saussure was known for one highly technical publication: *Memoir on the Primitive System of Vowels in Indo-European Languages* (1878). The importance of this otherwise obscure work is that it advanced the study of linguistics from *comparative linguistics* (comparing languages to see how they are historically related) to a technique of *internal reconstruction*, which explained how earlier sound changes in a language can explain apparent grammatical irregularities. Saussure's meagre publishing output does nothing to deny his towering influence. The linguist Anna Morpurgo Davies says of

the *Memoir* that it 'is full of unbelievable riches – most of which, sometimes in an altered form, have become part of what we now find in
our basic handbooks; some are still to be rediscovered'.

Saussure's structural linguistics

Saussure advances our understanding of language by proposing a series
of dualities, the first of which is the *signifier* and the *signified*, which
together compose a *sign*. A signifier is a word (a sound, represented
by the characters of an alphabet or other sign system) we use to refer
to a signified, which is the concept or meaning indicated by the signifier: a book, for instance. The connection between signifier and signified is arbitrary, having no absolute meaning. The meanings of signs
are arrived at by agreement in societies. So, a duck is called a 'duck',
rather than a 'fomgrat' (though it could be called a 'fomgrat' if the
usage became common). For Saussure language is 'a system of signs
that express ideas'. Meaning arises in the play of signifier and signified, which are the two essential components of the sign.

A second pair of dualities for Saussure is that of *langue* and *parole*.
Langue is language as a system of signs, while *parole* refers to speech
acts, the individual utterance of language. But language evolves from
the speech acts of individuals over time, so this leads to a third pair of
Saussurean dualities, what he called *synchronic* and *diachronic* linguistics. Synchronic linguistics looks at language as it is fixed at a point in
time. Diachronic linguistics studies speech acts (*parole*) to see how
language evolves over time through speech.

Saussure continues to focus on dualities when he says that 'linguistic
phenomena always present two complementary facets, each depending
on the other'. The first complementarity has to do with sound produc-

tion: the ear takes in the sounds of language that are produced by the vocal organs. A complementarity arises between ear and vocal chords. Consequently, 'one cannot equate the language simply with what the ear hears. One cannot divorce what is heard from oral articulation.' Sounds, then, are one part of the language system; however, 'Speech sounds are only the instrument of thought, and have no independent existence.' The structure of language is now seen to be made up of the 'auditory-articulatory' unit that combines with an idea, to form a unit which is now physiologically and psychologically complex. These sounds, these ideas, acquire yet another complementarity, consisting in their individual and social aspects, of which Saussure says: 'One is not conceivable without the other.' The fourth aspect of language is its historical character. Language is not a fixed 'thing', but rather a system that squirms and slips through our hands as we try to capture it. This is because 'Language at any given time involves an established system and an evolution'; it is mutable, protean, existing in the present while being informed by the past.

Structuralism as a methodological tool: Claude Lévi-Strauss

Saussure's discovery that language is a system of signs prompted other researchers to realize that systems other than language would be amenable to the structuralist method of investigation. Claude Lévi-Strauss's anthropological work *Tristes Tropiques* (1955) was among the first to apply structuralism as a methodological tool in a field beyond linguistics. He tried out its general utility by applying it to the problem of the 'savage mind', discovering that the savage mind uses the same thought processes as the 'civilized' mind. He borrowed Saussure's concepts of *langue* and *parole* to outline the theory of structuralist anthropology while practising it. Lévi-Strauss developed the structuralist method further in *Structural Anthropology* (1958) and applied it in *The Savage Mind* (1962), *The Raw and the Cooked* (1964) and *The Origin of Table Manners* (1968).

The development of structuralism and then post-structuralism – which began with Roland Barthes, was accelerated by the French psychoanalyst Jacques Lacan and found its ultimate expression in the work of Jacques Derrida put paid to the existentialist tendency in France, as epitomized by Jean-Paul Sartre and Simone de Beauvoir, and has provided the impetus for countless – if not always convincing or wholly intelligible – attempts to reduce the world to a series of a sign systems.

Languages are mostly known to us only through writing. Even in the case of our native language, the written form constantly intrudes. In the case of languages spoken in remote parts, it is even more necessary to have recourse to written evidence. The same is true for obvious reasons in the case of languages now dead. In order to have direct evidence available, it would have been necessary to have compiled throughout history collections . . . comprising recordings of spoken samples of all languages. Even then writing is necessary when it comes to publishing the texts thus recorded.

Ferdinand de Saussure, *Course in General Linguistics* (1916)

What we call structuralism in the field of linguistics, or anthropology, or the like, is nothing other than a very pale and faint imitation of what the 'hard sciences', as I think you call them in English, have been doing all the time.

Claude Lévi-Strauss, *Myth and Meaning* (1978)

What does Saussure mean by the arbitrary nature of the sign? In one sense the answer is quite simple. There is no natural or inevitable link between the signifier and the signified. Since I speak English I may use the signifier represented by *dog* to talk about an animal of a particular species, but this sequence of sounds is no better suited to that purpose than another sequence. *Lod*, *tet* or *bloop* would serve equally well if it were accepted by members of my speech community. There is no intrinsic reason why one of those signifiers rather than another should be linked with the concept of a 'dog'.

Jonathan Culler, *Ferdinand de Saussure* (1976)

42

A. J. Ayer

29 October 1910 – 27 June 1989

British apostle of logical positivism who argued for the verification principle of identifying meaning in language, and said all metaphysics is nonsense, including any discussion of God.

Alfred Jules Ayer took the logical positivism of Rudolf Carnap (1891–1970) and distilled it in an exceedingly clear form in *Language, Truth and Logic* (1936), a classic work of analytic philosophy and possibly the best-selling text by a British philosopher. A radical empiricist in the tradition of David Hume, Ayer made logical positivism and the principle of verification a dominant force in the English-speaking world in the second half of the twentieth century. He revered Bertrand Russell and assumed his mantle as 'Britain's greatest philosopher' – or at least its most visible one. Fiercely competitive and combative, Ayer was regularly in the media, challenging all-comers on philosophical and political issues. He was a man of the Left and a lifelong atheist; he particularly enjoyed debates on the existence of God, and famously battled the Jesuit historian of philosophy, Father Frederick Copleston (1907–94).

Ayer established a school around his ideas by taking over the moribund philosophy department of University College, London, where he was Grote Professor of the Philosophy of Mind and Logic (1946–59). His relationship with Oxford University was complicated by the fact that he had angered his tutors while an undergraduate by being the first to write on Ludwig Wittgenstein, whose ideas were unwelcome, not least because they emanated from Cambridge University; but in 1959 Ayer succeeded H. H. Price to the Wykeham Professorship in Logic at Oxford.

Militant atheism

Ayer's mother, Reine Citroën, was a Dutch Jew whose uncle founded the Citroën car company in France. His father, Jules Ayer, was a francophone Swiss Calvinist and a financier employed by the Rothschild family. Ayer's upbringing was rather solitary, and at Eton he crossed teachers and students alike with his sharp tongue and what his fellow philosopher Anthony Quinton called his 'militant atheism'. (Quinton said of Ayer: He was a philosopher of religion only in the sense that a dynamiter is an architect.) Precociously intellectual, Ayer won a Classics scholarship to Christ Church, Oxford, where he was tutored by Gilbert Ryle.

Logical positivism: Ayer and the Vienna Circle

Ayer considered British philosophy to have started with George Berkeley and David Hume, before it was refined by Bertrand Russell and the analytics. Ayer's own thinking about philosophy began with his reading of Russell. He was also influenced by Ludwig Wittgenstein, G. E. Moore, Rudolf Carnap, H. H. Price, Gilbert

Ryle, and W. V. Quine. He developed a fiercely reductive, empirical approach to philosophy (and everything else, for that matter). This focus led him to the logical positivism of the Vienna Circle, whose leading members included Moritz Schlick and Carnap. Ayer travelled to Vienna in 1932 and Schlick was particularly generous in welcoming him to the group. Though Schlick was the founder of the Vienna Circle, Carnap is its best-remembered member, and the one who had the greatest influence on Ayer; so much so that Ayer's first and most famous book, *Language, Truth and Logic*, is essentially a repackaging of Carnap's ideas about verification. The verification principle states that the meaning of a proposition must be able to be demonstrated empirically or by logical tautology. I can verify the statement that my desk measures six feet by four feet by means of a tape measure. A logically tautologous statement is one which is valid or true in all interpretations. The logical positivism of Carnap and the Vienna Circle was a position that understood all knowledge as strictly empirical – or experiential – and that the right method for understanding empirical knowledge was symbolic logic.

A crucial link between the analytic school and the logical positivists was Ludwig Wittgenstein, himself an Austrian, who decided to throw in his lot with Russell and the group of Cambridge analytic philosophers that included G. E. Moore. For a brief period between the world wars Wittgenstein would sit in on discussions with the Vienna Circle and Schlick was very keen to record and transcribe Wittgenstein's remarks at these meetings. Eventually Wittgenstein moved away from the group after growing mistrustful of Schlick. Wittgenstein would come to hold Ayer in low regard, remarking that he 'has something to say but he is incredibly shallow'. Anthony Quinton observed, more charitably: 'There was a certain narrowness to Ayer's mind which focused it sharply and contributed to its force.'

Language, Truth and Logic

Language, Truth and Logic is an admirably concise book that attempts two contradictory goals at the same time: it appears transparently to describe the subject at hand, while at the same time passing judgement upon it. So, in describing his method of examining premises, Ayer simultaneously lets it be known that metaphysics is enemy territory, and that philosophers who do metaphysics are the enemy. He offers handy tips for dealing with metaphysicians, such as: 'One way of attacking a metaphysician who claimed to have knowledge of a reality which transcended the phenomenal world would be to enquire from what premises his propositions were deduced.'

Carnap held that 'the sentences of metaphysics are pseudo-sentences which on logical analysis are proved to be either empty phrases or phrases which violate the rules of syntax. Of the so-called philosophical problems, the only questions that have any meaning are those of the logic of science. To share this view is to substitute logical syntax for philosophy.' Carnap's goal was to simplify philosophy by restricting its range by removing metaphysics, ethics and theology from the purview of philosophy. Ayer takes the position a little further to make the claim that there is no longer any need for conflicting schools of philosophy. In fact, he argues, there never were any conflicting schools. The belief that there were was simply the error of not understanding logic and the role of language. Ayer's goal in *Language, Truth and Logic* is to announce the end of philosophy: 'Consequently I maintain that there is nothing in the nature of philosophy to warrant the existence of conflicting philosophical "schools". And I attempt to substantiate this by providing a definitive solution of the problems which have been the chief sources of controversies between philosophers in the past.' A disgruntled housemaster at Winchester who thought *Language, Truth and Logic* a bad influence on young minds is reported to have hurled the book through an open window, demanding of Ayer: 'What next?' Ayer reportedly told him: 'There's no next. Philosophy has come to an end. Finished.'

Ayer's method in his attempt to limit the scope of philosophy was to use the verification principle as a kind of weed killer to clear the ground for what he considered a proper philosophical inquiry. The first thing was to eliminate metaphysics: 'Even the utterances of the metaphysician who is attempting to expound a vision are literally senseless; so that henceforth we may pursue our philosophical researches with as little regard for them as for the more inglorious kind of metaphysics which comes from a failure to understand the workings of our language.' For Ayer, the metaphysical can never be verified and therefore must be excised from the study of philosophy. 'It will be found that much of what ordinarily passes for philosophy is metaphysical according to this criterion, and, in particular, that it cannot be significantly asserted that there is a non-empirical world of values or that men have immortal souls or that there is a transcendent God.'

Ayer can be seen as a thinker whose genius lies in the way he combines and expresses ideas, rather than in conceiving original ones. Ayer's prose is exceedingly sparse and this economy lends his pronouncements an air of authority. For instance, defining philosophy, Ayer says that the function of a philosopher is 'to clarify the propositions of science by exhibiting their logical relationships, and by defining the symbols which occur in them'. Ayer borrowed heavily from Carnap in making these formulations. 'Philosophy is to be replaced by the logic of science,' Carnap wrote in his *Logical Syntax of Language* (1934). Anthony Quinton remarked that there is little that is original in Ayer's thought, but that its derivative quality did nothing to thwart its force.

Ayer – a very public philosopher

Ayer was a brilliant conversationalist and a cosmopolitan celebrity as well as a philosopher and university professor. He was a fine dancer and it was reputed he wanted to be a professional tap dancer as a child, an ambition that was crushed when he saw Fred Astaire dance and realized he could never be as good. He was also an inveterate partygoer and womanizer.

One of his four wives (three really, as he married one twice) observed that Ayer played women the way other men play golf. Ayer's biographer Ben Rogers relates how the Wykeham Professorship in Logic at Oxford reached a peak of notoriety in 1987 when Ayer, at a New York party filled with fashion models, responded to a woman's cry in an adjoining room. There, he found the boxer Mike Tyson manhandling the then unknown model Naomi Campbell. Ayer, a small but brave man, challenged Tyson.

'Do you know who the fuck I am?' Tyson replied. 'I'm the heavyweight champion of the world.'

'And I am the former Wykeham Professor of Logic,' Ayer said. 'We are both pre-eminent in our field. I suggest that we talk about this like rational men.'

In a sense, Ayer was England's answer to Jean-Paul Sartre. That is, he was the nation's first – and to date only – philosopher superstar. By contrast, France has had many: Claude Lévi-Strauss, Roland Barthes,

Michel Foucault and Jacques Derrida, to name but a few. In spite of his French and Swiss ancestry, Ayer was deeply opposed to continental philosophy, the French variety in particular. He spent time during the Second World War (1939–45) working for military intelligence in France, where he came to loathe existentialism, particularly the Sartrean form of it. Reviewing *Being and Nothingness* (1943) in 1945, Ayer concluded that the concept of being was meaningless, along with the concept of nothingness. He dismissed the philosophy of Sartre and the existentialists as the art of misusing the verb 'to be'.

The God Question revisited

Ayers's last days were marked by a peculiar event that has led to speculation that he may have revised his view about the existence of God. While being treated for pneumonia in hospital in 1988, Ayer choked on a piece of smoked salmon and was judged to have been clinically dead for four minutes. He gave numerous accounts of this experience, which ran in the popular press for some weeks. He recounted in the *Daily Telegraph* how he 'was confronted by a red light . . . Aware that this light was responsible for the government of the universe. Among its ministers were two creatures who had been put in charge of space.' These 'experiences' may have been influenced by the fact that just before the event Ayer had been reading *A Brief History of Time* (1988) by Stephen Hawking. While Ayer gave various accounts of his experience to the newspapers, his physician Dr Jeremy George at the Middlesex Hospital reported that Ayer told him: 'I saw a Divine Being. I'm afraid I'm going to have to revise all my various books and opinions.' If this account is true, Ayer finds himself in the company of his most loathed contemporary, Jean-Paul Sartre, who also experienced a deathbed conversion from atheism.

Ayer's philosophical legacy is meagre, though the store of anecdotes about him is large enough to keep him in the public mind at least for as long as his students are still alive. Ayer worked vigorously for the end of philosophy and in the narrow seam that he sought to mine it is probably fair to say that he exhausted it.

> The nature of the essence problem is closely connected with the concept of an *essential* relation. By this is meant that which connects the members of a relation 'essentially' or 'really' or 'actually', in contradistinction to the relation as a mere correlation which only points out the members that are so correlated . . . the problem of essential relations as well as the essence problem of a relation can, within (rational) science, neither be resolved nor even posed. It belongs to metaphysics.
>
> Rudolf Carnap, *The Logical Structure of the World and Pseudoproblems in Philosophy* (1928)
> (trans. Rolf A. George, 1967)

> What is important to us is to realize that even the utterances of the metaphysician who is attempting to expound a vision are literally senseless; so that henceforth we may pursue our philosophical researches with as little regard for them as for the more inglorious kind of metaphysics which comes from a failure to understand the workings of our language.
>
> A. J. Ayer, *Language, Truth and Logic* (1946)

I am deeply grateful for what I learnt from Freddie's [Ayers's] seminars. I reckon that I acquired from them whatever dialectical abilities I possess. But if you discount the high spirits, it could appear to be a bleak school. It was great to be a philosopher, but was philosophy, shorn of its ultimate attainment, a great thing? Whenever the Monday discussion reached a certain point, we would be told, 'And here we hand things over to the scientist, or to the historian, or to the psychologist.' This point often coincided with the moment at which the discussion got interesting, and at times the sacrifice appeared hard to make when anyhow the reward, what we could count on, seemed to be ever diminishing. There were nights when, waking up, I cursed philosophy.

Richard Wollheim, 'Ayer: The Man, The Philosopher, The Teacher' (1991)

43

Willard Van Orman Quine

25 June 1908 – 25 December 2000

American analytic philosopher whose scientific view of philosophy moved beyond logical positivism to develop a holistic approach to knowledge.

Quine was a Harvard philosopher who broke with the ideas of the Vienna Circle group of logical positivists to develop an original analytic approach to philosophy that attempted to ground philosophy in science. For Quine, philosophy *is* science, and vice-versa; he was the most prominent advocate of scientism in the twentieth century. He published two works that broadened the scope of analytic philosophy from its previously rather narrow agenda. In the essay 'Two Dogmas of Empiricism' (1951) he rejected the distinction between analytic and synthetic propositions, which was central to logical positivism, in favour of a holistic view. In *Word and Object* (1960) Quine developed his 'indeterminacy of translation' thesis, arguing that there can be no single, correct 'translation' of a subject's utterances, even within his own language. If Ludwig Wittgenstein was the most influential analytic philosopher of the first half of the twentieth century, Quine is his successor in the second half.

Quine had a lifelong association with Harvard University, doing his thesis there and finally taking the Edgar Pierce Chair of Philosophy. (1956–78). His thesis supervisor was A. N. Whitehead, co-author with Russell of *Principia Mathematica* (1910–13), a founding text of analytic philosophy (and which attempted to derive the rules of arithmetic from logic). In 1932 Quine travelled to Vienna, as had his contemporary A. J. Ayer, to attend meetings of the Vienna Circle of logical positivists. Like Ayer, Quine was impressed with the work of Rudolf Carnap, although he would later challenge Carnap's verification principle. In Europe Quine also made the acquaintance of the logician Alfred Tarski (1902–83). Quine arranged for Tarski, a Polish Jew, to be invited to an academic conference at Harvard; the invitation saved Tarski's life, as he sailed on the last ship leaving Gdansk before the Nazi invasion of Poland.

The influence of Otto Neurath

While Carnap was important for Quine, the logical positivist who had the greatest influence on him was the philosopher of science Otto Neurath (1882–1945). Quine's naturalism began to take form in Vienna in conversations with Neurath, who frequently used the metaphor of a boat to describe the business of science. Science, he taught, was like a boat to which alterations must be made while it is at sea; there is never the comfort or safety of returning to shore and a dry dock. He taught that the passengers in the boat (who were also its captains and engineers) were philosophers and scientists. Philosophy and science are in the same boat; their work is interchangeable. The philosopher of the day inherits a system of knowledge devised by his predecessors, and uses scientific methods to develop that system and modify it to suit new discoveries.

That is the essence of Quine's scientism. As a Jew and a socialist, Neurath was forced to flee the Nazis, and he eventually escaped to England by crossing the English Channel in an open boat with other refugees.

Beyond logical positivism: holism and the indeterminacy of translation

While Quine was a fierce empiricist, he disagreed with the logical positivists' distinction between analytic and synthetic statements, and also with their reductionism. He argued that their distinction was a matter of belief as opposed to knowledge, and famously referred to them as the two dogmas of empiricism – were not only unnecessary to philosophy, they were also wrong. It is here that Quine's main contribution to modern thought lies.

The differentiation between analytic and synthetic statements was first posited by Immanuel Kant and later adopted by Gottlob Frege and then the logical positivists. Put simply, an analytic statement is one whose truth is not dependent upon verification by experience. For example: *a square is a four-sided geometric figure*. A synthetic statement or proposition refers to what philosophers call a 'state of affairs'. For example: *my chair is blue*. The subject of the sentence is 'chair' and the predicate is 'blue'. 'Blue', the predicate, states more information than is contained in the definition of 'chair'; therefore the sentence is a synthetic proposition. Quine quarrels with the logical positivists' reductive use of sentence-by-sentence analysis because, in reality, these sentences do not occur in isolation, but as integral parts of a larger construct – for instance, a theory. The piecemeal (or atomistic) approach of the logical positivists was rejected by Quine in favour of a holistic approach.

Quine's holism is elegantly expressed in the Duhem-Quine thesis. Pierre Duhem was a French physicist and philosopher of science whose ideas presaged those of Quine, and so his name is joined to Quine's thesis. The Duhem-Quine thesis holds that scientific hypotheses cannot be tested in isolation, because other hypotheses will always be required to draw empirical conclusions from them. A single scientific hypothesis is always more complex than it might first appear because it carries with it a certain amount of baggage, of background assumptions. All of these come into play in any scientific experiment or philosophical inquiry. For Quine, scientific hypotheses are to be understood and tested in a contextual aggregate, as a whole.

Quine's indeterminacy of translation thesis, first elaborated in *Word and Object* (1960), may be seen as a development of his holistic approach. This thesis holds that words and sentences do not have unique, fixed meanings, but rather a multiplicity of meanings depending on the context in which they occur. In the argot of post-structuralism, language is polysemic; it admits of multiple meanings. In this way Quine might seem to have something in common with a post-structuralist thinker like Jacques Derrida. However, when Cambridge University proposed to bestow an honorary degree on Derrida in 1992, Quine joined a delegation of eighteen philosophers led by Professor Barry Smith, editor of *The Monist*, who opposed the honour.

Tolerating metaphysics

Quine's criticisms of logical empiricism led to major advances in analytic philosophy. He broadened its agenda — and its toolkit — to tolerate some metaphysical thinking. He even acknowledged that his work might have an idealist aspect. He would not, however, have subscribed to the more developed metaphysical views of two of his best-known students, Saul Kripke and David Lewis. Quine's influence on philosophical thinking, as measured by those he mentored, is very great. In addition to Kripke and Lewis, they include Daniel Dennett, Hilary Putnam, Donald Davidson and Dagfinn Follesdal. Despite his dislike of Derrida, Quine might be known in the future as an analytic philosopher whose work, thematically at least, partially bridged the continental divide.

Quality control is spotty in the burgeoning philosophical press. Philosophy has long suffered, as hard sciences have not, from a wavering consensus on questions of professional competence. Students of the heavens are separable into astronomers and astrologers as readily as are the minor domestic ruminants into sheep and goats, but the separation of philosophers into sages and cranks seems to be more sensitive to frames of reference. This is perhaps as it should be, in view of the unregimented and speculative nature of the subject.

W. V. Quine, 'Has Philosophy Lost Contact with People?' (1979)

If one pursues philosophy in a scientific spirit as a quest for truth, then tolerance of wrong-headed philosophy is as unreasonable as tolerance of astrology would be on the part of the astrophysicist.

W. V. Quine, *Quiddities: An Intermittently Philosophical Dictionary* (1987)

Ontology and epistemology are not popular topics, but Quine could render them fascinating through his use of clear prose, simple sentences and catchy expressions. Recall the discussion of the extent to which we can know private experience, both of ourselves and of others, which begins, 'As illustrated by "Ouch" . . . ,' and the reader's attention is captured. Quine's writings benefited us all by improving the intellectual climate, making epistemology and ontology accessible to ordinary people.

John C. Malone, 'Ontology Recapitulates Philology: Willard Quine, Pragmatism and Radical Behaviorism' (2001)

44

Jürgen Habermas

b. 18 June 1929

German critical theorist and proponent of communicative ration-
ality in the public sphere.

Contrary to the twenty-first century paradigms of postmodernism
and post-structuralism, Jürgen Habermas's main focus is on the explicit
continuation of what he calls the 'Enlightenment project'. His aim is
to ground philosophy, politics and law in the eighteenth-century principles of reason espoused by Immanuel Kant and descending through
G. W. F. Hegel and Karl Marx. In *The Structural Transformation of*
the Public Sphere (1962) Habermas defined the *public sphere* as a place
where rational dialogue can occur. Rational dialogue is conceived by
Habermas as *communicative rationality*, a concept he elaborates in *The*
Theory of Communicative Action (1981). Habermas has famously put
his own theory into practice, having carried on dialogues with holders
of positions ostensibly opposed to his. He engaged Michel Foucault
and Jacques Derrida, whom he accused of a dangerous relativism
with negative consequences for ethics; and in 2007 Habermas discussed
the issue of religion with Cardinal Joseph Ratzinger (*b.* 1927), now
Pope Benedict XVI, starting from his position as a self-confessed

'methodological atheist'.

The problem of Heidegger

Like most German teenagers growing up during the Second World War Habermas was a member of the Hitler Youth. At the age of fifteen he found himself deployed on Germany's western front during the final months of the war. Habermas was ill-suited to wearing the swastika, his left-leaning tendencies and his physical deformity (a harelip) making him the sort of person the Nazis wished to exterminate.

The Nuremberg Trials (1945–6) – the international tribunal that judged German war crimes – provided Habermas with an epiphany that resulted in his campaign to resurrect the values of the Enlightenment. Documentary film footage revealing the atrocities of the Nazi death camps so revolted Habermas that he became especially alert to any traces of totalitarianism that might remain in German culture.

While a PhD student at the University of Bonn from 1951 to 1954, Habermas found one such trace in the 1953 republication of Martin Heidegger's book *What is Metaphysics?* (1935). In it Heidegger wrote: 'The works that are being peddled about nowadays as the philosophy of National Socialism have nothing to do with the *inner truth and greatness of this movement* (namely the encounter between global technology and modern man) but have all been written by men fishing in the troubled waters of "values" and "totalities".' For Habermas (and countless others) here was the troubling fact of German philosophy: Heidegger was, for many, the greatest philosopher of the century – but he was also a Nazi (as were half of Germany's philosophy professors). Dealing with Heidegger was an essential element of Habermas's project as he picked through the ruins of German thought. The only hope for

German philosophy, as he saw it, was to promote liberal democracy, based on the principle of dialogue. In his essay 'Work and Weltanschauung: The Heidegger Controversy from a German Perspective' (1989) he observes that Heidegger's view of the Second World War was this: 'the victors were America and Russia, alike in their essence, who now divided up world hegemony. So the Second World War, in Heidegger's view, had decided nothing essential. That is why the philosopher prepared, after the war, to persevere quietistically in the shadows of a still unconquered destiny. In 1945 there remained for him only retreat from the disappointing history of the world.'

The centrality of dialogue

Habermas submitted his thesis *The Absolute and History: On the Schism in Schelling's Thought* in 1954. In 1956 he became an assistant to Theodor Adorno (1903–69), one of the leading lights of the Frankfurt School and its Marxist-orientated programme of critical theory. In 1962 Habermas became 'extraordinary professor' (that is, a professor without a chair) of philosophy at the University of Heidelberg and then in 1964 he took over from Max Horkheimer's chair in philosophy and sociology at Frankfurt. In 1971 Habermas became director of the Max Planck Institute in Starnberg and worked there until 1983, when he returned to his chair at Frankfurt and became director of the Institute for Social Research. He is also permanent visiting professor at Northwestern University in the United States, and Theodor Heuss Professor at The New School in New York. On top of his academic achievements, Habermas is also a well-known public intellectual.

Habermas's thought can be described as broadly Marxist, although he is perhaps better understood as a follower of Socrates (*c.* 469–399 BC). This is because for Habermas dialogue is everything, and like Socrates he is an advocate of public dialogue. Having staked out his early opposition to Holocaust revisionism, he weighed in during the 1986 *Historikerstreit* (historians' quarrel) in which right-wing historians argued that the Holocaust was unexceptional – just one more in a long line of European massacres. In this public debate, carried on in the press, Habermas fiercely challenged such views.

Habermas's career has been devoted to outlining strategies for dialogue, discovering the preconditions that create the kind of public sphere in which dialogue can occur, and giving these themes theoretical and practical consideration in sociology, law, politics and philosophy. Few living thinkers can match his fluency and mastery of so many disciplines. Richard Rorty, himself the leading US philosopher of the period, called Habermas 'the leading systematic philosopher of our time'.

Habermas's extension of the Enlightenment project into the twenty-first century has meant coming to grips with Hegel as if he were a contemporary. Where critics like Karl Popper find in Hegel an historicist tendency leading to totalitarianism (as with Plato and Marx, in Popper's view), Habermas, ever sensitive to the poison of tyranny, finds in Hegel the latest in a line of Enlightenment thinkers that began with Kant, and he inserts himself in that tradition, taking from Hegel (as he did from Heidegger) that which is useful to him. Habermas never descends into ideology; however, he is not averse to using the tools of Marxist analysis to make sense of the situation in which we find ourselves after the end of the Cold War and the fall of the Soviet Union.

Communicative action

Habermas borrows theories of intersubjectivity from metaphysics, and an understanding of linguistics and speech act theories from J. L. Austin, P. F. Strawson, Stephen Toulmin, John Searle and Ludwig Wittgenstein to try and explain how communication can occur in the public sphere. *Communicative action* is Habermas's recipe for the identification of goals that can be satisfactorily achieved by individuals and the groups of which they are members. *Strategic action* refers to acts in which actors seek to achieve solely individual goals. By contrast, communicative action involves speakers searching to define goals that can be the subject of a shared understanding. This understanding is based on the inherent reasonableness of the goal. Here we see the Enlightenment project in action in a practical way: not just the 'pure' reason of the Kantian mountain top, but a practical rationality that is the basis of building consensus and, ultimately, the creation of a peaceful society. Communicative action has five essential characteristics: (1) it is consensual, (2) socially coordinated, (3) rational, (4) based on ordinary language, and (5) it has agreement as its goal.

Discourse ethics

Habermas, along with Karl-Otto Apel (*b*. 1922) is the creator of *discourse ethics*. This is an ambitious programme to combine Kantian deontological ethics with the requirements of communicative rationality in its practical applications, such as in political discourse – e.g., policymaking or decision taking. To this end Habermas posits the *discourse principle*: 'the only moral rules that could win the assent of all affected as participants in a practical discourse can claim validity'. Once this has been established, the groundwork for communicative rationality has been laid: 'This explanation of the moral point of view privileges practical discourse as the form of communication that secures the impartiality of moral judgement together with universal interchangeability of participant perspectives.' (*Justification and Application: Remarks on Discourse Ethics*, 1991)

The Philosophical Discourse of Modernity: taking on Derrida

Habermas's early confrontation with Heidegger and his continuing suspicion of nihilistic tendencies in modern thought led him to criticize postmodernism and post-structuralism as movements that had abandoned the reasoned, scientific Enlightenment project in favour of a series of relativistic positions of questionable ethical value. In *The Philosophical Discourse of Modernity* (1985) Habermas takes on Foucault and Derrida. While hoping to provoke dialogue, he offers a crushing assessment of Derrida's continuation of Heidegger's late philosophy: 'The human being as the being toward death has always lived in relation to its natural end. But now it is a matter of the end of its humanistic self-understanding: in the homelessness of nihilism it is not the human being but the essence of the human that wanders blindly about.' In Habermas's view, Derrida's philosophy is not only nihilistic but also ultimately destructive: 'Heidegger prepares the completion of an epoch that will perhaps never end in a historical-ontic sense. The familiar melody of the self-overcoming of metaphysics also sets the tone for Derrida's enterprise; destruction is renamed deconstruction.' Derrida replied in 'Is There a Philosophical Language?' (1992) that Habermas had 'visibly and carefully avoided reading me'.

Religion and reason revisited

In January 2004, fifteen months before he became the Pope, Cardinal Joseph Ratzinger engaged in a written dialogue with Habermas about the role of religion in society. It was published as *The Dialectics of Secularization: On Reason and Religion* (2005). Habermas has always followed Hegel's insistence on philosophy's right to 'methodological atheism', the presupposition of nothing in the way of religious belief. He also describes himself as a student of Max Weber in that he is 'tone deaf in the religious sphere'. However, 9/11 caused Habermas to observe that secular society needed to have a new understanding of religious conviction. (Previously, as with perhaps most philosophers, he had regarded religion as a subject to be studied with regard to stages of human development.)

In *The Dialectics of Secularization* Habermas argues that the secular state is founded on practical reason. Ratzinger argues that there is a pre-political moral foundation that justifies the state. He concludes that reason and faith need each other: faith informs reason to help humankind avoid the kind of hubris that leads to the creation of nuclear weapons or the view of people as products. Habermas concludes that the existence of believers and unbelievers will continue, and each must accept that fact about the other. What both groups must confront is the destruction of old ethical certainties by science, and the existence of a new kind of terrorism that requires a global dialogue.

Ultimately Habermas takes us back to the very place where we started. Two and a half millennia after the Pre-Socratics reached for reason, looking for answers other than those offered by mythology, reason and religion are still in the frame; but in the communicative rationality of Habermas, and the philosophically sophisticated thought of Pope

Benedict XVI, they can be viewed less as polar opposites and more as complementary to each other.

> All attempts at discovering ultimate foundations, in which the intentions of First Philosophy live on, have broken down. In this situation, the way is opening to a new constellation in the relationship of philosophy and the sciences. As can be seen in the case of the history and philosophy of science, formal explication of the conditions of rationality and empirical analysis of the embodiment and historical development of rationality structures mesh in a peculiar way. Theories of modern empirical science, whether along the lines of logical empiricism, critical rationalism or constructivism, make a normative and at the same time universalistic claim that is no longer covered by fundamental assumptions of an ontological or transcendental-philosophical nature.
>
> Jürgen Habermas, *The Theory of Communicative Action*, Volume 1 (1981) (trans. Thomas McCarthy, 1984)

> I think that a certain form of unrestrained communication brings to the fore the deepest force of reason, which enables us to overcome egocentric or ethnocentric perspectives and reach an expanded view.
>
> Jürgen Habermas, interview with Mitchell Stephens (1994)

> If we imagine the philosophical discussion of the modern period reconstructed as a judicial hearing, it would be deciding a single question: how is reliable knowledge (*Erkenntnis*) possible?
>
> Jürgen Habermas, *Knowledge and Human Interests* (1968)

45

Roland Barthes

12 November 1915 – 25 March 1980

French post-structuralist who proclaimed the death of the author
and regarded the world as a text to be interpreted.

Roland Barthes took Ferdinand de Saussure's structuralist position that the meaning of signs in language was arbitrary and not fixed, and developed it to (perhaps) its logical conclusion: that texts are social, semiological artefacts, and that the author's production of them is not, as previously thought, the result of an omniscient, God-like, entirely self-generated literary (or other) production. If it fell to Saint Augustine (354–430) in his *Confessions* (397–8) to proclaim the birth of the 'I', the first-person authorial voice, it was Roland Barthes's job to put it to death in his seminal essay 'The Death of the Author' (1967). What did he mean by the death of the author? For Barthes, books, films, photographs, advertisements – all of them, he argued, are the products of various historical, social and generic precedents whose meaning is to be gleaned through 'reading'. The author is no longer in control of the text, the reader is: 'The birth of the reader must be at the cost of the death of the Author.' So the key question Barthes asked when starting an investigation was *qui parle*? Who is speaking?

In *Mythologies* (1957) Barthes illustrates his view of the world as text and demonstrates how this text can be decoded. In *Writing Degree Zero* (1953) and *S/Z* (1970) he laid the foundations for the work of post-structuralists like Jacques Derrida and Julia Kristeva, as well as the less-easily pigeonholed Michel Foucault.

Decoding texts

Barthes begins with the basic notion of structuralism that significance arises in the play between the signifier (the sign) and the signified (that to which the sign refers). But he goes beyond the possibility of a certain arbitrariness between signifier and signified to develop a methodology that exposes a multitude of hidden factors at work in any of the representations that he called 'texts'. The texts that most interest Barthes are what he saw as the modern myths that arise as a result of the prevailing value system of a given society.

In *Mythologies* (1957) Barthes gives two examples of how to identify and decode the texts of modern myths. One is the representation of red wine in French culture. He shows how wine, as presented in French advertising, is portrayed as the national drink, using references to the divine and the secular. The advertisements Barthes decodes borrow from Roman Catholic symbolism, giving the signified (wine) a near-sacramental status, referring (perhaps unconsciously on the part of the advertisers) to the process of transubstantiation in the Catholic ritual, in which wine becomes the blood of Christ. As red wine is also the preferred drink of the French proletariat, its red *robe* – the technical term for a wine's colour and overall visual appearance – can refer to the red flag of Europe's revolutionaries of 1848 (and the colour red continues to be associated with present-day socialism and communism).

So much for what is *present* in the text. Barthes also points up what is *absent* in the text: and that is any suggestion that wine can be unhealthy or is associated with widespread alcoholism in France. Barthes shows that red wine, as portrayed in French advertising, is sold as a quintessentially French product. Its purchase and consumption identifies the consumer as French. The adverts work by tugging at the diverse but audience-inclusive symbols of religion and revolution; they offer the consumer an opportunity to fly the flag of nationalism, while enjoying a product that is advertised as *good for you*.

The other famous example from *Mythologies* is Barthes's decoding of the front cover of a copy of *Paris Match* magazine, which he picks up while at the barber's one day. 'On the cover, a young Negro in a French uniform is saluting, with his eyes uplifted, probably fixed on a fold of the tricolor. All this is the meaning of the picture. But, whether naively or not, I see very well what it signifies to me: that France is a great Empire, that all her sons, without any colour discrimination, faithfully serve under her flag, and that there is no better answer to the detractors of an alleged colonialism than the zeal shown by this Negro in serving his so-called oppressors. I am therefore again faced with a greater semiological system: there is a signifier, itself already formed with a previous system (a black soldier is giving the French salute); there is a signified (it is here a purposeful mixture of Frenchness and militariness); finally, there is a presence of the signified through the signifier . . . In myth (and this is the chief peculiarity of the latter) the signifier is already formed by the signs of the language . . . Myth has in fact a double function: it points out and it notifies, it makes us understand something and it imposes it on us.'

Structuralism, post-structuralism and the decline of existentialism

Barthes's proclamation of the death of the author had significance for Western thought beyond the boundaries of linguistics and literary criticism. The theoretical *Zeitgeist* represented by Barthes was in the process of surpassing the radical status quo represented by Jean-Paul Sartre's brand of existentialism and Marxism. The existentialism of Sartre, Simone de Beauvoir and Maurice Merleau-Ponty (1908–61) was all about the subject (author); the inevitable development of structuralist views of language towards the emerging post-structuralism spearheaded by Barthes was to identify an absence where the subject used to be. The ramifications were enormous. Literature (and the text in general) was to be liberated from the 'tyranny' of authorship. The meaning of texts would no longer be located in a God-like author and his history. Meaning would become the responsibility of the reader, a newly empowered constituency. In place of the traditional author figure, Barthes introduced the concept of the scriptor – the person whose name may be on the cover of the book and is advertised as author, but who is in reality someone who recombines or rearranges pre-existing texts. In academic circles, at least, this is the real legacy of the revolutionary fervour that swept France in 1968.

The death of Roland Barthes

Barthes was a modest and retiring man whose bouts of tuberculosis had interrupted his formal education and exempted him from military service during the Second World War. His father died in a First World War naval battle in 1916 and Barthes lived with his mother all of his life. Perhaps it was the absence of a father that made it easier for Barthes to accept the death of the author (of whom the father, starting with God, is the ultimate example), and so set in train ideas that found further development in feminism and queer theory. Ironically, Barthes's own death was hastened by an arbitrary and capricious event: in 1980 he was run over in the street by the drunk driver of a laundry delivery van. Barthes had been walking home from a lunch given by François Mitterrand, who would be elected president of France the following year. Barthes died from his injures one month later.

How then posit the value of a text? How establish a basic typology of texts? The primary evaluation of all texts can come neither from science, for science does not evaluate, nor from ideology, for the ideological value of a text (moral, aesthetic, political, alethiological) is a value of representation, not of production (ideology 'reflects', it does not do work). Our evaluation can be linked only to a practice, and this practice is that of writing. On the one hand, there is what it is possible to write, and on the other, what is no longer possible to write: what is within the practice of the writer and what has left it: which texts would I consent to write (or re-write), to desire, to put forth as a force in this world of mine? What evaluation finds is precisely this value: what can be written (rewritten) today: the writerly. Why is the writerly our value? Because the goal of literary work (of literature as work) is to make the reader no longer a consumer, but a producer of the text.

Roland Barthes, *S/Z* (1970) (trans. Richard Miller, 1974)

Barthes is famous for contradictory reasons. To many, he is above all a structuralist, perhaps *the* structuralist, advocate of a systematic, scientific approach to cultural phenomena. The most prominent promoter of semiology, the science of signs, he also outlined a structuralist 'science of literature'. To others, Barthes stands not for science but for pleasure: the pleasures of reading and the reader's right to read idiosyncratically, for what pleasure he or she can get. Against a literary criticism focused on authors – interested in recovering what authors thought or meant – Barthes champions the reader and promotes literature that gives the reader an active, creative role.

Jonathan Culler, *Barthes* (1983)

46

Michel Foucault

15 October 1926 – 25 June 1984

*French philosopher and social theorist who explored the archae-
ology of knowledge and discourses of power.*

Michel Foucault moved beyond French structuralism and its phenomenological and existential traditions to create a new method of inquiry
that he first described as an *archaeological* approach to texts, and then,
in the 1970s, a *genealogical* one. By texts Foucault intended the structuralist or hermeneutical meaning of a text to include subjects as diverse
as the penal system or human sexuality.

Foucault's work did much to unseat existentialism as the reigning
philosophical attitude in France. In *Madness and Civilization* (1961) he
explored the uses of the insanity diagnosis as a means of excluding
'otherness' from society, and he exposed the unscientific nature of psychiatric discourse. *The Birth of the Clinic* (1963) continued his critique of
the history of medicine, and in *The Order of Things* (1966) Foucault
turned his critical gaze on the human sciences, Marxism and phenomenology. *The Archaeology of Knowledge* (1969) is an attempt to understand how meaning arises in discourse through what Foucault calls
discursive formations, the significance of which are determined by the

historical conditions under which they are spoken or written. All of these works are examples of Foucault's archaeological period, in which he uncovered the unconscious rules that govern discourse.

With *Discipline and Punish* (1975), a look at the prison system in France, Foucault begins his genealogical period, in which he attempts to identify how one dominant way of thinking (discourse of power) gives way to a succeeding one. He continued this approach in his unfinished three-volume *History of Sexuality* (1966), which comprises *The Will to Knowledge*, *The Use of Pleasure* and *The Care of the Self*.

Foucault was notorious for rejecting the disciplines in which he worked: philosophy, history, critical theory. Because Foucault questioned the very existence of those subjects as believed in by the majority of their practitioners, he is infuriating to those who want to classify thinkers and their ideas in neat categories. Foucault challenges the very activity of historical ordering and classification as a power relation that always serves other interests.

The birth of a radical

Foucault was raised in Poitiers. His father was a prominent surgeon who wanted his son to follow in the profession, but acute depression dogged Foucault throughout his youth and besides his interests lay elsewhere. It was not a good time to be a homosexual in France. Foucault's experience with depression may have focused his attention on the history of insanity and confinement, the subjects of his first major work, *Madness and Civilization*.

Foucault attended the academically prestigious Lycée Henri IV in Paris, where he was taught by the Hegelian philosopher Jean Hyppolite (1907–68). In 1952 he took degrees in psychology and philosophy at the École Normale Supérieure, where he studied under Maurice Merleau-Ponty (1908–61). Both teachers were products of the Kantian and Hegelian traditions that placed the subject at the centre of the world. Foucault rejected this notion and set out to describe a world that was not based on subjectivity, but rather was based on organizing linguistic structures that he called *epistemes*, and characterized by power relations that determine social orders. Foucault foreshadowed the post-structuralist position by arguing that language takes primacy over authors in the study of texts. Foucault eventually rejected the concept of the episteme; instead, he borrowed and adapted the notion of *genealogies* from Nietzsche's *On the Genealogy of Morals* (1887): to study history in such a way as to account for what he termed 'knowledges' and 'discourse'. He identified and elaborated the concept of 'discourse of power' to explain what 'history' is.

Foucault did not feel comfortable in France. One of his mentors was the philologist Georges Dumézil (1898–1986), who arranged for Foucault to get a job through the French embassy's cultural department at the University of Uppsala in Sweden in 1954. There, Foucault flourished. He did not hide his homosexuality. While he found himself in several scrapes with the authorities in Sweden, the result of a fondness for alcohol and sexual encounters, he was more than tolerated by the French consular officials. Foucault stayed four years in Uppsala, and spent the period from 1958 to 1960 at Warsaw University, then at the University of Hamburg.

Discourse(s) of power

Foucault rejected the orthodoxies of Marxism and psychoanalysis, along with the phenomenological tradition that had defined much of French philosophy after Heidegger's *Being and Time* (1927), Sartre's *Being and Nothingness* (1943) and Merleau-Ponty's *Phenomenology of Perception* (1945). Foucault argued that there is no subjectively constituted history. What we had thought of as 'history' is in reality a series of histories that are the product of larger forces beyond the control of (or even the cognizance of) the subject. Indeed, for Foucault, history is the identification and description of discourses of power behind the operations of social control over populations at various moments and places in time. Foucault rejected attempts to pin him down as a thinker. He rejected the labels 'postmodern' and 'post-structuralist'. If he had to be anything, Foucault preferred to be identified as someone working in the vein of Friedrich Nietzsche (1844–1900), with whom he shared a birthday. It is in his sense of turning things upside down (inverting the role of the subject), of posing questions in other ways, that Foucault can be said to be Nietzschean.

Foucault developed a set of tools for thinking with which he could conduct what he called 'the archaeology of knowledge'. His work differed from that of most post-Kantian thinkers – apart from Freud and the scientists – in that each of his projects was an ambitious study of a major historical subject: insanity, the prison system, sexuality. Analytic philosophers do not regard Foucault as a philosopher; yet Foucault used philosophy to develop sets of tools specific to various tasks of understanding, and so demonstrated its relevance and usefulness. His greatest contribution may not be the actual studies he completed, but rather the example he provided for future work.

Madness and Civilization

Foucault's first book, *Mental Illness and Psychology* (1954), was written under the influence of Marxist theory and the phenomenological psychiatry of Ludwig Binswanger (1881–1966). In *Madness and Civilization* (1961) Foucault broke with the new orthodoxies of phenomenology and existentialism almost at the moment of their birth to offer an original analysis of how society viewed (or created) 'madness' at different moments in history. Thus, madness moves from its revered status as divine ecstasy in ancient Greece to its post-Enlightenment manifestation as a medical diagnosis of an illness that must be treated: segregated, confined, drugged.

Foucault further developed his idea that the subject was no longer the centre of the world (the post-structuralist idea of the 'decentred subject') in *The Birth of the Clinic* (1963). Here, the object of study was modern medicine, which Foucault viewed as being composed of a series of linguistic and conceptual structures. Following Roland Barthes, he believed that the essence of literature resided in the text, not the author; Foucault broadened this idea to include any subject he might choose to study as a 'text'. He took from the philosophers of science Gaston Bachelard (1884–1962) and Georges Canguilhem (1904–95) the sense of a world of objects that stood in contradiction to the subjectively constituted world of the phenomenologists (which Foucault condemned as a world of 'narcissistic transcendentalism'). The influence of Fernand Braudel (1902–85) and the *Annales* school of history is also evident, with its focus on the influence of extra-subjective phenomena, such as climate and topography, upon history.

Epistemes

Foucault's genius was to combine aspects of these various theoretical sources and fashion tools for his own use – tools specific to the job in hand. In *The Order of Things* (1966) he charted the linguistic structures (*epistemes*) that lie behind the organization of academic disciplines and official knowledge, and showed that 'progress' from one period and its epistemes to another is not always a smooth, evolutionary process, but may be characterized as a rupture known as an 'epistemic break'. The American philosopher of science T. S. Kuhn would describe a similar movement in his book *The Structure of Scientific Revolutions* (1962). For Foucault, an example of an epistemic break or rupture would be the replacement of Jean-Baptiste Lamarck's theory of the inheritance of acquired characteristics with Charles Darwin's theory of the origin of species and the mechanism of evolution. The movement from Lamarckism to Darwinism is not a smooth transition, but rather a violent epistemic rupture.

Power and sexuality

In his later work Foucault identified and described the power relations that characterize government and institutions, and whose purpose is to exercise social control. Perhaps nowhere is this more apparent than in criminal justice systems, and Foucault's *Discipline and Punish* (1975) shows how modes of social control operate not only in prisons, but also in schools, the workplace and other arenas. Foucault then turned his attention to human sexuality, planning a four-volume work of which three have been published so far: *The Will to Knowledge* (1976), *The Use of Pleasure* (1984) and *The Care of the Self* (1984). In *The Will to Knowledge* Foucault rejects the 'repressive hypothesis' which argues that sexuality is driven underground and out of sight by repressive societies such as that of Victorian England. On the contrary, he argues, any attempts at repression lead to discourses that emphasize rather than repress sexuality. In *The Use of Pleasure* Foucault revisits Classical

Greece to explore its tolerance – indeed, celebration – of a full range of sexual practices. In *The Care of the Self* Foucault moves towards a description of how the Christian tradition has led us to be dominated by the 'sciences of sexuality'.

A playful iconoclast

Foucault's work is characterized by a sense of adventure, of play, of daring. It is also disrespectful; Foucault proudly and defiantly took up an anti-foundationalist position with regard to his own work (that is, he refused to base it, or its results, upon the 'solid' footing of a system of reason). Foucault's genealogies, his archaeologies of knowledge and his articulation of discourses of power were seen as dangerous by Jürgen Habermas (*b*. 1929). As the foremost proponent of communicative rationality (an assertion of the importance of reason and rationality in language, with implications for social order), Habermas feared that post-structuralism would lead to uncertainty, relativism and the end of philosophy. One can only imagine how Habermas's dismay must have delighted Foucault, for whom uncertainty, relativism and the end of philosophy were already a reality.

Foucault loved the United States and from 1980 he was a regular visiting professor at the University of California at Berkeley. His lectures drew crowds as large as 2,000, and Foucault was able to reach an audience that was knowledgeable in philosophy, but which did not carry the heavy baggage of competing ideologies and schools as in France.

There was another reason Foucault loved California: it had a thriving gay scene. He was a regular at gay bathhouses in the early 1980s and was a frequenter of leather and sadomasochistic establishments. This was the period when the little-known AIDS virus was becoming an epidemic. Foucault, on occasion, would scoff at the notion of a 'gay cancer', but an AIDS-related illness would be the cause of his death in 1984. After Foucault's death, his partner of twenty-one years, the sociologist Daniel Defert (*b.* 1937) became a prominent AIDS activist.

While Foucault's work rejects the central role of the subject and refuses to honour philosophy's orthodoxies – be they Hegelian, Marxist, or Freudian – his attitude is anything but nihilistic. Rather, it is joyful, creative, impish. In his essay 'On the Genealogy of Ethics' (1983) he observed: 'From the idea that the self is not given to us, I think that there is only one practical consequence: we have to create ourselves as a work of art.'

If sex is repressed, that is, condemned to prohibition, non-existence and silence, then the mere fact that one is speaking about it has the appearance of a deliberate transgression. A person who holds forth in such a language places himself to certain extent outside the reach of power; he upsets established law; he somehow anticipates the coming freedom. This explains the solemnity with which one speaks of sex nowadays.

Michel Foucault, *The History of Sexuality, Volume 1* (1976)

It is possible to speculate that before Foucault reached a stage in his conceptualization of 'discourse' in which the privileged term of his opus is capable of bearing its full political weight – a stage that would lead from the archaeological method to the genealogical one and embroil him in a consideration of the operations of power and knowledge – he needed first to void it entirely of human intentionality and 'personal' meaning. This message is given in the striking closing words of the conclusions of the *Archaeology*

[*of Knowledge*], a conclusion which takes the form of an imaginary dialogue between Foucault and one of his detractors. The final sentences, which both echo and modify the closing words of *The Order of Things*, announce the foolishness of failing to realize the non-individuality of discourse, its function as impersonal system:

Discourse is not life: its time is not your time; in it, you will not be reconciled to death; you may have killed God beneath the weight of all that you have said; but don't imagine that, with all that you are saying, you will make a man that will live longer than he.

Lisa Downing, *The Cambridge Introduction to Michel Foucault* (2008)

47

Noam Chomsky

b. 7 December 1928

*American linguistic theorist who established generative grammar
and became a leading voice of left-wing intellectual dissidence
in the United States.*

Noam Chomsky is a thinker with two careers. In the first he is a theorist of linguistics who created transformational grammar (which then became generative grammar) and made important contributions to analytic philosophy. In the other he is an anarcho-syndicalist political dissident, whose criticism of United States foreign policy from 1968 to the present makes him the most prominent left-wing voice in the American public sphere.

The roots of Chomsky's twin passions can be traced to his youth in Philadelphia. He is the son of Jewish immigrants who were socialists. At home he heard Hebrew and Yiddish, which, combined with his own English, made him comfortable with the sounds and differences of language – and curious about them. His parents' and uncle's left-wing politics were an obvious influence, but so was his own experience of anti-Semitic taunting and bullying in a predominantly Catholic neighbourhood.

From transformational to generative grammar

Chomsky's early contribution to linguistics was to challenge the primacy of structural linguistics as developed by Ferdinand de Saussure, the notion that language is a system in which meaning is composed of signifier and signified and other dualities. In *Syntactic Structures* (1957) Chomsky introduced the concept of *transformational grammar*. This approach resonated with the tradition of Gottlob Frege, Bertrand Russell and Ludwig Wittgenstein, because it sought to uncover logical structures governing language.

In identifying *surface structures* and *deep structures* of grammar Chomsky showed how relations such as subject and object are not absolute, but are relative to levels of grammatical structure. Surface structure describes a sentence as it is spoken and heard. Deep structure refers to an abstract representation of a sentence, and Chomsky argues that deep structures contain properties shared by all languages. Transformational grammar understands that utterances have a syntax, and that syntax is 'a context-free grammar extended with transformational rules'. By creating a model of language using transformational grammar Chomsky was able to demonstrate how, beginning with a finite set of terms and rules of grammar, a speaker has the possibility to speak and comprehend an infinite number of utterances.

Chomsky's transformational grammar developed into *generative grammar*, which is how he explains a child's facility for language. Children start with an innate *universal grammar* and they only need to acquire a knowledge of grammatical features specific to their native language. In Chomsky's later work he identifies what he calls an *empty category*, an implied, non-phonetic element of grammar. Chomsky defines it thus: 'If some element is "understood" in a particular proposition, then it is *there* in syntactic representation, either as an overt category that is phonetically realized or as an empty category assigned no phonetic form.' (*Knowledge of Language*, 1986)

Chomsky argues that empty categories are an essential part of the structure of the human mind. In *Language and Problems of Knowledge* (1988) he makes the very large claim that: 'The discovery of empty categories and the principles that govern them and that determine the nature of mental representations and computations in general may be compared with the discovery of waves, particles, genes, valence and so on and the principles that hold of them, in the physical sciences.' Chomsky says that by exploring the subsystems of grammar 'we are beginning to see into the deeper hidden nature of the mind and to understand how it works, really for the first time in history'. For Chomsky, the study of linguistics is not simply an attempt to map how language works. He considers language to be the evidence by which we come to an understanding of the mind and the brain. In *Language and Problems of Knowledge* he writes: 'we are approaching a situation that is comparable with the physical sciences in the seventeenth century, when the great scientific revolution took place that laid the basis for the extraordinary accomplishments of subsequent years and determined much of the course of civilization since.'

Chomsky's political stance

Chomsky's political stance is unique in American public life. His anarcho-syndicalism derives from his youthful experience of his parents' left-wing politics – his father William Chomsky was a Hebrew scholar and a member of the Industrial Workers of the World (IWW). Popularly called 'the Wobblies', the IWW is an international trade union that unites workers irrespective of their trade or local union representation and advocates abolition of the wage system. In a 1976 interview, Chomsky described his view of anarchism 'as a kind of voluntary socialism, that is, as libertarian socialist or anarcho-syndicalist or communist anarchist, in the tradition of, say [Mikhail] Bakunin [1814–76] and [Peter] Kropotkin [1842–1921]'. By that Chomsky refers to a kind of social and community organization of organic units, represented by delegates who look after the community's interests in a wider national and international context.

Chomsky's chief criticism of representative democracies like those of Great Britain and the United States is that while voters have a say in the political sphere, they have no say in the management of the economic sphere. For Chomsky, 'democratic control of one's productive life is at the core of any serious human liberation . . . as long as individuals are compelled to rent themselves on the market to those who are willing to hire them, as long as their role in production is simply that of ancillary tools, then there are striking elements of coercion and oppression that make talk of democracy very limited'.

Chomsky's outspoken criticism of United States foreign policy began with the Vietnam War (1964–70) and continues unabated into the second decade of the twenty-first century. He is a fierce critic of the undeclared imperialism of the United States – its exercise of power by economic and military might – as particularly evidenced by its wars in Iraq (2003–11) and Afghanistan (2001–). For Chomsky, the United States, 'the world's hegemonic power accords itself the right to wage war at will, under a doctrine of "anticipatory self-defence" with unstated bounds. International law, treaties and rules of world order are sternly imposed on others with much self-righteous posturing, but dismissed as irrelevant for the United States.'

Q. Is the nation's so-called war on terrorism winnable? . . .

CHOMSKY: If we want to consider this question seriously we should recognize that in much of the world the US is regarded as a leading terrorist state, and with good reason. We might bear in mind, for example, that in 1986 the US was condemned by the World Court for 'unlawful use of force' (international terrorism) and then vetoed a Security Council resolution calling on all states (meaning the US) to adhere to international law. Only one of countless examples.

Noam Chomsky, *9/11: Was There An Alternative?* (2001)

[Chomsky] relentlessly pursues what he sees. No one has exposed more forcefully the self-righteous beliefs on which America's imperial role is based, or delineated more effectively the appalling actions which maintain it. No one has focused more compellingly on the violence of our world, or conveyed more directly the responsibility of the United States for much of it. Few have so carefully dissected how America's acclaimed freedoms mask its irresponsible power and unjustified privilege.

James Peck, from the Introduction to
The Chomsky Reader (1987)

48

Jacques Derrida

15 July 1930 – 8 October 2004

French thinker who forwarded the philosophical projects of the Enlightenment, building on the work of Husserl and Heidegger to create deconstructionist methods.

It is said of Wittgenstein that he read nothing and of Heidegger that he read everything. Jacques Derrida possessed the raw originality of Wittgenstein, while reading deeper than his master Heidegger. He is the most original of the twentieth-century philosophers whose work spilled over into the twenty-first; and he is also the most controversial. Beginning with a completely original reading of Plato, Derrida embarked on a lifelong exploration of the entire canon of Western thought that culminated in a deeply disturbing yet compelling view of what justice is and how it works. Derrida's style of interpreting texts has been called *deconstruction*. For those who follow Derrida's method a 'deconstructionist' style of reading is a powerful tool for getting at the root causes of ideas and misunderstandings; to Derrida's critics, it is nothing but smoke and mirrors and he is the greatest charlatan ever to call himself a philosopher.

A French Jew in Algeria

Jacques Derrida (his given name was 'Jackie') was a *pied noir*, a French colonial living in Algeria before it became independent. As a teenager during the Second World War Derrida developed a consciousness of himself as 'other', this sense of alienation compounded by the fact that he was a Jew living in an Arab country (this was further increased by his being a member of the minority Sephardic sect). As an adolescent, Derrida would face yet sterner challenges. France fell to Germany in June 1940 and Algeria came under the control of the collaborationist Vichy regime.

Anti-Semitic laws imposed by the regime not only disrupted Derrida's education, but threatened his very existence. In October 1940 French Jews in Algeria were stripped of their French citizenship. After the war Derrida emigrated to France. It took him two attempts to pass the examination to enter the École Normale Supérieure (ENS). Eschewing symbols of success, Derrida did not earn his doctorate until 1980, though he actually began his thesis in the early 1950s.

This was a golden age for the ENS. Derrida's teachers and contemporaries included some of the most gifted individuals in modern French history. His thesis was supervised by Jean Hyppolite (1907–68) and his fellow students included Michel Foucault, Jean-François Lyotard, Roland Barthes and Louis Marin.

The first and greatest friend Derrida made while at the ENS was Louis Althusser. One of the chief interpreters of Marx, Althusser was also a *pied noir*. He was further alienated by the fact of his persistent mental illness; and he would become an extreme outsider after a bout of madness in which he fatally strangled his wife in 1980. Derrida's relationship with Althusser is significant because in his thought Derrida is perhaps more sensitive to 'otherness' than any thinker of his generation.

The origins of deconstruction

In his ability to describe, to understand without judging (several judgements are already attached to the thing that is described, he would say), Derrida employs a version of the phenomenological method laid down by Husserl. By putting brackets around our preconceptions about objects under study (including our own consciousness of things) Derrida examined the *cogito* of René Descartes – 'I think therefore I am' – at the dawn of the Enlightenment. The beginning of deconstruction – a term Derrida was uncomfortable with and which is often misused – was Derrida's examination of Descartes' *Meditations on First Philosophy* (1641). Descartes' method is to strip away all his assumed knowledge until he can find a foundation on which it can rest, the *cogito*: I think. The 'I', first introduced by Augustine (354–430) in his *Confessions* (AD 397–8), was raised to the level of a foundation by Descartes, but was subsequently chipped away at by Heidegger and Derrida.

Derrida imagines Descartes' epistemological edifice as a building, and his method consists in a 'de-construction' of that building. Husserl had outlined his phenomenological method of *eidetic reduction* in *Cartesian Meditations* (1931), a series of lectures he gave at the Sorbonne in 1929. The lectures never appeared in a German edition in Husserl's lifetime, but they were translated into French by Gabrielle Peiffer and Emmanuel Levinas.*

---

* Though Derrida and Levinas would publicly disagree, they remained lifelong friends.

Husserl's influence on Derrida

The importance of Husserl in Derrida's thought cannot be overstated. Derrida's most elegant interpreter in English, Leonard Lawlor, describes Derrida's relation to Husserl and phenomenology like this: 'Only phenomenology can . . . give us knowledge of sense as the possibility of the appearing of Being or History . . . Only the phenomenological light allows us to speak.' (*Derrida and Husserl*, 2002). Derrida's *mémoire* (his master's thesis) was *The Problem of Genesis in Husserl's Philosophy* (submitted in 1954, but not published until 1990). Derrida returned to Husserl with a French translation of *The Origin of Geometry* (1962) to which he contributed a long introduction. In it, Derrida observes: 'The mathematical object seems to be the privileged example and most permanent thread guiding Husserl's reflection. This is because the mathematical object is *ideal*. Its being is thoroughly transparent and exhausted by its phenomenality. Absolutely objective, i.e., totally rid of empirical subjectivity, it nevertheless is only what it appears to be.'

Derrida marvels at the purity of the mathematical object, maybe because he is about to undertake an ontological journey the main discovery of which will be that in language (which infects all our realities) nothing is pure. There is no ideal Garden of Eden and no *simply* fallen Adam or Eve. The first couple left a permanent trace in the garden; the garden existed in them, and that trace is bequeathed to all their progeny.

Writing vs speaking

The second, post-Cartesian stage of Derrida's construction of deconstruction is Plato. Plato's thought is defined in a hierarchy of opposed pairs – visible/invisible, essence/appearance, body/soul and so on – but Derrida rejects these by reversing their importance. Essence and appearance are no longer separate, because each is marked by a trace of the other. We find essence *in* appearance and vice-versa. How did he arrive at this view?

As Derrida tells it, Western thought has privileged the spoken word above the written text since at least the time of Plato – Plato's master Socrates was a talker, not a writer. In *Speech and Phenomena* (1967) Derrida attacks this perceived over-valuing of the spoken word by describing how it is that we speak, and what role speech plays in relation to our constitution of ourselves, and our understanding of ourselves as temporal beings. When we speak, there is an infinitesimal lag between the speech utterance and our hearing of what we just said. What we hear ourselves saying already belongs to the past, but we fold it into our present, while at the same time looking forward to the future that, in the blink of an eye, is already the past.

Différance

Speech and Phenomena also engages with Husserl as Derrida develops the idea of *différance*. He builds on Husserl's description of how we perceive time. There is *retention* (of the immediate past); and *protention* (anticipation of the future). Derrida interprets this phenomenon as a hiatus that separates us from ourselves, as being both speakers of and listeners to language. This hiatus is the source of Derrida's concept of *différance*. In typically dense style, Derrida would describe *différance* in his late work *Spectres of Marx* (1993): 'In the incoercible differance the here-now unfurls. Without lateness, without delay, but without presence, it is the precipitation of an absolute singularity, singular because differing, precisely, and always other, binding itself necessarily to the form of the instant, in *imminence and in urgency*: even if it moves towards what remains to come, there is the *pledge*.'

This gap or delay – this *différance* – is similar to the constitutive lag that occurs when we see 'ourselves' in a mirror. There is a hesitation, a moment of recognition, and then a kind of identification with the reflection that is a part of our self-constitution or *auto-affection*, as Derrida describes it (borrowing from Aristotle's definition of God as 'thought thinking itself').

In the act of speaking there is a moment of hesitation in which we cannot decide whether we are in the past or the present. Derrida uses the term *undecided* to indicate this state of affairs (as opposed to *indecision*, which would imply some failing on our part; undecided is simply the nature of things). For Derrida, the old Platonic hierarchies fall away in this moment and we find ourselves in the position of Heraclitus (*c.* 535 – *c.* 475 BC) when he observed that time is like a river one cannot enter in the same place twice. In Heidegger, the essential arguments in *Being and Time* (1927) identify *Dasein* or Being as situated in time, as *thrown* into it, with Being-towards-death its very definition. Perhaps Derrida's best explanation of *différance* – a furthering of Husserlian and Heideggerian notions of time – came in the last interview he gave before his death in 2004. He told Jean Birnbaum of *Le Monde*, 'I am never more haunted by the necessity of dying than in moments of happiness and joy. To feel joy and to weep over the death that awaits are for me the same thing. When I recall my life, I tend to think I have had the good fortune to love even the unhappy moments of my life, and to bless them.' (*Learning to Live Finally: The Last Interview*, 2007).

Death is of central importance in Derrida, and he links it to the concept of the *pledge* or promise that comes in the unfurling of *différance*. Leonard Lawlor identifies this key understanding that is a result of the deconstructionist attitude: 'The ghost of my dead father demands of me to avenge his unjust murder; this demand can only be an aporia: how can I avenge my father's murder? I must have faith. But having nothing but faith, I can never know when I have completely finished with the keeping of the promise; I must keep on living for the promise. For Derrida, therefore, we have a religious experience in which death is "refinished" in the moment of life, which is more than one life (equivocal); life is the refinition of death: death in life.' (*Thinking Through French Philosophy*, 2003).

Hospitality, judgement and 'messianism without religion'

Derrida's concern with justice focuses on the problem of globalization and the plight of the poor. Derrida identifies themes within the context of US hegemony and global terrorism which are central to his discussion of justice: *hospitality* and what the he calls *the worst* (*le pire*). Derrida's entire corpus is about noticing that finite borders do not exist in language or in nature; they are, rather, porous and mutable constructions erected by those who wield power, with the purpose of excluding others. This, in itself, Derrida argues, is unjust. By excluding others we violate hospitality, which should be a governing principle of inclusion. In *Of Hospitality* (1997) Derrida asks if there could be 'A politics, an ethics, a law that thus answer to the new injunctions of unprecedented historical situations, that do indeed correspond to them, by changing the law, by determining citizenship, democracy, international law, etc., in another way?' In the context of the post-9/11 world and the new terrorism, Derrida asked an age-old ontological question, 'What is the worse, the worst? Is there an essence of the worst? And does it mean anything else, for worse, than evil?' (*The Work of Mourning*, 2001).

At one level, Derrida's consideration of the law is a highly technical philosophical one in which the deconstructionist principle of *différance* is brought to bear. In a court of law or a tribunal judgment must eventually be rendered, which is to say, at the given moment, *immediately*. No matter how much deliberation is involved, the moment at which a case is decided is a moment that like all others, is tainted with the past and already hurrying into the future. There is, paradoxically, a singularity about the moment as well as a mechanically repetitive aspect. In this moment, a judge can be *right* in terms of following the law as it is written (and, we know, those texts are highly problematical for Derrida); but the judgement may well not be *just*.

In one of his last interviews, a conversation with Lieven De Cauter of the radical think tank The BRrussells Tribunal (an appropriately Derridean reference to the self-appointed Russell-Sartre Tribunal that sat in judgement of American war crimes in Vietnam), Derrida spoke of the excluded, who, in his view, will inherit the earth. He sees messianism without religion in the heterogeneous, unformed anti-globalization movement, which, while full of contradictions, serves the purpose of gathering 'together the weak of the earth, all those who feel themselves crushed by the economic hegemonies, the liberal market, by sovereignism, etc.' Among his last words: 'I believe it is these weak who will prove to be strongest in the end and who represent the future.'

The problem with reading Derrida

It is said by Derrida's critics that his work is unintelligible. Reading Derrida is less difficult if one has an encyclopaedic knowledge of Western thought, in particular the technical language of phenomenology.* When critics complain that Derrida's work is unintelligible, he would argue it is because they are unfamiliar with the subject matter and terminology of the tradition; they do not speak the language.

Analytic and continental philosophers find themselves in a *dialogue de sourds*: the former are intent on establishing the linguistic foundations of truth, while the latter (at least Derrideans) are convinced this is impossible. For Derrida there is no pessimism or nihilism in this understanding. It is simply an ontological truth, and one that makes him particularly sensitive to the nuances of whatever he chooses to study. His obituary in *The Times* noted: 'what can be said of his work is that each publication is a singular demonstration of a patient response to the contours, rhythms and turns of the subject being addressed.'

The German philosopher Jürgen Habermas, the proponent of communicative rationality, feared that Derrida was leading the world into an ethical morass of deconstructed disconnection and relativism. As Derrida succinctly remarked in 'Is There a Philosophical Language?': 'Those who accuse me of reducing philosophy to literature or logic to rhetoric (see, for example, the latest book by Habermas, *The Philosophical Discourse of Modernity*) have visibly and carefully avoided reading me.'

Now, 'everyday language' is not innocent or neutral. It is the language of Western metaphysics, and it carries with it not only a considerable number of presuppositions of all types, but also presuppositions inseparable from metaphysics, which, although little attended to, are knotted into a system.

Jacques Derrida, *Positions* (1972)

---

* Something this author does not claim for himself.

Along with Ludwig Wittgenstein and Martin Heidegger, Jacques Derrida . . . will be remembered as one of the three most important philosophers of the twentieth century. No thinker in the last 100 years had a greater impact than he did on people in more fields and different disciplines. Philosophers, theologians, literary and art critics, psychologists, historians, writers, artists, legal scholars and even architects have found in his writings resources for insights that have led to an extraordinary revival of the arts and humanities during the past four decades. And no thinker has been more deeply misunderstood.

Mark C. Taylor, 'What Derrida Really Meant',
New York Times (14 October 2004).

49

Richard Rorty

4 October 1931 – 8 June 2007

American post-analytic philosopher who revived pragmatism as a distinctly American philosophical response to the late twentieth century.

The work of Richard Rorty heralded the end of analytic philosophy as the sole trend in late twentieth-century American philosophy. In rejecting the analytic tradition in which he had been trained, Rorty reinterpreted the uniquely American tradition of pragmatism to develop neopragmatism – a set of tools for investigating problems that concern ordinary people, and not just professors of philosophy. His most important book is *Philosophy and the Mirror of Nature* (1979) in which he rejects the representationalist tradition which holds that we can only be aware of objects through the mediation of the ideas that represent them, (as in Descartes and Locke). Rorty challenged the notion of objectivity, eventually concluding that there is no such thing as universal truths. Rorty became so critical of philosophy's narrowness of thought that he gave up the Stuart Chair of Philosophy at Princeton to become Kenan Professor of Humanities at the University of Virginia. (In 'The Philosopher as Expert' (2009), Rorty noted dismissively,

'Philosophy in America is just one more academic speciality.') Of thinkers writing in English after the Second World War he is among the clearest of prose stylists, along with the early pragmatists William James and George Santayana.

Influence of Dewey

The pragmatist who most influenced Rorty is John Dewey – the first American thinker to address problems of democracy using philosophy as a tool to help build a more desirable outcome in politics. He did this largely by examining the importance of informed dialogue in politics (including the role of journalism), but premised the entire concept of democracy on effective education. At fifteen, Rorty attended Hutchins College at the University of Chicago, an experimental school that had been set up by Dewey's colleague and intellectual sparring partner, the educational reformer Robert Maynard Hutchins (1899–1977). The *New Yorker* journalist A. J. Liebling famously referred to Hutchins College as a 'collection of juvenile neurotics'.

Rorty was an unusually sensitive boy who was bullied enough as a child to remember Hutchins College as his escape from persecution. The concept of personal freedom was thus established early and permanently for Rorty, both of whose parents were communists. Rorty's larger sense of political freedom may have derived from the fact that both his parents left the American Communist Party in 1932 to become Trotskyists. Rorty tells how his father 'almost, but not quite, accompanied John Dewey to Mexico as PR man for the Commission of Inquiry which Dewey chaired' ('Trotsky and the Wild Orchids', 1992). Rorty was referring to the 1940 inquiry held by American Marxists into whether or not Leon Trotsky (1879–1940) was guilty of treason in the

Soviet Union. The Dewey Commission decided he was innocent, but Trotsky was assassinated in Mexico on the orders of the Soviet leader Joseph Stalin. The bloody consequences of thought were further impressed on the consciousness of the nine-year-old Rorty when Trotsky's assistant John Frank escaped assassination in Mexico and came to live incognito for a time at the Rorty home in Flatbrookville, New Jersey. Just three years later Carlo Tresca (1879–1943), a leading anarcho-syndicalist and member of the Industrial Workers of the World or 'wobblies' (another friend of the Rorty's) was assassinated in New York, possibly by Stalin's NKVD secret police.

Darwinian naturalism

In his autobiographical essay 'Trotsky and the Wild Orchids' (1992) Rorty achieves in the compass of only 7,000 words an outline of the genesis of his thought, which is not only philosophical and political: it also has a scientific component. Rorty describes his boyhood fascination with the wild orchids that flourished near his New Jersey home. Their significance for him was that they 'are the latest and most complex plants to have been developed in the course of evolution'. Here we find the germ of Rorty's naturalism, which derives from Charles Darwin's work on the origin of species. Rorty used Darwin to support his position that no one vocabulary of science or philosophy is innately more important than the other; that these 'vocabularies' only gain significance through their proven efficacy when employed in scientific or philosophical inquiry. In other words, they do not constitute, in themselves, absolute knowledge or truth.

Perception, truth and ironism

In *Philosophy and the Mirror of Nature* Rorty took on two cornerstones of empiricism: the representational theory of perception and the correspondence theory of truth. The former theory holds that the mind acts in such a way as to mirror what exists in nature, an idea found in the work of Descartes, Locke and Kant. The correspondence theory of truth says that 'truth' is in agreement with 'reality'; that a statement can correspond with a state of affairs, with 'the way things are'.

Rorty says that 'truths' elicited in this fashion are simply the result of tricks we do with language to get the result we want. He believes that philosophers and scientists too often 'force' language to perform the trick of 'proving' the point they wish to make. He challenges the *raison d'être* of analytic philosophy, arguing that it poses and 'solves' only the questions it believes are relevant to philosophy, in a language created for that specific purpose. This, he argues, has nothing to do with reality.

Rorty proposes we understand that the vocabularies of science and philosophy are contingent. We pick them up and put them down according to how useful they are in framing questions and giving answers. Words, paradigms, philosophical doctrines are all, in Rorty's view, useful as tools for the investigation of problems. But they should not be fetishized or mistaken for 'the truth'. The idea of 'truth', understood as a fixed thing *out there* in the world, is no longer possible. In *Contingency, Irony and Solidarity* (1989) Rorty argues that 'Truth cannot be out there – cannot exist independently of the human mind – because sentences cannot so exist, or be out there. The world is out there, but descriptions of the world are not.' He calls his position *ironism*.

Irony is a defining factor of the inquiring mind and Rorty identifies it in the work of Proust, Nietzsche and Heidegger. In Proust's *In Search of Lost Time* (1913–27) the main character constantly reinterprets events as he encounters characters – and his own memory – over a period of time. It is this unwillingness to give fixed interpretations that characterizes the ironist. For Rorty, the ironic stance has three defining characteristics: 'radical and continuing doubts' about one's own vocabulary, and those of others; the realisation that arguments phrased in one's own vocabulary 'can neither underwrite nor dissolve these doubts'; and an understanding that one's own vocabulary is not 'closer to reality than others' (*Contingency, Irony and Solidarity*).

Rorty's thought is original in its revival and reworking of pragmatism, and courageous in its pugnacious refusal of the analytic philosophical agenda. He rejects the convenient and easy 'truths' of representationalism in favour of the more difficult exploration of contingent truths. His thinking encourages a multiplicity of conversations about the nature of human freedom, conducted in a spirit of reasoned disagreement. In *Achieving Our Country: Leftist Thought in Twentieth-Century America* (1998) Rorty defines his neopragmatic political philosophy in contrast to that of what he calls the 'critical Left', exemplified by the post-structuralist Michel Foucault. The critical Left, he argues, fails to provide practical answers to social problems it may identify. By contrast, the progressive Left – best represented by John Dewey – is attached to the idea of progress through pragmatic action by which democracy can be achieved. Pragmatic action, for Rorty, is participation in the democratic process, which, he argues, declined in America after the Vietnam War.

As Rorty observes in 'Trotsky and the Wild Orchids': 'I wanted a way to be both an intellectual and spiritual snob and a friend of humanity – a nerd recluse and a fighter for justice.'

Pragmatists hope to break with the picture which, In Wittgenstein's words, 'holds us captive' — the Cartestian-Lockean picture of a mind seeking to get in touch with a reality outside itself. So they start with a Darwinian account of human beings as animals doing their best to cope with the environment — doing their best to develop tools which will enable them to enjoy more pleasure and less pain. Words are among the tools which these clever animals have developed.

Richard Rorty, *Philosophy and Social Hope* (1999)

Rorty's enduring appeal has a number of sources. One is the scope and urgency of his views, for he was never shy about presenting his call for the abandonment of objective truth against the grand backdrop of the cultural progress of the West.

James Tartaglia (ed.), *Richard Rorty* (2009)

50

Julia Kristeva

b. *24 June 1941*

Bulgarian-French thinker who synthesized Marxism, phenome-
nology, structuralism and psychoanalysis to create a range of
interpretative tools.

Julia Kristeva is the leading heir to the structuralist and post-structuralist traditions. Her unique style of thinking uses insights gained
from phenomenology, Marxism, psychoanalysis and semiotics. She
introduced two important terms into popular intellectual discourse:
intertextuality and *abjection*. Intertextuality, a fundamental element of
post-structuralist theory, refers to the way in which the meaning of a
text is informed by other texts and our own accumulated reading of
them. *Abjection* or the *abject* describes the condition of marginalized
persons: women, people of colour, the mentally ill, criminals. Kristeva's
work includes philosophical writings, biography and novels. An early
student (and critic) of Jacques Lacan, she is a practising psychoanalyst. Following her reading of psychoanalysis and the Swiss linguist
Ferdinand de Saussure, she developed an original concept of the *semi-*
otic, which describes an aspect of language that is pre-symbolic, before
grammar.

Bulgaria and the Tel Quel group

Like many leading French thinkers of the twentieth century – Albert Camus, Jacques Derrida, Louis Althusser, Hélène Cixous (*b*. 1937) and Luce Irigaray (*b*. 1932) – Kristeva is a naturalized French citizen, which may explain in part her concern for the marginalized, the *abject*. She was born and educated in communist-ruled Bulgaria, as was her colleague, the Bulgarian-French philosopher and literary critic Tzvetan Todorov (*b*. 1939). In 1960 Kristeva joined the *Tel Quel* group of philosophers that formed around the journal of the same name and which lasted until 1982. Founded by Kristeva's husband, the novelist Phillipe Sollers (*b*. 1936), the focus of the *Tel Quel* movement was on radical social and literary criticism; its members included Foucault, Derrida and Barthes.

Abjection

In *Powers of Horror: An Essay on Abjection* (1980) Kristeva uses the term abjection to describe the complex situation of the subject who is not simply alienated, but who is 'radically excluded' and drawn 'towards the place where meaning collapses'. In abjection, 'A certain "ego" that merged with its master, a superego, has flatly driven it away. It lies outside, beyond the set, and does not seem to agree to the latter's rules of the game.' The abject includes anyone who is alienated in society: immigrants, people of colour, but also homosexuals and transgendered persons, single mothers, criminals and the mentally ill. Kristeva uses the image of the corpse – a person who once was, but is no longer – to describe the status of the abject. Not fully recognized as a subject (a person) and regarded more as an object, the abject inhabits a twilight world of partial existence. Kristeva's psychoanalytic interpretation of the abject leads her to conclude that we all experience abjection in our rejection of the maternal. She argues that we need to reject the mother with whom we have a shared identity from the moment we are conceived, in order to create a new, separate identity for ourselves.

Intertextuality

Intertexuality offers a new understanding of our own subjectivity and its relation to texts. Saussure uncovered the structure of language to show the arbitrary nature of the signifier and the signified. Barthes declared the death of the author, giving primacy to the text. In one sense, these developments are a challenge to a line of thinking that descends from the idealist tradition starting with Kant and culminating in the phenomenological tradition of Husserl, in which we, the *subject*, ascribe meaning to the world. In thinkers as diverse as Hegel and Karl Jaspers we find an elaboration of the mechanisms by which subjects are not locked in a solipsistic world of their own making, but rather recognize each other's subjectivities and by mutual agreement arrive at intersubjectivity – a shared world of meaning.

Kristeva derives the notion of intertextuality from her reading of the Russian philosopher and critic Mikhail Bakhtin (1895–1975). In *Desire in Language* (1977) she presented this fundamental discovery of Bakhtin's: 'any text is constructed as a mosaic of quotations; any text is the absorption and transformation of another.' Following on from Bakhtin, Kristeva claims that 'any text is the absorption and transformation of another. The notion of *intertextuality* replaces that of inter-subjectivity and poetic language is read as at least *double*.' At least double. Authors borrow – consciously or not – from other texts.

Readers bring to the reading of each new text a whole personal history of reading, which incorporates the read texts and – consciously or not – the entire tapestry of which those already-read texts are an unavoidable part. In *Revolution in Poetic Language* (1974) Kristeva says, with characteristic obscurity, that the mechanism of intertextuality is the 'transposition of (or several) sign-system(s) into another'.

Semiotic

Kristeva's use of the term semiotic is not be confused with its use by either Saussure or C. S. Peirce. She marries insights gained from the practice of psychoanalysis with her own reading of philosophy to identify two essential components of language: the *symbolic* and the *semiotic*. The symbolic is governed by grammatical and social rules. Part of the experience of abjection is to be excluded from this symbolic world. It is to this world that Saussure's theory of language belongs, in which words (the signifier) and things (the signified) exist in a relation of arbitrary meaning.

More important for Kristeva is the semiotic, which enriches our understanding of language by focusing on its vocal expression. This contains pre-verbal elements, the source of which are bodily rhythms – not only those of the subject as a separate person – but also our pre-linguistic experiences in the womb. Kristeva borrows from Plato the term *chora* to describe this phenomenon. She argues that even after the child acquires language, with its paternally dominated system of signs, a maternal, pre-linguistic self continues after birth. This pre-linguistic self existed apart from rules (grammatical or social) and has an aspect that is wild and untameable. It finds its ultimate expression in poetic language, which often challenges linguistic rules.

Kristeva's concern for language and her statement that intertextuality is the new intersubjectivity does not mean the death of the subject. It is just that the subject is expressed in language and deeply influenced by it. The subject is essential (texts don't read themselves!) and Kristeva tries to relocate subjectivity amidst the debris of the post-empirical, post-analytic, post-structuralist world. Here, Kristeva finds that subjectivity comes in a variety of pluralities: masculine, feminine, stranger, psychotic, and a multiplicity of sexualities. What these diverse subjects have in common is that their subjectivity is grounded in the body. That is why Kristeva pays so much attention to the semiotic; to the primordial, physical articulations of language.

According to Kristeva we all (irrespective of gender) learn the rhythm of life, the music of being, in the womb. Separation from the womb and birth into a world dominated by the institutions of paternalism particularly alienates the female subject. As a result, her experiences, actions, utterances are different from those of men. So, while Kristeva recognizes and describes female alienation, she is nevertheless famous (or infamous) for not aligning herself with mainstream feminism. Feminists may object to Kristeva's work because she puts so much emphasis on the maternal and on the subject's experience both within in the womb and outside it – the rejection of the mother in search for a separate identity. This is at odds with the thinking of Simone de Beauvoir,* who denounced motherhood in *The Second Sex* (1949), the bible of second-wave feminism.

A believer in words

Interviewed by the *Guardian* newspaper in 2006, Kristeva said: 'I am not a believer, I believe in words. There is only one resurrection for me

* Ironically, Kristeva is a co-founder of the Simone de Beauvoir Prize for work in gender equality.

– and that is in words.' The context for her remarks was the publication of *This Incredible Need to Believe* (2009). In her introduction she writes, 'Unlike Freud, I do not claim that religion is just an illusion and a source of neurosis. The time has come to recognize, without being afraid of "frightening" either the faithful or the agnostics, that the history of Christianity prepared the world for humanism.' Kristeva's work is never 'merely' aesthetic or merely technical: it always implies an ethical discovery, and it always notices the political context in which it occurs.

In her study *Hannah Arendt* (1999) Kristeva considers the work of another refugee from totalitarianism and another student of the Christian tradition. Arendt was Heidegger's student and Kristeva places Heidegger at the centre of her inquiries. Describing Arendt, Kristeva could be talking about herself: 'Today we find it hard to accept that life, a sacred value in both Christian and post-Christian democracies, is the recent product of a historical evolution . . . It is precisely the questioning of this fundamental value – its formation in Christian eschatology as well as the dangers it faces in the modern world – that quietly unifies Arendt's entire work.' The same could be said of Kristeva's work; in all its variety, complexity and explorations in diverse disciplines, it brings philosophy and thinking to bear on life as a sacred value.

> The child king becomes irredeemably sad before uttering his first words; this is because he has been irrevocably, desperately separated from the mother, a loss that causes him to try to find her again, along with other objects of love, first in the imagination, then in words.
>
> Julia Kristeva, *Black Sun: Melancholia and Depression* (1987)

Postscript

Philosophy is dead, according to the British physicist Stephen Hawking (*b.* 1942). 'How can we understand the world in which we find ourselves?' he asks in *The Grand Design: New Answers to the Ultimate Questions of Life* (2010). 'Did the universe have a creator? Traditionally these are questions for philosophy, but philosophy is dead.' In his view scientists have taken over the 'real' questions of philosophy and are busy answering them. Eventually they will answer all of them, leaving philosophy with nothing to do. Philosophy is a dinosaur.

But claiming that philosophy is dead is the same as saying that thinking is dead. Martin Heidegger (1889–1976) said that philosophy *is* thinking; and where science is concerned, philosophers do plenty of thinking about it. Indeed, the philosophy of science is one area that has grown dramatically since R. V. Quine (1908–2000) questioned logical positivism and T. S. Kuhn (1922–96) identified the means by which scientific paradigms rise and fall.

In fact, science and scientific revolutions provide us with a useful comparison for the state of professional philosophy today (not all thinking that shapes our world is done by philosophers, and we will address that fact in a moment). In science, says Kuhn, we have a prevailing paradigm or ruling concept that creates an entire worldview that includes man's popular view of himself in relation to the universe, and also how scientists 'do' science. A good example of a ruling paradigm would be the theory of the Egyptian mathematician Ptolemy (second-century AD) that the Sun moves around the Earth: the geocentric picture of the universe. Along comes the Polish astronomer Copernicus (1473–1543), who inverts the paradigm. No, he says, it is the *Earth* that revolves around the *Sun*. At first there is chaos and disbelief. People are tortured and burned at the stake by the Church because this heliocentric picture seems to go against God. After a while, however, the Copernican Revolution doesn't seem quite so revolutionary any more and the scientists go back to work, doing what they do.

Bench science

And what do scientists do? They experiment. Scientists – hundreds of thousands (if not millions) of them around the world develop hypotheses and test them experimentally. When an experiment seems to work – when it can be repeated by diverse investigators and results can be replicated – then we have established an incremental building block of the ruling paradigm. And so scientists go on experimenting until a revolutionary scientist like Albert Einstein comes along and says, 'No, I don't think this is how it works at all. It's more like *this*.' But your average scientist is a workaday experimenter, doing what Kuhn calls 'bench science'. Scientists like Einstein or Richard Feynman (1918–88) are rare. And maybe getting rarer as science becomes more and more corporatized.

In philosophy, when Immanuel Kant made his so-called 'Copernican turn' there was a similar paradigm shift in modern thought. He argued that human knowledge not only consisted of *more* than the simple receptions of sense impressions, but also that it was *different in kind*. Instead of sense impressions being 'written' on a passive *tabula rasa* (or blank slate), as philosophers from Aristotle to John Locke would have it, knowledge comes from the power of human subjectivity in the act of perception. Kant gave primacy to the subject over the object: that was his Copernican turn.

Philosophy's progress

The subject's ascendancy over the object almost inevitably led to someone like the German philosopher Friedrich Nietzsche declaring that God is dead. And it was equally inevitable, perhaps, that someone like Ludwig Andreas von Feuerbach would come to assert the divinity of man. Then Karl Marx would search for the values of man in terms of his economic and material history and relations; Jean-Paul Sartre would call man a 'useless passion'; Roland Barthes would declare the death of the author; and Jacques Derrida would deconstruct language until we found ourselves naked in front of it, exposed by our attempts at meaningful utterances, confronted by what is present by virtue of its absence in the words that use us.

So, philosophers have been busy.

But how will they be busy in the twenty-first century? And who will they be? Let's try to answer the second question first. The new thinkers may no longer be professional philosophers, since economic pressures in universities mean there will be fewer of them. How many are there now? The American Philosophical Association has more than 11,000 paying members. This fact evokes in me a major *here-to-there* moment, as in how did we get from a handful of Greek philosophers in Miletus 2,500 years ago to 11,000 American ones today? And that number doesn't begin to take into account philosophers in Britain and the rest of the Anglophone world; it omits the whole of Europe. That's a lot of philosophers. What do they all do?

Death of the philosophical superstar

We may have seen the last of the philosophical superstars. Jacques Derrida is probably the last philosopher whose name might ring a bell with the general public (though they almost certainly won't have read him). Sartre was a recent one, as was Bertrand Russell. Charles Darwin, Karl Marx and Sigmund Freud are perennial giants (and two of them were primarily scientists). Why is it that yesteryear had more big-name thinkers? Who are the thinkers of tomorrow, in our midst today?

In his essay 'The Future of Philosophy' John Searle (*b.* 1932) says the age of the philosophical giant is over because we now have more well-trained philosophers than ever before, and that they are busy solving philosophical problems. In Searle's view they are all so good at what they do that nobody stands out. From one perspective this is a very generous stance to take, rather like a general surveying his divisions and claiming that every one of his soldiers is a hero. But, just as we may have more military hardware than enemies, so we may have more philosophers than problems. Rather like the general who wants the government to keep upping the military budget to protect the jobs of himself and his soldiers, so the professor of philosophy needs more funding to keep his staff of philosophers, all of whom are busy solving philosophical problems.

Old problems

Which problems? J. L. Austin once observed that the Greeks had identified about a thousand philosophical problems, and that after Ludwig Wittgenstein they were on the way to being solved. A. J. Ayer said that the work of solving philosophical problems was nearly done. On the other hand, John Searle thinks there is much more to do. 'I would estimate that about 90 per cent of the philosophical problems left us by the Greeks are still with us,' he says, 'and that we have not yet found a scientific, linguistic or mathematical way to answer them.'

Richard Rorty suspected that much of modern philosophy's concern with language was, at bottom, make-work. Problems are what philosophers say they are, and they are solved when philosophers say so (but only in the world of language games that some philosophers share with others of their persuasion). Rorty was speaking as a neo-pragmatist whose hero was John Dewey, but he may have had George Santayana in mind when he gave up his chair of philosophy at Princeton for one in the humanities at the University of Virginia. Santayana left his post at Harvard in favour of a wandering existence in Europe, finally settling in Mussolini's Italy, where he became ill and died. Santayana left academia full of contempt for a garden overgrown with the 'thistles of trivial and narrow scholarship'.

Rorty's relinquishing of his chair didn't mean he gave up philosophy; it was just that he no longer earned his money working as a philosophy professor. He was a professor of humanities and, at Stanford, he even worked in a literature department (perhaps confirming the view of some analytic philosophers that anyone who so much as flirts with continental philosophy is not a philosopher, but a mere littérateur).

New problems

What will thinkers work on as the twenty-first century proceeds? Some will teach the history of philosophy and science – a job that needs to be done. Understanding the full range of questions that past philosophers philosophized about – which, in the case of Aristotle, Kant and Hegel, means *everything* – will provide clues as to how present and future problems might be solved. And those problems will not be ones solely of language or mathematics. They will also include new problems arising from the things that are happening to us in our world today. Terrorism raises important questions about belief and reason. How can dialogue be possible between the fundamentalist point of view and a post-Enlightenment one?

Our responses to terrorism cry out for philosophical study and guidance: pre-emptive war; the use of torture; respect for international boundaries in pursuit of those we deem our enemies. What is an acceptable calculus of civilian deaths? What about indefinite detention without habeas corpus? The 'war on terror': what does that mean? What is 'terror'? Who is a terrorist? Should the West borrow the values of its enemies in their pursuit? And, if so, how does that affect us? Should governments restrict our civil liberties in order to fight terrorism (in order to protect our civil liberties . . .)?

War aside, globalization raises questions of scarcity for tens of millions of people around the world. Should we challenge the views of climate-change deniers? Do governments have a duty to protect the Earth's resources? Do corporations have a right to exploit these resources until they are depleted?

There are plenty of other ethical issues for philosophers to tackle, from abortion to advances in biotechnology. Nuclear war has now threatened humankind for more than sixty-five years. Some experts believe that within the lifetime of most readers of this book a terrorist group will detonate a crude nuclear device.

While that's hardly an exhaustive list of issues for modern philosophers to think about, it should keep them busy for a while.

Acknowledgements

Peg Culver, director of the Bancroft Public Library in Salem, New York, was a constant and ever-agreeable companion during my research for this book. She obtained dozens of volumes on interlibrary loan to the little upstate New York village where the first draft of this book was written, and helped make it possible for me to work outside of a major city or institution. Thank you doesn't begin to express my gratitude. Peg was ably assisted by Susan Getty, Rebecca Brown and Julie Brown.

I completed this work in London, and I owe an enormous debt of gratitude to Rachel and David Allison, and to Ginny Goudy. Their steadfast friendship and support is invaluable.

During the editing process I enjoyed the hospitality of Oliver Ray, Chris Sauer, Jennifer Donofrio and Sarah Johnson in Tucson, AZ. My brother, Brian Trombley, was a gracious host in Nashua, NH; and I concluded the work at the home of Angela Kaset and Bruce McGaw in Nashville, TN.

The following people helped in many ways for which I am grateful: Babette Babbich, Professor of Philosophy, Fordham University; Jürgen Braungardt, psychotherapist, Oakland, CA; Al Budde and Nancy Flint-Budde; Charles Carlson, Department of Philosophy, Texas A&M University; Felicia Dougherty; Professor Sigrid Close, Department of Astronautics and Aeronautics, Stanford University; Nancy Fitzpatrick; Hans Herlof Grelland, Professor of Quantum Chemistry (Physics) and Philosophy, University of Agder; Professor Pete Gunter, University of North Texas Department of Philosophy and Religion; Laureen Jean Harrington; Dr Charles Krecz, Department of Philosophy, University of Texas at Austin; Irma Kurtz; Professor Leonard Lawlor, Department of Philosophy, Pennsylvania State University; William L. McBride, Arthur G. Hansen Distinguished Professor of Philosophy, Purdue University; John J. McDermott, Distinguished Professor of Philosophy and Humanities, Texas A&M University; Professor David Mowry, University Distinguished Teaching Professor, SUNY Plattsburgh; Dr Paul Nnodim, Associate Professor, Department of Philosophy, Massachusetts College of Liberal Arts; Rabbi Norman and Naomi Patz; Fred and Norene Russo; Sean Sayers, Professor of Philosophy, University of Kent; Matthew Silliman, Professor of Philosophy, Massachusetts College of Liberal Arts; Dr Caren Steinlight; Beth Steves; Glenn Stokem; Dr Robin Waterfield.

I am grateful to the following university and public libraries for providing books through interlibrary loan: Clifton Park-Halfmoon Public Library; College of Saint Rose; Crandall Public Library, Glens Falls, NY; Gloversville NY Free Library; New York State Library; Rensselaer Polytechnic Institute Library; Saratoga Springs Public Library; Schenectady Public Library; Skidmore College Library; SUNY Albany; SUNY Plattsburgh; SUNY Stony Brook; Union College Library; Waterford Public Library.

Richard Milbank suggested I write this book, and we have enjoyed many hours of stimulating discussion from conception to final editing; I do not think an author could ever find a more agreeable editor. Ian Pindar is an extraordinarily attentive copy editor, and he has improved this text enormously. Toby Mundy, CEO of Atlantic Books, is a great friend and for several decades I have enjoyed his constant support and wise counsel.

Glossary of Terms

abjection Julia Kristeva uses abjection, or the abject, to describe the condition of the marginalized: women, people of colour, the mentally ill, the criminal.

absolute, the (see **spirit**)

absolutism The political theory that government has absolute, unchecked power to act.

absurd, the Albert Camus's *The Myth of Sisyphus* (1942) characterized man's position as that of Sisyphus, in Greek mythology condemned to spend eternity pushing a rock up a mountain, only for it to roll down again. The absurd is created in the impossible conflict between our desire for meaning and the indifference of the universe. Camus proposes recognition of this fact, rather than suicide or the Kierkegaardian leap of faith.

active citizenship Term coined by British idealist T. H. Green, who advocated the practical application of idealist and liberal principles in public life. He believed the proper end of philosophy was action.

alienation Karl Marx's description of the worker's predicament under capitalism. The object of the worker's labour, the product, was alienated from him (i.e., it was not for his use). Additionally, the worker was alienated from himself by his work, because it was not part of what Marx called his 'species-life' or 'species-being'.

American transcendentalism A tendency among New England intellectuals in the mid-nineteenth century who believed in the individual's ability to achieve spiritual (transcendental) knowledge through intuition – without recourse to organized religion or departments of philosophy at universities like those at Harvard. Prominent representatives were Ralph Waldo Emerson and Henry David Thoreau.

analytic philosophy The broad tendency in Anglophone philosophy that started with Gottlob Frege's work grounding arithmetic in logic. It was taken up by Bertrand Russell and G. E. Moore, along with Ludwig Wittgenstein, to make a style of philosophy that reduced problems to their component parts, dismissing metaphysical approaches as meaningless.

anarchism Position advocating abolition of all government and its replacement by free association, voluntary groups or collectives. It was proposed in various forms by William Godwin, Pierre-Joseph Proudhon and Mikhail Bakunin.

animal faith George Santayana's view that reasoning is not the source of knowledge and belief; rather, they result from the fact of our animal existence (animal faith). The fact that I am hungry and there is food proves the existence of the self and the external world.

Annales school A group that arose around Lucien Fevre and Marc Bloch and their journal *Annales: économies, sociétés, civilizations*. They were concerned less with political narrative and chronology than analysis of long-term trends and structures. Ferdinand Braudel is an *Annales* historian.

Anomie In the thought of Emile Durkheim, the situation of detachment from shared social norms that can result from an alienating division of labour under capitalism, and the chief sociological (as opposed to individual, psychological) reason for suicide.

anxiety Søren Kierkegaard characterized the position of humankind in the face of death as anxiety or dread. This theme was further elaborated by Martin Heidegger as being-towards-death.

a posteriori/ a priori Two types of knowledge. *A posteriori* knowledge is derived empirically, after experience of it. *A priori* knowledge is derived before experience. Immanuel Kant said that the truths of geometry are given to us a priori.

arc theory John Dewey's reflex arc theory states that 'sensory stimulus, central connections and motor responses shall be viewed not as separate and complete entities in themselves, but as divisions of labour, function factors, within the single concrete whole.'

associationism Epistemological doctrine which says that association of ideas or experiences with things or events in memory accounts for our understanding of them. It was held by the British empiricists John Locke, David Hume, James Mill and J. S. Mill.

authenticity In Martin Heidegger's *Being and Time* (1927) the condition of **Dasein** or the human being coming to terms with its defining nature as **being-towards-death**. It is also used by Jean-Paul Sartre and the existentialists.

being-towards-death In Martin Heidegger's philosophy, the defining condition of our existence, **Dasein**. Death is destiny and our lives are lived in the context of embracing that fact (or not, which would be inauthenticity). See **authenticity**.

Bradley's Regress Argument employed by T. H. Bradley in *Appearance and Reality* (1893) to claim that relations – including thought – are contradictory. They are appearance only and not reality.

category mistake An error identified by Gilbert Ryle in *The Concept of Mind* (1949). A category mistake 'represents the facts of mental life as if they belonged to one logical type or category . . . when they actually belong to another.'

chora Term borrowed from Plato and used by Julia Kristeva to describe pre-linguistic experience that is maternal, because much of it occurs at the foetal stage of development.

class (1) In *mathematics*, class appears in set theory as a collection of sets (or sometimes other mathematical objects), which is identified by a property that all its members share. (2) In *sociology* and *political theory*, a term to denote the status of an individual. It can be determined by birth (nobility, common) or, in the sense used by Karl Marx, to describe a person's relationship to an economic power matrix; for instance, bourgeoisie (owners of capital) or working class (labourer).

coherence theory of truth Theory put forward by T. H. Bradley in *The Nature of Truth* (1906), which holds that a proposition is true to the extent that it is a necessary constituent of a systematically coherent whole.

communicative rationality In the work of Jürgen Habermas the argument that human rationality is a necessary outcome of successful communication.

communitarianism As opposed to liberalism, with its focus on the role of the individual in achieving social good, communitarianism looks to the collaborations of groups with a state in achieving social good.

consequentialism In ethics, the position that the value of an action is to be determined from its consequences.

constitution Term in the philosophy of Edmund Husserl to describe the creative act by which an object is brought into consciousness.

Copernican turn In the *Critique of Pure Reason* (1781) Kant argued that space, time and causal relations are to be attributed to the perceiving mind. This was to philosophy what Nicolaus Copernicus's declaration that the Earth revolves around the Sun (and not vice versa) was to astronomy, in that it upset the prevailing paradigm.

critical rationalism Term used by Karl Popper to reject the reliance on verifiability as a test of meaning by the Vienna Circle. Instead he argued that falsifiability should be the criterion for scientific work; hypotheses should be designed to attract attempts to falsify them.

critical theory Its original meaning referred to a method of interpretation developed by members of the Frankfurt School, including Theodore Adorno, Max Horkheimer and Herbert Marcuse, which employed Marxist and Freudian ideas. Latterly it is used loosely to describe the activities of post-structuralists.

Dasein Term used by the German philosopher Martin Heidegger to refer to the human condition of being. He defined it in his inaugural address as rector of Freiburg in 1933 as 'the power of the beginning of our spiritual-historical being (*Dasein*). This beginning is the setting out of Greek philosophy.'

decentred subject The concept that the individual person, the 'I', is not the sole author of texts; that they are the result of historical/linguistic/structural forces, of writing itself. An early elaboration was Roland Barthes's essay 'The Death of the Author' (1967). It is a key concept in the work of Jacques Lacan, Michel Foucault, Jacques Derrida and other post-structuralists.

demarcation, problem of Term used by Karl Popper to denote the crucial question in the philosophy of science, which is identifying the differences between science and non-science.

demythology Style of interpreting the Gospels set out by the existentialist theologian Rudolf Bultmann in his essay 'New Testament and Mythology' (1941), which sought to translate in a non-mythological way what the New Testament authors were only able to translate mythologically.

deontology/deontological ethics A position which entails acting according to a code of ethics or a sense of duty regardless of the consequences. It is the opposite of **consequentialism**.

dialectic Term usually associated with G. W. F. Hegel, whose dialectical method involved the positing of a thesis, countered by an antithesis, yielding a synthesis.

dialectical materialism Term used by Joseph Dietzgen to describe a method of understanding reality through the combination of Feuerbach's materialism and Hegel's dialectic. It was the official philosophy of the Soviet Union and other communist states.

discourse ethics An ambitious programme in the philosophy of Jürgen Habermas to combine Kantian deontological ethics with the requirements of **communicative rationality** in its practical applications, such as in political discourse – for example, policymaking or decision-taking.

dualism The view that mind and body are separate (as opposed to **monism**, in which they are a unity). Plato was a dualist, as was René Descartes.

Duhem-Quine thesis Argument in work of Pierre Duhem and W. V. Quine that scientific hypotheses cannot be tested in isolation, because other hypotheses will always be required to draw empirical conclusions from them. It was part of Quine's **holism**.

eidetic reduction Method employed in the **phenomenology** of Edmund Husserl and his followers in which contingent and empirical preconceptions are 'bracketed out', so that reflection may give access to essences.

élan vital In Henri Bergson's *Creative Evolution* (1907), a term to refer to those aspects of life and evolution that cannot be reduced to mechanical explanation.

elective affinity Term coined by Max Weber in *The Protestant Ethic and the Spirit of Capitalism* (1905) to describe the fact that the worldview of Protestantism had an inbuilt sympathy with the aims of capitalism, so facilitating their joint ascendancy.

embodiment/embodied subject Philosophical concern with the fact of the human subject being embodied. The problem of embodiment is central to the work of existentialists such as Søren Kierkegaard, Jean-Paul Sartre, Maurice Merleau-Ponty and, latterly, Julia Kristeva.

empiricism The position that knowledge derives from experience.

encompassing, the In the work of Karl Jaspers, the indefinite horizon beyond our own perspective: '*being* itself, which always seems to *recede* from us, in the very manifestation of all the appearances we encounter'. The encompassing appears during the course of human interaction he describes as the **loving struggle**.

episteme Term used by Michel Foucault to signify sets of relation or rules of formation that govern the production of knowledge.

eternal recurrence/eternal return A concept in the work of Friedrich Nietzsche, premised on the idea that each moment should be lived as if it will occur again and again in an endless circle.

existentialism European philosophical tendency (beginning with Søren Kierkegaard and descending through Martin Heidegger and Karl Jaspers to Jean-Paul Sartre, Maurice Merleau-Ponty and others) to describe a concern with the ontological status of the subject after the death of God (although Kierkegaard was a Christian, as was the leading existentialist Gabriel Marcel).

facticity In the work of Jean-Paul Sartre and Simone de Beauvoir facticity is the situation in which the subject finds himself: gender, parentage, nationality, abilities, etc. It is in the context of this situation that the subject confronts his freedom, limited by facticity. This situation gives rise to the **absurd**.

feminism, second wave A period commencing with the publication of Simone de Beauvoir's *The Second Sex* (1949), which offered an historical examination of woman's situation using Marxist and phenomenological analyses. First-wave feminism was the period of the suffragettes in the nineteenth and early twentieth centuries. Third-wave feminism is concerned with issues including reproductive rights, race and class as they relate to women.

foundationalism Idea of knowledge having to be built on secure foundations. Modern foundationalism begins with René Descartes and his *cogito ergo sum*: 'I think, therefore I am.'

foundheretism Term coined by Susan Haack to avoid the logical problems of both pure foundationalism (infinite regress) and pure coherentism (circularity). She uses the example of a crossword puzzle solution: arriving at an answer from a clue is like using a foundational source, i.e., one grounded in empirical evidence; solving the puzzle by interconnecting the words is like justification through coherence. Haack holds that both **foundation-alism** and coherentism are necessary to knowledge.

Frankfurt School The Institute for Social Research – more popularly known as the Frankfurt School – is also a catch-all term to encompass the Marxist critical theory for which it became famous through the work of Max Horkheimer, Theodor Adorno, Erich Fromm and Herbert Marcuse. During the Second World War the school moved to Columbia University in New York.

game theory An attempt mathematically to describe subjects' behaviour in real-life games, like economics and politics, a sort of calculus of choices.

greatest happiness principle In the utilitarianism of Jeremy Bentham and J. S. Mill a term to define a morally correct action: that which brings the greatest amount of happiness to the greatest number of people. See **utilitarianism**.

hermeneutics/hermeneutic circle Originally a term to describe the interpretation of biblical texts, it became in the hands of German nineteenth-century scholars like Friedrich Schleiermacher and Wilhelm Dilthey a tool for the analysis of larger 'texts', such as groups or societies. Hermeneutics was developed in the twentieth century by Martin Heidegger, Hans-Georg Gadamer and Paul Ricoeur. The hermeneutic circle refers to the analysis of texts by relating parts to the whole, and in an historical context that accounts for the subject.

historical materialism Karl Marx's material view of history. In *A Contribution to the Critique of Political Economy* (1859) he wrote: 'The mode of production determines the social, political and intellectual life processes in general.'

historicism The view that outcomes are historically determined. This view was famously challenged by Karl Popper in *The Poverty of Historicism* (1957) and *The Open Society and Its Enemies* (1945). By believing in all-encompassing 'laws' of history, Plato, Hegel and Marx were the forerunners of **totalitarianism**.

holism The thesis that wholes are greater than the sum of their parts. It is an essentially anti-reductive position.

instrumentalism The view that a concept or theory's value should be determined by its ability to explain and predict phenomena (as opposed to its ability to describe objective reality).

intentionality In the **phenomenology** of Edmund Husserl, the means by which objects of consciousness are constituted (see **constitution**). Husserl's master Franz Brentano had reintroduced the term to modern philosophy, borrowing it from the Scholastic Augustine. But the term may also be traced back to Parmenides' fifth-century BC poem *On Nature*, and the discussion of the problem of what *is*.

intersubjectivity Refers to mechanisms or conditions under which our experience and perception of the world can be confirmed by and shared with others. It is a particularly significant theme in **phenomenology** and **existentialism**.

intertextuality Term coined by Julia Kristeva in her essay 'Word, Dialogue and the Novel' (1966) to refer to the endless interconnectedness of texts: 'Any text is constructed as a mosaic of quotations; any text is the absorption and transformation of another.'

intuition A slightly fuzzy term often used to refer to the phenomenon of becoming immediately aware of something. It is specifically defined by Henri Bergson in *Creative Evolution* (1907): 'By intuition I mean instinct that has become disinterested, self-conscious, capable of reflecting upon its object and of enlarging it indefinitely.'

jouissance Term central to the work of Jacques Lacan, who uses it to mean a kind of orgasmic pleasure that exceeds phallogocentrism (Jacques Derrida's term for male-dominated discourse). *Jouissance* is a kind of maverick, outlaw, bliss-seeking tendency, an *id* left unsupervised by the male parent, free to do as it wishes without interference from ego or superego.

labour theory of value Theory important to Karl Marx, though developed by Adam Smith and David Ricardo, which holds that only labour can contribute to the value of a product. By contrast neo-classical economic theory holds that a product's value is determined by its value in consumption and its relative use-value.

Lamarckism Theory in evolutionary biology promulgated by Jean-Baptiste Lamarck that the acquired characteristics of a species could be inherited by succeeding generations. It was superseded by the researches of Gregor Mendel, who provided the genetic basis for evolution.

law of three stages Evolutionary idea of man's intellectual development put forth by Auguste Comte in his *Course on Positive Philosophy* (1830–42) that 'each branch of our knowledge, passes successively through three different theoretical conditions: the Theological or fictitious; the Metaphysical or abstract; and the Scientific or positive.'

limit-situation Drawing upon his early work in psychiatry, a term used by Karl Jaspers to refer to a moment when the human subject faces extremes of guilt or anxiety. In these moments the human being's potential for undetermined freedom manifests itself as the possibility for transcendence.

linguistic philosophy A programme of thinking that identifies philosophical problems as ones that can be solved (or dissolved) by a proper understanding and application of language.

logical atomism Position which holds that philosophical problems may be solved by breaking them down into atoms of meaning. It is espoused in Bertrand Russell's paper 'The Philosophy of Logical Atomism' (1918) and Ludwig Wittgenstein's *Tractatus Logico-Philosophicus* (1921).

logical empiricism A development of **logical positivism** in which thinkers like W. V. Quine abandoned its original anti-metaphysical stance.

logical positivism Doctrine developed principally by Moritz Schlick and Rudolf Carnap (leaders of the Vienna Circle) which held metaphysics to be without meaning, and which judged a meaningful statement as one being verifiable using logical analysis.

logicism School of mathematics which holds that the fundamental concepts of mathematics can be deduced from the laws of logic. This was the task of both Bertrand Russell and A. N. Whitehead in *Principia Mathematica* (1910–13).

Look, the A theme introduced by Simone de Beauvoir in her novel *She Came to Stay* (1943) and used by Jean-Paul Sartre in *Being and Nothingness* (1943) to denote the gaze that appropriates the other, always with sexual content, because for Sartre to be is to be a sexual being.

loving struggle Concept at the heart of Karl Jaspers's work, which refers to the manner in which each human being or *Existenz* confronts the other in dialogue: 'In Existenz, the man who is himself present speaks. He speaks to another *Existenz* as one irreplaceable individual to another' (*Philosophy of Existence*, 1956).

materialism The ontological position that everything that exists does so in material form, that it occupies space.

mirror phase In the work of Jacques Lacan, a term that refers to the child's assumption of an (imaginary) unity with his or her body image. This sets in motion a tendency of the subject always to seek imaginary wholeness.

monism Literally, 'oneness' from the Greek *monos* (single), it signifies the notion of unity, as in the indivisibility of mind and body. It is the opposite of **dualism**, where mind and body are conceived as separate.

multiplicity Term devised by Henri Bergson and defined by Gilles Deleuze in *Bergsonism* (1966) as a characteristic of that which cannot be counted or accounted for by logic or reductive methodologies. Bergson developed his theory of multiplicity after studying the mathematician Georg Friedrich Bernhard Riemann; the Riemann singularity theorem identifies the multiplicity of a point.

natality Term used by Hannah Arendt to describe the situation from which the subject proceeds towards its future, full of possibilities for freedom. It is posited to supplement the view of her teacher Martin Heidegger that we are characterized by being-towards-death.

naturalism The belief that all phenomena are ultimately accountable for by the methods used in the natural sciences.

naturalistic fallacy In G. E. Moore's *Principia Ethica* (1903) the idea that 'goodness' can be defined in terms of natural properties, such as 'pleasant', 'desired' or 'evolved'. Moore believed that goodness is not analyzable. Good is 'one of those innumerable objects of thought which are themselves incapable of definition, because they are the ultimate terms by reference to which whatever is capable of definition must be defined'.

nihilism A term first used by Ivan Turgenev in his novel *Fathers and Sons* (1862) to describe an attitude that denies all traditional values and moral truths. It is often used to describe the condition of believing in nothing. Friedrich Nietzsche is erroneously described as a nihilist, but he wanted to rediscover new values after the 'death of God', not to continue without any.

ontology That branch of philosophy which is concerned with questions of being: what does is mean to *be*? What is existence? It is the first question of philosophy, and in his *Metaphysics*, Aristotle defined metaphysics as the study of 'being qua being'.

ordinary language philosophy (see **linguistic philosophy**)

Other, the In **phenomenology** (and particularly in the **existentialism** of Jean-Paul Sartre and Simone de Beauvoir) the Other is a necessary but threatening subject. On the one hand, by recognizing me, the Other confirms my existence and creates an intersubjective (see **intersubjectivity**) bond. On the other hand, the gaze of the Other reduces me to the status of an object and denies my subjectivity.

overman (*Übermensch*) Concept introduced by Friedrich Nietzsche in *Thus Spoke Zarathustra* (1883) to describe the man who attempts to get past his present position, through exertion of his will. The overman must also be the creator of his own values.

phenomenological method/phenomenological reduction (see **phenomenology**)

phenomenology School of philosophy developed by Edmund Husserl that uses the method of eidetic reduction to eliminate preconceptions (bracketing them out) and so perceive the essences of phenomena under study. It is the dominant trend of twentieth-century thinking and it continues to inform **post-structuralism**.

picture theory of language Developed by Ludwig Wittgenstein in his *Tractatus Logico-Philosophicus* (1921). In the picture theory of meaning, a sentence shares a pictorial form with a state of affairs. To illustrate his point Wittgenstein likens language to musical notation, which he describes as the pictorial form of the state of affairs that is the musical composition.

positivism Term coined by Auguste Comte to describe the view that all phenomena can be understood by scientific method. Comte used his positivist method to study subjects that would now fall under the heading of sociology. It was on foundations laid by Comte that Émile Durkheim created sociology as an academic discipline.

post-structuralism The tendency to view meaning as indeterminate, because it is produced through the interrelationships of texts and not (as Enlightenment philosophy would have it) by an authorial 'I'. The movement succeeded phenomenology, existentialism and structuralism in France, borrowing liberally from all three while surpassing them. Prominent post-structuralists include Roland Barthes, Jacques Derrida and Julia Kristeva.

praxis Literally, 'action' from the Greek *prattein* (do). In the thought of Karl Marx it refers to the unity of theory and practice in socialism.

psychologism A tendency to derive facts or laws in one area (usually logic or mathematics) from those found in psychology. Both John Locke and David Hume did this. In establishing **logicism** in the early twentieth century Gottlob Frege famously accused Edmund Husserl of psychologism in his *Philosophy of Arithmetic* (1891). Husserl criticized psychologism in 'The Prolegomena of Pure Logic' (1900).

public sphere Term used by Jürgen Habermas in *The Structural Transformation of the Public Sphere* (1962) to describe the Enlightenment 'place' of public discourse, be it parliament or coffee house. He sees modernization as having compromised the public sphere, but is optimistic that a democracy-driven activist tendency will reinvent it.

punctuated equilibrium Term introduced by Stephen Jay Gould and Niles Eldredge in their paper 'Punctuated Equilibria' (1972), which argues that the gap in fossil records in the theory of evolution exists because evolution occurs in fits and starts rather than at a constant rate.

queer theory Discipline in **critical theory** that explores the socially constructed nature of sexualities.

radical empiricism William James's term for investigations which take into account not only that which is experienced empirically, but also the relations that obtain among the objects of study (including the observer and the act of observing).

reflex arc (see **arc theory**)

repressive tolerance In his essay *Repressive Tolerance* (1965) Herbert Marcuse identified the mechanism which governs unfreedom as the 'ideology of tolerance, which, in reality, favours and fortifies the conservation of the status quo of inequality and discrimination'.

Russell's Paradox A flaw exposed by Bertrand Russell in the first volume of Gottlob Frege's *Basic Laws of Arithmetic* (1893). It involves the concept of the set of all sets that are not members of themselves. If such a set existed, it would be a member of itself only if it was not a member of itself. Russell found a solution to the paradox by developing the theory of types, which allowed for the segregation of properties, relations and sets. Frege's error, Russell argued, was to assume that classes and their members conformed to a single, homogeneous type, instead of a number of types that conformed to a hierarchy.

Scholasticism The medieval philosophy of the Church Fathers developed to define orthodoxy and to train theologians in the logical skills necessary for the defence of orthodoxy against heresy, and against the arguments of 'infidels'. The high point of Scholastic philosophy was the work of St Thomas Aquinas.

scientism The philosophical view that only scientific claims to knowledge are meaningful.

second-wave feminism (see **feminism, second wave**)

semiotics/theory of signs Area of study developed by Ferdinand de Saussure to study systems. Saussure used it to study the system of language, but his work soon led to structuralism and the application of semiotics to a broader range of systems (social, political, textual, etc.). The units of meaning studied by semioticians are called signs.

set theory Sets are collections of objects and set theory is the branch of mathematics that studies sets. It is important to philosophy because sets are considered the purest of mathematical objects, and provide a ground for the rest of mathematical knowledge. The theory of infinite sets developed by Georg Cantor paved the way for the **logicism** of Gottlob Frege and Bertrand Russell.

signifier/signified In the structuralist theory of Ferdinand de Saussure, the two elements of a sign. The signifier is the sound-image or written form, while the signified is the mental component of the sign. So, the signifier 'chair' will bring to mind the concept of a chair. However, Saussure pointed out, the relation between signified and signified is arbitrary.

scepticism View advanced by Pyrrho of Elis, who said that all attempts at knowledge are inconclusive. It has since come to represent the view that knowledge or rational belief is impossible.

social fact In the *Rules of Sociological Method* (1895) Émile Durkheim defined social facts as 'facts with very distinctive characteristics: they consist of ways of acting, thinking and feeling, external to the individual, and endowed with a power of coercion, by reason of which they control him'.

solipsism The position that only one's self and one's experiences exist. It is the opposite of **intersubjectivity**.

spirit In the work of G. W. F. Hegel there are three types of spirit: subjective, objective and absolute. Subjective spirit is the physical and psychological existence of individual human beings. Objective spirit describes the structure of the communal world outside. Absolute spirit refers to knowledge and freedom accrued over time and expressed in religion, art and philosophy. World history is directed to absolute spirit.

structuralism A broad term to describe a range of interdisciplinary activities that derive from the work of Ferdinand de Saussure, who argued that language was to be understood as a system with a particular structure, rather than a given set of words with fixed meanings. Gradually this methodology grew to include the study of everything – from historical movements to movies – that could be construed as a system whose signs could be identified and decoded. Early structuralists included Claude Lévi-Strauss and Roland Barthes, although Barthes soon became a post-structuralist (see **post-structuralism**).

superman (see **overman**)

surplus value, theory of Theory of Karl Marx that when a worker produces goods from raw materials they acquire a new value that creates profit for the capitalist, at the expense of the unpaid labour of the worker.

teleology The study of 'ends'. The belief that events and phenomena occur to some 'end' and therefore are explicable (and have meaning). The creationist position that God created the world in six days and put all life on it is a teleological one that is negated by evolutionary science. Aristotle's philosophy is based on the teleological premise that a prime mover is responsible for putting the world in motion. That view was superseded by Isaac Newton's discovery of gravity.

theory of signs (see **semiotics**)

thrownness In Martin Heidegger's *Being and Time* (1927) the situation of our existence in which we find ourselves 'thrown' into the world according to circumstances that are peculiarly ours (our **facticity**), over which we have no choice.

totalitarianism A system of government whereby the state has control of all institutions, public and private. The fascist (Germany, Italy, Spain) and communist (Soviet Union, China) examples of totalitarianism in the twentieth century were characterized by one-party rule and the use of military and police forces to keep order and punish deviation. Totalitarian regimes require adherence to dogma and discourage free thought, argument or disagreement. As a result they become intellectually weak. The discouragement of free thought leads to stagnation in science and philosophy.

transcendental idealism Immanuel Kant's doctrine that objects of perception do not just give themselves to consciousness, but that the subject plays an active role in perceiving them.

transcendentalism (see **American transcendentalism**)

transformative method Ludwig Feuerbach showed Karl Marx a device for criticizing Hegel, who argued that thought was the subject and existence was the predicate, establishing the possibility of materialism. The transformative method takes the human and the subject and thought as the predicate. Feuerbach 'turns Hegel on his head'.

types, theory of Bertrand Russell's solution of the self-referential paradox that arises from the notion of 'the class of all classes that are not members of themselves', which involves hierarchy of types in which items are defined by reference to a lower type, thereby avoiding self-reference.

Übermensch (see **overman**)

unitarianism A sect of Christianity that rejects the concept of the Holy Trinity of God as simultaneously Father, Son and Holy Spirit.

utilitarianism Ethical theory proposed by Jeremy Bentham, James Mill and J. S. Mill, summarized by the latter thus: 'actions are right in proportion as they tend to promote happiness, wrong as they tend to promote the reverse of happiness.'

will to power Concept advanced by Friedrich Nietzsche in *Thus Spoke Zarathustra* (1883–5) referring to a life force that not only precedes and drives human existence, but all things, including the inanimate world.

Bibliography

Anonymous, *No Subject: Encyclopedia of Lacanian Analysis*, http://nosubject.com/Main_Page.

Adamson, Robert, *Fichte* (London: Wm. Blackwood and Sons, 1881).

Allison, Henry E., *Kant's Transcendental Idealism: An Interpretation and Defense* (New Haven: Yale University Press, 1983).

Amery, Colin, 'Wittgenstein's Poker: A Moment of Destiny', http://www.philosophos.com/philosophy_article_11.html.

Ayer, A. J., *Bertrand Russell* (Chicago: University of Chicago Press, 1972).

Babich, Babette, 'On the "Analytic-Continental" Divide in Philosophy: Nietzsche and Heidegger on Truth, Lies and Language', in *A House Divided: Comparing Analytic and Continental Philosophy*, ed. C. G. Prado (Amherst: Prometheus/Humanity Books, 2003), pp. 63–103.

Bailly, Lionel, *Lacan: A Beginner's Guide* (Oxford: Oneworld Publications, 2009).

Baldwin, Thomas, *G. E. Moore* (London: Routledge, 1990).

Barrett, William, *Irrational Man: A Study in Existential Philosophy* (New York: Doubleday, 1958).

Berkowitz, Roger, 'Bearing Logs on Our Shoulders: Reconciliation, Non-Reconciliation and the Building of a Common World', *Project MUSE – Theory & Event*, Volume 14, Issue 1 (2011).

Berkowitz, Roger, et al., eds, *Thinking in Dark Times: Hannah Arendt on Ethics and Politics* (New York: Fordham University Press, 2010).

Berkowtiz, Roger, 'Why We Must Judge', *Democracy Journal*, Autumn 2010.

Berlin, Isaiah, *Freedom and Its Betrayal: Six Enemies of Human Liberty* (London: Chatto, 2002).

Boas, George, 'Review of History of Western Philosophy', *Journal of the History of Ideas*, Volume 8 (1947), pp. 117–123.

Bohman, James, 'Jürgen Habermas', in *Stanford Encyclopedia of Philosophy*, http://plato.stanford.edu/entries/habermas/ (17 May 2007).

Bohman, James, *Public Deliberation: Pluralism, Complexity and Democracy* (Cambridge: MIT Press, 2000).

Boucher, David, ed., *The British Idealists* (Cambridge: Cambridge University Press, 1997).

Bowie, Andrew, 'Obituary of Hans-Georg Gadamer', *Radical Philosophy* (July/August, 2002).

Bowler, Peter J., *Evolution: The History of an Idea* (Berkeley: University of California Press, 2003).

Bowler, Peter J., *Monkey Trials and Gorilla Sermons: Evolution and Christianity from Darwin to Intelligent Design* (Cambridge: Harvard University Press, 2007).

Brent, Joseph, *Charles Sanders Peirce: A Life* (Bloomington: Indiana University Press, 1998).

Candlish, Stewart, 'The Truth About F. H. Bradley', *Mind*, Volume 98, No. 391 (1989), pp. 331–48.

Capra, Fritjof, *The Tao of Physics* (Boston: Shambhala, 1975).

Cartwright, David E., *Schopenhauer: A Biography* (New York: Cambridge University Press, 2010).

Caygill, Howard, *A Kant Dictionary* (Oxford: Blackwell, 1995).

Chodorow, Nancy, *The Reproduction of Mothering: Psychoanalysis and the Sociology of Gender* (Berkeley: University of California Press, 1978).

Chomsky, Noam, *The Chomksy Reader* (New York: Pantheon, 1987).

Chomsky, Noam, 'The Relevance of Anarcho-syndicalism', *The Jay Interview* (25 July 1976) http://www.chomsky.info/interviews/19760725.htm.

Cladis, Mark, ed., *Durkheim and Foucault: Perspectives on Education and Punishment* (Oxford: Durkheim Press, 1999).

Cohen-Solal, Annie, *Jean-Paul Sartre: A Life* (New York: New Press, 2005).

Critchley, Simon, and Schroeder, William, R., eds, *A Companion to Continental Philosophy* (Oxford: Blackwell, 1998).

Culler, Jonathan, *Barthes* (London: Fontana, 1983).

Culler, Jonathan, *Ferdinand de Saussure* (Ithaca: Cornell University Press, 1976).

Damrosch, Leo, *Jean-Jacques Rousseau: Restless Genius* (New York: Houghton Mifflin, 2005).

Davies, Anna Morpurgo, 'Saussure and Indo-European linguistics', in *The Cambridge Companion to Saussure*, ed. Carol Sanders (Cambridge: Cambridge University Press, 2004).

Deleuze, Gilles, *Bergsonism* (New York: Zone Books, 1988).

Deleuze, Gilles, and Guattari, Félix, *What Is Philosophy?* (New York: Columbia University Press, 1996).

Dennett, Daniel C., 'Dennett and Carr Further Explained: An Exchange', *Emory Cognition Project*, Report No. 28, Department of Psychology, Emory University (April 1994).

Derrida, Jacques, 'For a Justice to Come', interview with Lieven De Cauter (5 April 2004) http://archive.indymedia.be/news/2004/04/83123.html.

Derrida, Jacques, *Learning to Live Finally: The Last Interview*, with Jean Birnbaum (Brooklyn: Melville House, 2007).

Desmond, Adrian, and Moore, James, *Darwin: The Life of a Tormented Evolutionist* (London: Norton, 1994).

Detmer, David, *Sartre Explained: From Bad Faith to Authenticity* (Peru, IL: Carus, 2008).

Dilthey, Wilhelm, 'The Rise of Hermeneutics', in *Hermeneutics and the Study of History: Selected Works, Volume IV*, eds, R. A. Makkreel and F. Rodi (Princeton, NJ: Princeton University Press, 1996).

Downing, Lisa, *The Cambridge Introduction to Michel Foucault* (Cambridge: Cambridge University Press, 2008).

Dykhuizen, George, *The Life and Mind of John Dewey* (Cardondale: Southern Illinois University Press, 1978).

Dynes, Wayne R., et al., eds, *Encyclopedia of Homosexuality* (New York: Garland, 1990).

Eagleton, Terry, *Marx* (New York: Routledge, 1999).

Eco, Umberto, *Kant and the Platypus* (New York: Harvest, 1999).

Edmundson, Mark, *The Death of Sigmund Freud: The Legacy of His Last Days* (New York: Bloomsbury, 2007).

Eliot, T. S., *Knowledge and Experience in the Philosophy of F. H. Bradley* (New York: Farrar Strauss, 1964).

Embree, Lester, 'A Representation of Edmund Husserl (1859–1938), Husserl Circle (June 1988).

Eribon, Didier, *Michel Foucault* (Cambridge: Harvard University Press, 1992).

Feenberg, Andrew, *Heidegger and Marcuse: The Catastrophe and Redemption of History* (New York: Routledge, 2005).

Fernández-Armesto, Felipe, *1492: The Year the World Began* (New York: HarperOne, 2010).

Ferrarello, Susi, 'On the Rationality of Will in James and Husserl', *European Journal of Pragmatism and American Philosophy*, Volume 1, No. 1 (2009).

Ferreira, Phillip, *Bradley and the Structure of Knowledge* (Albany: State University of New York Press, 1999).

Fox, Michael, *The Accessible Hegel* (Amherst: Humanity Books, 2005).

Freadman, Richard, *Threads of Life: Autobiography and the Will* (Chicago: University of Chicago Press, 2001).

Fussell, Paul, *The Great War and Modern Memory* (New York: Oxford University Press, 1975).

Garff, Joakim, *Søren Kierkegaard: A Biography* (Princeton: Princeton University Press, 2005).

Glassman, Peter, *J. S. Mill: The Evolution of a Genius* (Gainesville: University of Florida Press, 1985).

Glazebrook, Trish, *Heidegger's Philosophy of Science* (New York: Fordham University Press, 2000).

Glendinning, Simon, *The Idea of Continental Philosophy* (Edinburgh: Edinburgh University Press, 2006).

Glock, Hans-Johann, *What is Analytic Philosophy?* (Cambridge: Cambridge University Press, 2008).

Golumbia, David, 'Quine, Derrida and the Question of Philosophy', *The Philosophical Forum*, Volume 30, No. 3 (September 1999).

Graef, Hilde, *Scholar and the Cross: The Life and Works of Edith Stein* (Westminster: Newman Press, 1958).

Grelland, Hans H., 'Husserl, Einstein, Weyl and the Concepts of Space, Time and Space-Time', in *Space, Time and Spacetime*, ed. Vesselin Petkov (New York: Springer, 2010).

Guerlac, Suzanne, *Thinking in Time: An Introduction to Henri Bergson* (Ithaca: Cornell University Press, 2006).

Gunter, Pete A. Y., 'Bergson, Mathematics and Creativity', *Process Studies*, Volume 28, No. 3–4 (1999), pp. 268–88.

Guyer, Paul, ed., *The Cambridge Companion to Kant* (Cambridge: Cambridge

University Press, 1992).

Haack, Susan, *Evidence and Inquiry: A Pragmatist Reconstruction of Epistemology* (Amherst: Prometheus, 2009).

Habermas, Jürgen 'America and the World', conversation with Eduardo Mendieta, *Logos*, issue 3.3 (Summer 2004).

Habermas, Jürgen, *Jürgen Habermas on Society and Politics: A Reader*, ed. Steven Seidman (Boston: Beacon Press, 1989).

Habermas, Jürgen, 'Work and Weltanschauung: The Heidegger Controversy from a German Perspective', *Critical Inquiry*, Volume 15, No. 2. (Winter 1989), pp. 431–56.

Hamlyn, D. W., 'Gilbert Ryle and *Mind*', *Revue Internationale de Philosophie*, No. 223 (2003), pp. 5–12.

Hanna, Robert, *Kant and the Foundations of Analytic Philosophy* (New York: Oxford University Press, 2004).

Hannay, Alastair, *Kierkegaard: A Biography* (Cambridge: Cambridge University Press, 2001).

Harding, Walter, *The Days of Henry Thoreau: A Biography* (New York: Knopf, 1965).

Hawking, Stephen and Mlodinow, Leonard, *The Grand Design* (New York: Bantam Books, 2010).

Herbstrith, Waltraud, *Edith Stein: A Biography* (San Francisco: Ignatius Press, 1992).

Hill, Claire Ortiz, and Haddock, G. E. R., *Husserl or Frege? Meaning, Objectivity and Mathematics* (Peru, IL: Carus Publishing Co., 2000).

Hodges, Michael P. and Lachs, John, *Thinking in the Ruins: Wittgenstein and Santayana on Contingency* (Nashville: Vanderbilt University Press, 2000).

Irvine, Andrew D., 'Principia Mathematica', *Stanford Encyclopedia of Philosophy* (2010) http://plato.stanford.edu/entries/principia-mathematica.

Irvine, Andrew D., 'Russell's Paradox', *Stanford Encyclopedia of Philosophy* (2009) http://plato.stanford.edu/entries/russell-paradox/#SOTP.

Isaacson, Walter, *Einstein: His Life and Universe* (New York: Simon & Schuster, 2007).

Jones, Robert Alun, *Emile Durkheim: An Introduction to Four Major Works* (Beverly Hills: Sage Publications, 1986).

Jung, Joachim, 'The Future of Philosophy', paper given at Twentieth World

Congress of Philosophy, Boston (10–15 August 1998) http://www.bu.edu/wcp/Papers/Cont/ContJung.htm.

Kaelin, E. F. and Schrag, Calvin O., eds, *American Phenomenology: Origins and Developments* (Dordrecht: Springer, 1988).

Kahn, Michael, *Basic Freud: Psychoanalytic Thought for the 21st Century* (NY: Basic Books, 2002).

Kellner, Douglas, 'Radical Politics, Marcuse, and the New Left', *Introduction to Collected Papers of Herbert Marcuse, Volume 3* (Abingdon: Routledge, 2001).

Kenny, Anthony, *Frege: An Introduction to the Founder of Modern Analytic Philosophy* (Chichester: Wiley-Blackwell, 2000).

Kim, Sung Ho, 'Max Weber', *Stanford Encyclopedia of Philosophy* (2007) http://plato.stanford.edu/entries/weber.

Kim, Sung Ho, *Max Weber's Politics of Civil Society* (Cambridge: Cambridge University Press, 2004).

Kirk, G. S. and Raven, J. E., *The Presocratic Philosophers* (Cambridge: Cambridge University Press, 1962).

Kirkbright, Suzanne, *Karl Jaspers: A Biography – Navigations in Truth* (New Haven: Yale University Press, 2004).

Kretzmann, Norman, et al., eds., *The Cambridge History of Later Medieval Philosophy* (Cambridge: Cambridge University Press, 1982).

Kristeva, Julia, 'Interview with John Sutherland', *Guardian* (14 March 2006).

Kuehn, Manfred, *Kant: A Biography* (Cambridge: Cambridge University Press, 2001).

Lacan, Jacques, '*Les Clefs de la Pyschanalyse*', *L'Express* (31 May 1957).

Lachs, John, 'George Santayana', in *The Cambridge Dictionary of Philosophy*, ed. Robert Audi (Cambridge: Cambridge University Press, 1995).

Lane, Christopher, *The Burdens of Intimacy: Psychoanalysis and Victorian Masculinity* (Chicago: University of Chicago Press, 1998).

Lawlor, Leonard, *Derrida and Husserl: The Basic Problem of Phenomenology* (Bloomington: Indiana University Press, 2002).

Lawlor, Leonard, 'Intuition and Duration: an Introduction to Bergson's "Introduction to Metaphysics"', in *Bergson and Phenomenology*, ed. Michael R. Kelly (Basingstoke: Palgrave Macmillan, 2010).

Lawlor, Leonard, 'Jacques Derrida', *The Stanford Encyclopedia of Philosophy*

(2006) http://plato.stanford.edu/entries/derrida/#Rel.

Lawlor, Leonard, *Thinking Through French Philosophy: The Being of the Question* (Bloomington: Indiana University Press, 2003).

Malone, John. C., 'Ontology Recapitulates Philology: Willard Quine, Pragmatism and Radical Behaviorism', *Behavior and Philosophy*, No. 29 (2001), pp. 63–74 (2001).

Liszka, James Jakób, *A General Introduction to the Semiotic of Charles Sanders Peirce* (Bloomington: Indiana University Press, 1996).

Luscombe, David, *Medieval Thought* (Oxford: Oxford University Press, 1997).

Macey, David, *The Lives of Michel Foucault* (New York: Vintage, 1995).

McAfee, Noëlle, *Julia Kristeva* (New York and London: Routledge, 2004).

McBride, William Leon, *Sartre's Life, Times and Vision du Monde* (London: Routledge, 1996).

McCormick, John, *George Santayana: A Biography* (New York: Knopf, 1987).

MacIntyre, Alasdair, *Edith Stein: A Philosophical Prologue, 1913–1922* (Lanham: Rowman & Littlefield, 2006).

McClintock, John, and Strong, James, *Cyclopaedia of Biblical, Theological and Ecclesiastical Literature*, Supplement, Volume 1 (New York: Harper & Brothers, 1885).

McLellan, David, *Karl Marx* (Harmondsworth: Penguin, 1975).

McLellan, David, *Karl Marx: His Life and Thought* (New York: Harper & Row, 1973).

Madison, G. B., 'Hermeneutics: Gadamer and Ricoeur', in *The Columbia History of Western Philosophy*, ed. Richard H. Popkin (New York: Columbia University Press, 1999).

Maier-Katkin, Daniel, *Stranger from Abroad: Hannah Arendt, Martin Heidegger, Friendship and Forgiveness* (New York: Norton, 2010).

Malpas, J. E., *Heidegger's Topology: Being, Place, World* (Cambridge: MIT Press, 2007).

Manser, Anthony, and Stock, Guy, *The Philosophy of F. H. Bradley* (New York: Oxford University Press, 1987).

Marcuse, Herbert, *Eros and Civilization: A Philosophical Inquiry into Freud* (London: Routledge, 1987).

Marcuse, Herbert, *One Dimensional Man* (Boston: Beacon Press, 1964).

Marcuse, Herbert, 'The Problem of Violence: Questions and Answers' (1967) http://www.marxists.org/reference/archive/marcuse/works/1967/questions-answers.htm.

Mikics, David, *Who Was Jacques Derrida?: An Intellectual Biography* (New Haven: Yale University Press, 2009).

Miller, James, *The Passion of Michel Foucault* (New York: Simon and Schuster, 1993).

Misak, C. J., *Truth and the End of Inquiry: A Peircean Account of Truth* (New York: Oxford University Press, 2004).

Mises, Ludwig von, *Marxism Unmasked: From Delusion to Destruction* (Irvington-on-Hudson, NY: Foundation for Economic Education, 2006).

Mitchell, Juliet, *Psychoanalysis and Feminism: A Radical Reassessment of Freudian Psychoanalysis* (London: Allen Lane, 1974).

Moi, Toril, *Simone de Beauvoir: The Making of an Intellectual Woman* (Oxford: Oxford University Press, 2008).

Monk, Ray, *Bertrand Russell: The Spirit of Solitude 1872–1921* (New York: Free Press, 1996).

Monk, Ray, *Bertrand Russell: The Ghost of Madness 1921–1970* (New York: Free Press, 2001).

Monk, Ray, *Ludwig Wittgenstein: The Duty of Genius* (New York: Free Press, 1990).

Mullarkey, John, *Bergson and Philosophy* (Edinburgh: University of Edinburgh Press, 1999).

Mullarkey, John, and Lord, Beth, eds, *The Continuum Companion to Continental Philosophy* (New York: Continuum, 2009).

Murray, Michael, 'Heidegger and Ryle: Two Versions of Phenomenology', *The Review of Metaphysics*, Volume 27, No. 1 (September 1973), pp. 88–111.

Mussolini, Benito, 'The Doctrine of Fascism', *Enciclopedia Italiana* (Rome: Treccani, 1932).

Natanson, Maurice, *Husserl: Philosopher of Infinite Tasks* (Evanston: Northwestern University Press, 1973).

Naugle, David K., *Worldview: The History of a Concept* (Grand Rapids: Wm. B. Eerdmans, 2002).

Norton, David Fate, and Taylor, Jacqueline, eds, *The Cambridge Companion to Hume* (Cambridge: Cambridge University Press, 1993).

Oliver, Kelly, 'Julia Kristeva's Feminist Revolutions', *Hypatia*, Volume 8, No. 3. (Summer 1993), pp. 94–114.

Parr, Adrian, ed., *The Deleuze Dictionary* (Edinburgh: University of Edinburgh Press, 2005).

Pax, Clyde, *An Existential Approach to God: A Study of Gabriel Marcel* (The Hague: Martinus Nijhoff, 1972).

Perry, Ralph Barton, *The Thought and Character of William James* (Cambridge: Harvard University Press, 1948).

Pickering, Mary, *Auguste Comte: An Intellectual Biography*, Volume I (Cambridge: Cambridge University Press, 1993).

Plant, Raymond, *Hegel* (New York: Routledge, 1999).

Pollock, Griselda, 'Dialogue with Julia Kristeva', *Parallax*, Issue 8 (July–September 1998), pp. 5–16.

Poole, Roger, *Kierkegaard: The Indirect Communication* (Charlottesville: University of Virginia Press, 1993).

Porter, Roy, *The Creation of the Modern World: The Untold Story of the British Enlightenment* (New York: Norton, 2000).

Prado, C. G., *A House Divided: Comparing Analytic and Continental Philosophy* (Amherst, NY: Humanities Press, 2003).

Preucel, Robert W., *Archaeological Semiotics* (Malden: Wiley-Blackwell, 2010).

Preston, Paul, *Comrades! Portraits from the Spanish Civil War* (London: HarperCollins, 1999).

Quammen, David, *The Reluctant Mr Darwin: An Intimate Portrait of Charles Darwin and the Making of His Theory of Evolution* (New York: Norton, 2006).

Quinton, Anthony, 'Alfred Jules Ayer 1910–1989', *Proceedings of the British Academy*, Volume 94 (1997).

Reston, Jr., James, *Dogs of God: Columbus, the Inquisition and the Defeat of the Moors* (New York: Anchor, 2006).

Richardson, Robert D., *Nietzsche's New Darwinism* (New York: Oxford University Press, 2004).

Richardson, Robert D., *William James: In the Maelstrom of American Modernism* (Houghton Mifflin, 2006).

Richman, Sheldon, 'Fascism', in *Fortune Encyclopedia of Economics*, ed., David R. Henderson (New York: Time, Inc., 1993).

Ringer, Fritz, *Max Weber: An Intellectual Biography* (Chicago: University of Chicago Press, 2004).

Rockmore, Tom, *Kant and Idealism* (New Haven: Yale University Press, 2007).

Rockmore, Tom and Margolis, Joseph, eds, *The Heidegger Case: On Philosophy and Politics* (Philadelphia: Temple University Press, 1992).

Rorty, Richard, interview with Josefina Ayerza in *Flash Art* (November/December 1993).

Ross, Kelly. L., 'Ludwig Wittgenstein (1889–1951)', http://www.friesian.com/wittgen.htm.

Russell, Bertrand, 'Some Replies to Criticism', in *My Philosophical Development* (London: Unwin, 1959).

Russell, Bertrand, 'The Cult of "Common Usage"', *The British Journal for the Philosophy of Science*, Volume 3, No. 12 (1953), pp. 303–7.

Sacks, Jonathan, *The Politics of Hope* (London: Jonathan Cape, 1997).

Safranksi, Rüdiger, *Martin Heidegger: Between Good and Evil* (Cambridge: Harvard University Press, 1998).

Safranksi, Rüdiger and Frisch, Shelley, *Nietzsche: A Philosophical Biography* (New York: Norton, 2002).

Safranksi, Rüdiger and osers, Ewald, *Schopenhauer and the Wild Years of Philosophy* (Cambridge: Harvard University Press, 1991).

Sandel, Michael J., *Justice: What's the Right Thing to Do?* (New York: Farrar, Straus & Giroux, 2009).

Sayers, Sean, 'F. H. Bradley and the Concept of Relative Truth', *Radical Philosophy*, No. 59 (Autumn 1991), pp. 15–20.

Seymour-Jones, Carole, *A Dangerous Liaison: A Revelatory New Biography of Simone De Beauvoir and Jean-Paul Sartre* (New York: Overlook, 2009).

Shabel, Linda, 'Kant's "Argument from Geometry"', *Journal of the History of Philosophy*, Volume 42, No. 2 (2004), pp. 195–215.

Shin, Sun-Joo, 'Peirce's Logic', *Stanford Encyclopedia of Philosophy* (2011) http://plato.stanford.edu/entries/peirce-logic/.

Simon, Linda, *Genuine Reality: A Life of William James* (New York: Harcourt Brace, 1998).

Singer, Peter, *Hegel: A Very Short Introduction* (Oxford: Oxford University Press, 1983).

Skorupski, John, *Why Read Mill Today?* (London: Routledge, 2006).

Sluga, Hans, *Heidegger's Crisis: Philosophy and Politics in Nazi Germany* (Cambridge: Harvard University Press, 1993).

Sluga, Hans and Stern, David. G., eds, *The Cambridge Companion to Wittgenstein* (Cambridge: Cambridge University Press, 1996).

Specter, Matthew G., *Habermas: An Intellectual Biography* (New York: Cambridge University Press, 2010).

Spiegelberg, Herbert, *The Phenomenological Movement: A Historical Introduction* (Dordrecht: Kluwer, 1984).

Spurling, Hilary, 'The Wickedest Man in Oxford', *The New York Times* (24 December 2000).

Steiner, George, *Martin Heidegger* (New York: Viking, 1979).

Stephens, Mitchell, 'Jacques Derrida and Deconstruction', *New York Times Magazine* (23 January 1994).

Stephens, Mitchell, 'Jürgen Habermas: The Theologian of Talk', *Los Angeles Times Magazine* (23 October 1994).

Taylor, Charles, *Hegel* (Cambridge: Cambridge University Press, 1975).

Thornhill, Christopher J., *Karl Jaspers: Politics and Metaphysics* (London: Routledge, 2006).

Turner, Stephen P., ed., *The Cambridge Companion to Weber* (Cambridge: Cambridge University Press, 2000).

Turner, Stephen P., *Emile Durkheim: Sociologist and Moralist* (London: Routledge, 2003).

Wartofsky, Marx W., *Feuerbach* (Cambridge: Cambridge University Press, 1977).

Waterfield, Robin, *The First Philosophers: The Presocratics and the Sophists* (Oxford: Oxford University Press, 2000).

Webster, Richard 'The Cult of Lacan: Freud, Lacan and the Mirror Stage' (1994) http://www.richardwebster.net/thecultoflacan.html.

Westphal, Kenneth, 'G. W. F. Hegel', in *A Dictionary of Continental Philosophy*, ed. John Protevi (New Haven: Yale University Press, 2006).

Wheen, Francis, *Marx's Das Kapital: A Biography* (New York: Atlantic Monthly Press, 2007).

Wicks, Robert, *Schopenhauer* (Malden: Blackwell, 2008).

Wiener, Norbert, *Ex-Prodigy: My Childhood and Youth* (Cambridge: MIT Press, 1964).

Wittgenstein, Ludwig, *Wittgenstein in Cambridge: Letters and Documents, 1911–1951*, ed. Brian McGuinness (John Wiley and Sons, 2008).

Wolin, Richard, *Heidegger's Children: Hannah Arendt, Karl Lowith, Hans Jonas and Herbert Marcuse* (Princeton: Princeton University Press, 2001).

Wolin, Richard, *The Seduction of Unreason: The Intellectual Romance with Fascism from Nietzsche to Postmodernism* (Princeton: Princeton University Press, 2004).

Wollheim, Richard, 'Ayer: The Man, The Philosopher, The Teacher', in *A. J. Ayer: Memorial Essays*, ed. A. Phillips Griffiths (Cambridge: Cambridge University Press, 1991).

Young, Julian, *Friedrich Nietzsche: A Philosophical Biography* (New York: Cambridge, University Press, 2010).

Young-Bruehl, Elisabeth, *Hannah Arendt: For Love of the World* (New Haven: Yale University Press, 2004).

Stephen Trombley is a writer, editor and Emmy Award-winning film-maker. He collaborated with Alan Bullock on the second edition of *The Fontana Dictionary of Modern Thought*, and was editor of *The New Fontana Dictionary of Modern Thought*. His books include *A Short History of Western Thought* (Atlantic, 2012); *The Execution Protocol*; *Sir Frederick Treves: The Extraordinary Edwardian*; *The Right to Reproduce*; and *'All That Summer She Was Mad': Virginia Woolf and her Doctors*.